MW00489563

"*The Gospel of John in Modern Interpretation* is a wonderful introduction to the fascinating world that is the New Testament study of John's gospel. Tracing the general history of the gospel's treatment, and focusing on the contribution of several key scholars, this book also traces the discussions that drive the gospel's study and how best to read it. The gospel of John has been an outlier in Jesus studies. This work explains why that should not be so, and what one must pay attention to in reading this crucial gospel. It is well worth a careful read."

—Darrell L. Bock,
Senior Research Professor of New Testament Studies,
Dallas Theological Seminary

"This is a very worthwhile volume, because instead of viewing 'modern interpretation' as an abstraction, it looks at eight, carefully chosen modern *interpreters*, with their whole careers and scholarly contributions in view—not merely their work on John's gospel. Three of them (Rudolf Bultmann, C. H. Dodd, and Raymond E. Brown) are obvious choices. Five others have been either half-forgotten (B. F. Westcott), unfairly neglected or underappreciated (Adolf Schlatter and Leon Morris), dismissed as idiosyncratic (John A. T. Robinson), or pigeonholed as a 'mere' literary critic (R. Alan Culpepper). They all deserve better, and this collection calls attention, once again, to their substantial contributions. A much needed and promising correction. Thank you, Stan Porter and Ron Fay, and your authors!"

—J. Ramsey Michaels,
Professor of Religious Studies Emeritus,
Missouri State University, Springfield

"Here is an extremely well-chosen collection of vignettes of major Johannine scholars from the late 1800s to the present. Not only do we learn of their contributions and significance, but we get a feel for their lives and social contexts. This is exemplary scholarship modeled in a fashion not quite paralleled anywhere else. If the series this volume inaugurates can continue this quality of offering, it will be of extraordinary value."

—Craig L. Blomberg,
Distinguished Professor of New Testament,
Denver Seminary

"In these valuable treatments of eight leading scholars over the last century or more, diverse approaches to the gospel of John in modern scholarship are here laid out in clear and helpful ways. Given the hugely diverse ways that top scholars have engaged and addressed John's notorious riddles (theological, historical, literary), a collection such as this provides interpreters a helpful guide in sorting out such subjects as John's authorship, composition, relation(s) to the Synoptics, situation, and meaning. New Testament readers and scholars alike are thus indebted to Stanley Porter and Ron Fay for gathering this fine collection, which shows that as much as some things change in biblical scholarship, many others remain the same."

—Paul N. Anderson,
Professor of Biblical and Quaker Studies,
George Fox University

THE
GOSPEL OF JOHN
IN MODERN
INTERPRETATION

Stanley E. Porter and Ron C. Fay

EDITORS

The Gospel of John in Modern Interpretation
© 2018 by Stanley E. Porter and Ron C. Fay

Published by Kregel Publications, a division of Kregel Inc., 2450 Oak Industrial Dr. NE, Grand Rapids, MI 49505–6020.

The Hebrew font, NewJerusalemU, and the Greek font, GraecaU, are available from www.linguistsoftware.com/lgku.htm, +1-425-775-1130.

ISBN 978–0–8254–4510–1

Printed in the United States of America

18 19 20 21 22 / 5 4 3 2 1

To All Those Johannine Scholars
Who Have Gone Before Us

CONTENTS

SERIES INTRODUCTION

The *Milestones in New Testament Scholarship* (MNTS) series fills a necessary place between a proper biography and a dictionary entry. Each person chosen as a subject of a chapter has had a major influence upon how scholarship, and usually along with it lay readers, have thought about a specific book, group of books, or topic in the New Testament. The history of scholarship leaves certain fingerprints that stand out more than others; yet many times some important makers of fingerprints are overlooked due to the time period in which they lived, the circumstances in which they wrote, or the influence of one of their contemporaries. MNTS will often shine a light on significant scholars who have been overlooked, while also giving space to those whose names are nearly synonymous with the books they studied.

The vision for this series is to cover numerous books and topics in the New Testament, with each volume providing a small snapshot of milestones in New Testament scholarship. We seek to balance canonical studies with textual and theological studies. This series will produce brief biographies of scholars who have had an impact on the study of a given book, corpus, or major issue in New Testament studies, and thereby established a milestone in the area. By looking at the lives of these scholars, the impact of their work can be felt. We have intentionally utilized an extended chronology for the chosen scholars, in order to show how their impact is felt by subsequent generations. Each article tells the story of a single person. It communicates the life circumstances, the influences on the person, and how that person impacted the specific area in New Testament studies. In turn, each volume of this series then tells multiple stories forming a timeline, and thus a narrative of the subject of each volume can be seen through the intellectual progression within the topic.

These volumes will then create a history of New Testament studies. In order to see how work in the Johannine literature has progressed, one would read the volume on John. To see how New Testament studies in general have progressed and to diagnose general trends, the entire series would be necessary. This allows both a deeper understanding of each individual subject and a more comprehensive view of how change in each subfield of New Testament studies has occurred. This makes MNTS perfect for those studying for comprehensive exams; those examining why certain trends in specific fields have occurred, wanting to understand the history of New Testament studies; or those wishing to see ideas embodied in the stories of the participants rather than simply in didactic material.

Our goal for MNTS, to fit in scope between a single biography of a certain scholar and an encyclopedia or dictionary of various New Testament interpreters, means that these volumes allow for a quicker read than a biography[1] but greater depth than a dictionary.[2] Each volume also allows the reader to approach each chapter individually, as each is a story with a beginning and an end. Since the chosen scholars are treated separately, researchers have a place to start when working on bibliographies. Since each chapter is written by someone working in the field, the nonspecialist gains a glimpse at how an expert understands and assesses an important scholar.

The purpose of MNTS is to open historical vistas normally closed to non-experts, without having to dig into sources not readily available. This approach gives the student shoulders on which to stand, the expert a quick reference tool, and the biographer a short sample. Our hope is that MNTS brings joy and information to all who use the series.

—Stanley E. Porter and Ron C. Fay

---

1. For example, Konrad Hammann, *Rudolf Bultmann: A Biography* (Farmington, MN: Polebridge Press, 2012).
2. For example, William Baird, *History of New Testament Research*, 3 vols. (Minneapolis: Fortress Press, 1993–2013).

PREFACE

Stanley E. Porter and Ron C. Fay

W e are pleased to be able to present these essays on milestones in the history of Johannine scholarship. These essays originated in the invited papers of the Johannine Literature Consultation (now Section) delivered at the Evangelical Theological Society annual meetings in 2014 and 2015. We were very pleased that the individual contributors were willing to include their papers in revised form in this volume. Johannine scholarship has not received as much notice as other areas of New Testament scholarship have over the last century or so. However, there are positive and encouraging signs that Johannine scholarship is gaining interest, with significant research being done by a number of important scholars. This scholarship promises not only to once again bring to the fore a number of major topics already discussed over the course of Johannine scholarship, but also to bring to scholarly attention new topics for exploration. We look forward to that continuing research and writing.

This volume, however, is not geared toward the future of Johannine scholarship, but to its past. We have included eight scholars who rightly belong in a volume that attempts to represent milestones in previous Johannine interpretation. The scope of their work extends well over a century and a half, from the mid-nineteenth century to the twenty-first. We do not believe that any of these scholars requires justification, even if some of them are more widely known than others, some of their positions are more positively viewed than others, and some of them may fit more widely known or endorsed theological paradigms. Brooke Foss Westcott will always be remembered as one of the major English scholars of the nineteenth century, and his work in the Johannine literature is only a part of a wide range of important scholarly research. Adolf Schlatter, though less well known in English-language scholarship, was in many ways a German counterpart to Westcott, as he tended to argue for traditional positions in the face of strong opposition from his colleagues within mainstream German New Testament scholarship. C. H. Dodd, another Englishman, was also a scholar of widespread interest and expertise, often translating ideas developed in German scholarship for an English audience. However, his views in Johannine studies pushed the discipline forward in a number of ways that have endured to the present. Rudolf Bultmann is simply Rudolf Bultmann—a scholar to whom most scholarship still must react, not because his conclusions have necessarily endured, but because the force of his scholarship has cast a long and enduring shadow over all of New Testament studies. This includes especially his Johannine studies, where his commentary on John's gospel continues to arouse deeply felt responses. John A. T. Robinson is known as a theological liberal who argued for conservative critical biblical positions. These are seen most significantly perhaps in his view of John's gospel and its relationship to other traditions about Jesus. Raymond E. Brown was also a scholar of wide-ranging interests, but some of his most important work was saved for the Johannine literature, where he was one of the formative figures in thinking about the notion of a Johannine community and its influence. Even though this position has been widely criticized in recent scholarship, it has been a dominating paradigm for more than fifty years in Johannine studies. Leon Morris represents the finest of evangelical scholarship. Not known as a critical innovator, he was a thorough and dedicated advocate of traditional conservative conclusions on the basis of detailed knowledge. He continues to represent what evangelical scholarship at its best can look like. Finally, R. Alan Culpepper marks a major change in Johannine studies, when he brought literary criticism to bear on the fourth gospel. He was at the forefront of a movement that has continued to provide an alternative to historical-critical readings.

We of course realize that there are many other worthy and able scholars who could have been included in this discussion. This is not the place to list such names. We realize that any books similar to this one—and the editors involved—will have various opinions on what constitutes true milestones in Johannine scholarship, but the list of worthy scholars would far exceed the confines of a single volume such as this one. We, however, are more than satisfied with our list of major scholars. These scholars represent a variety of methods, some of them innovators and others solidifiers. They represent various current issues in Johannine scholarship of their times, some of them on the avant-garde and others in defensive response to the onslaught. They represent some new departures and some well-established paths of endeavor. They also represent some new findings and able defenses of traditional viewpoints. One of the common threads that emerges in this series of essays is that each of these scholars endeavored to interpret the Johannine literature for his day and age, and as a result brought insights to the discussion. Our contributors are to be commended for their efforts to capture the sense of each of these scholars, whose work represent milestones in Johannine scholarship.

The editors wish to thank the contributors for their chapters in this volume. We wish also to thank those of the steering committee of the Johannine Literature Consultation/Section for their developing this program of papers over the years. We finally wish to thank those who attended our sessions, for their probing and critical questions that have helped to make these individual papers better representations of the work of these milestone figures in Johannine interpretation.

LIST OF CONTRIBUTORS

Bryan R. Dyer, Calvin College, Grand Rapids, Michigan

Ron C. Fay, Liberty School of Divinity, Lynchburg, Virginia

Joshua W. Jipp, Trinity Evangelical Divinity School, Deerfield, Illinois

Andreas J. Köstenberger, Southeastern Baptist Theological Seminary, Wake Forest, North Carolina

Stanley E. Porter, McMaster Divinity College, Hamilton, Ontario, Canada

Beth M. Stovell, Ambrose University College and Seminary, Calgary, Alberta, Canada

Robert Yarbrough, Covenant Theological Seminary, St. Louis, Missouri

INTRODUCTION TO
THE GOSPEL OF JOHN
IN MODERN INTERPRETATION

Stanley E. Porter and Ron C. Fay

INTRODUCTION

S everal histories of Johannine scholarship have been written, although not as many as is perhaps warranted by the intriguing scholarly history that attaches to the Johannine corpus, and in particular John's gospel.[1] This volume attempts to be one of those historical volumes. In this volume, we include scholarly presentations of eight scholars whose work constitutes milestones in the history of Johannine scholarship. We recognize that others might have chosen an entirely different group of scholars for consideration, and if we were to

---

1. See, for example, the older works of Benjamin Wisner Bacon, *The Fourth Gospel in Research and Debate: A Series of Essays on Problems concerning the Origin and Value of the Anonymous Writings Attributed to the Apostle John* (New York: T. Fisher Unwin, 1910) and Wilbert Francis Howard, *The Fourth Gospel in Recent Criticism and Interpretation*, 4th ed., rev. C. K. Barrett (London: Epworth, 1955 [1931]); the more recent Klauss Scholtissek, "The Johannine Gospel in Recent Research," in *The Face of New Testament Studies: A Survey of Recent Research*, eds. Scot McKnight and Grant R. Osborne (Grand Rapids: Baker, 2004), 444–72; and Stanley E. Porter and Andrew K. Gabriel, *Johannine Writings and Apocalyptic: An Annotated Bibliography*, JOST 1 (Leiden: Brill, 2013). The account we offer here is coordinated with the modern interpreters recounted in this volume.

produce further volumes on milestones in Johannine scholarship we would wish to include many other scholars as well. However, we make no apology for those who are presented here. Each of them clearly represents a significant figure in the development of Johannine scholarship. We recognize, nevertheless, that scholarship does not exist without context. Context in this volume indicates the personal context of the given Johannine scholar and the wider contexts of Johannine and New Testament scholarship and the world in which such scholarship is undertaken, both as a response to these factors and as a provocation to others. As a result, rather than simply presenting a variety of different ideas that have emerged in Johannine discussion—ideas related to dating, audience, historicity, origins, sources, community, relation to the Synoptics, theology, etc.—we have chosen to represent the development of Johannine scholarship through the work of particular scholars so that we may take their personal and larger scholarly contexts into consideration. The ideas that are central to Johannine scholarship are all to be found embedded within the work of individual scholars, and some of those scholars are the ones that form the content of this volume. In order to understand the history of Johannine scholarship more clearly—and with it, to place the individual scholars included in this volume within it—in this introduction we present a brief history of some of the major figures within Johannine studies, especially study of John's gospel. For the sake of discussion, we divide this history into seven periods, recognizing that these are not firmly fixed categories but represent general movements and trends within Johannine scholarship, especially as it is focused upon John's gospel. This framework will provide a suitable context into which to place the eight scholars who are represented in more detail in the essays presented in this volume.

THE EARLY CHURCH

At the outset, the early church recognized the place of John's gospel and its importance as a witness to the life, teaching, and ministry of Jesus Christ. From the earliest evidence that we have, John's gospel was placed together with the Synoptic Gospels, constituting the fourfold Gospel. However, the early church also recognized that there were differences between John's gospel and the Synoptic Gospels, even if these were not a hindrance to its being accepted as a reliable source for understanding of Jesus.[2] From the second century on, there is evidence, even if it is not as abundant as one would like, of the early church fathers knowing John's gospel, as evidenced through their various types of citations of it (e.g., Ignatius, *Magn.* 8.2; Justin Martyr, *1 Apology* 61), to the point that Irenaeus (AD 130–202)[3] places John's gospel with the other three gospels as reflecting the four directions of the compass (*Adv. Haer.* 3.11.8). It is only natural that their similarities and differences incited thought regarding their relationship. Clement of Alexandria (AD 150–215), probably writing soon after Irenaeus, inadvertently identifies three features of John's gospel that have persisted as critical questions regarding that gospel: authorship, date, and characteristics. Clement states "that John, last of all, conscious that the outward facts had been set forth in the [Synoptic] Gospels, was urged on by his disciples, and divinely moved by the Spirit, composed a spiritual Gospel" (*apud* Eusebius, *Hist. eccl.* 6.14.7 LCL). Clement is also attributed with saying that, of the gospel writers, John "at last took to writing," after the "three gospels which had been written down before were distributed to all including himself" (*Hist. eccl.* 3.24.7 LCL). The belief that John, the son of Zebedee and disciple of Jesus, was the author of the gospel, had a direct bearing upon the possible date of composition. Irenaeus states the influential view that John lived in Ephesus (*Adv. Haer.* 3.3.4) until the reign of the emperor Trajan (AD 98–117) (*Adv. Haer.* 2.22.5, both cited in Eusebius, *Hist. eccl.* 3.23.3–4), and that he published his gospel last from Ephesus (*Adv. Haer.* 3.1.1). Jerome (347–420) adds that John died in the sixty-eighth year after Jesus's death (*De vir. Ill.* 9).[4] On the basis of this evidence, the date for composition of John's gospel from early on was interpreted as occurring around AD 80–100, what has come to be identified as the traditional or middle date, although with some early church writers perhaps suggesting a slightly earlier date. However, its differences in some characteristics, in particular its theol-

---

2. For a concise and helpful history of discussion of John's gospel among the church fathers, see D. Moody Smith, *John among the Gospels*, 2nd ed. (Columbia: University of South Carolina Press, 2001), 6–10; and also Stanley E. Porter, "The Date of John's Gospel and Its Origins," in *The Origins of John's Gospel*, JOST 2, eds. Stanley E. Porter and Hughson T. Ong (Leiden: Brill, 2015), 11–29, esp. 13; cf. also D. A. Carson, *The Gospel according to John* (Leicester, UK: Inter-Varsity, 1992), 23–29; and Ruth Edwards, *Discovering John* (London: SPCK, 2003), 8–12.

3. We provide dates of birth and death for those writers other than contemporaries, so far as we can determine them, to help establish the relative chronology of the various movements that we are recounting.

4. See John A. T. Robinson, *Redating the New Testament* (Philadelphia: Westminster, 1976), 257, who disputes whether these references to John, Ephesus, and his age mandate a late date of composition.

ogy (as a spiritual gospel), resulted in a number of different proposals about how John related to the other gospels. Clement, as noted above, posited that John's gospel was written last, and took the Synoptics into account in writing a gospel inspired by the Spirit. Eusebius later wrote, reflecting the opinions of others, that the Synoptics as a whole were to be welcomed but that they did not contain the material about Jesus from before he began his preaching—something that John's gospel captured (Eusebius, *Hist. eccl.* 3.24.7–13). Origen (AD 185–254) took the occasion of differences between John and the Synoptics as an opportunity to reinforce the spiritual nature of John's gospel by noting how these discrepant passages could be interpreted anagogically, in which a mystical sense of the passage was found (Origen, *Commentary* 10.2). This view of John's gospel as written by John the son of Zebedee—and at a time that necessitated some understanding of a relationship between John and the Synoptics—was generally held both by the church and by scholarship at least until the first half of the nineteenth century, and by many still after that date.

On the basis of the reception of John's gospel among the early church fathers—including the supposition that it is mentioned less frequently among various writers compared to the Synoptics—the history of Johannine scholarship has for the most part endorsed the notion that John's gospel was early on cited and, more importantly, authoritatively used by heterodox Christians, in particular the Gnostics and Valentinians. It therefore was, so it is said, at first widely neglected by the early church until the time of Irenaeus and some other early church fathers. The reasons for this would revolve in particular around the spiritual character of John's gospel, as well as other dimensions of its thought such as its soteriology and eschatology. The major scholarly proponent of this viewpoint was the German scholar Walter Bauer (1877–1960). Charles Hill has traced the course of this scholarly discussion, which he calls "orthodox Johannophobia," dividing it into three periods: "Foundations: Bauer to Braun (1934–1955),"[5] "Heyday: Schnackenburg to Koester (1959–90),"[6] and "Uneasy Supremacy: Hengel to Nagel (1989–2000)."[7] The only

---

5. Including Walter Bauer, J. N. Sanders, and C. K. Barrett.
6. Including Rudolf Schnackenburg, Melvyn Hillmer, Hans von Campenhausen, T. E. Pollard, Ernst Haenchen, Raymond Brown, D. Moody Smith, Harry Gamble, F. F. Bruce, and Helmut Koester.
7. Including Jean-Daniel Kaestli, Jean-Michel Poffet, Jean Zumstein, R. Alan Culpepper, Michael Lattke, James H. Charlesworth, and Gerard Sloyan.

major scholars that Hill cites who call this consensus into question are F. M. Braun, Martin Hengel, Wolfgang Röhl, René Kieffer, and Titus Nagel, before Hill's own effort to show that the Johannine writings, including John's gospel, were not overlooked by the early church but were in fact rising in acceptance during the second century and not the source or possession of those within various gnostic circles.[8] Hill's work has had a strong effect on calling the previous consensus into question. The scholars he cites as advocates of the disputed hypothesis are not themselves early church authors, but their understanding and reconstruction of the Johannine church within early Christianity has had an important effect on critical scholarship, to the point of influencing scholarly engagement with the early church authors.

THE RISE OF HISTORICAL CRITICISM

As mentioned above, the state of discussion of John's gospel remained relatively consistent throughout the ensuing several hundreds of years, with traditional authorship of John's gospel being endorsed, and with it a date within the lifetime of an early follower of Jesus. The situation changed radically with the rise of historical criticism within Enlightenment thought. The seeds of historical criticism were laid with the rise of Deism and then the emergence of theological liberalism, with historical criticism as the eventual triumph of this philosophical reorientation. Deism created an intellectual vacuum that required filling with new theological, philosophical, and scientific thought. Encouraged by the Renaissance, a broad range of human intellectual exploration resulted, such as the rise of rationalism, naturalism, revived interest in classical knowledge, a distinction between dogmatic theology and the study of ancient texts, interest in recently discovered ancient texts other than the Bible, and advances in other areas of human learning that influenced questions of understanding and interpretation. Some of the areas that were most directly affected were: the nature of interpretation, textual criticism, the rise of the historical-grammatical method that ushered in historical criticism, questions of canon, the development of the field of "introduction" in biblical studies as an area

---

8. See Charles E. Hill, *The Johannine Corpus in the Early Church* (Oxford: Oxford University Press, 2004), esp. 13–55, for the discussion of the categories above. See Hill for reference to the particular works by these scholars.

concerned with questions of dating, provenance, and authorship, the Bible as literature movement, and the rise of biblical theology, among others. There were two major responses to such developments. The first was development of historical criticism and the other was a pietist response, with each of them evident in various forms in the responses to historical-critical thought regarding John's gospel.[9]

The result for textual interpretation was the desire to apply the same critical standards to the biblical texts as were being applied to other realms of human knowledge. Two major figures stand out in the transformation generated by historical criticism. In many ways, the history of Johannine scholarship has been a series of responses, both for and against, to their reconsiderations of the Johannine literature. The first major figure to argue for a major reconception of John's gospel in light of historical-critical thought was David Friedrich Strauss (1808–1874) in first his *The Life of Jesus Critically Examined*, and then his *A New Life of Jesus*. He placed John's gospel in the mid-second century and dismissed its historical value, along with any supernatural elements. He saw early affinity between John's gospel and various gnostic authors (as have many since; see above), as well as with developments in Hellenistic thought, and treated John's gospel as not historical but mythical, a work of what he called "fiction."[10] Strauss's work caused such controversy that he was fired from his university position and ended up in German politics after a career as a popular writer.[11] Nevertheless, his views were highly influential not only because of the boldness of his statements, but because he captured the tenor of the increasingly skeptical times. However, in some ways more important were the similar findings of Ferdinand Christian Baur (1792–1860), the first major scholar to argue rigorously for such a position and who functioned within the mainstream of academic theology. Baur examined the various levels of tradition and dated John's gospel to the mid-second

---

9.   This paragraph is dependent upon Stanley E. Porter, "The History of Biblical Interpretation: An Integrated Conspectus," in *Pillars in the History of Biblical Interpretation*, 2 vols., McMaster Biblical Studies Series 2, eds. Stanley E. Porter and Sean A. Adams (Eugene, OR: Pickwick Publications, 2016), 1–70, esp. 3–4 (the same pagination in either volume 1 or 2); cf. also 12–23 on historical criticism.

10. See David Friedrich Strauss, *The Life of Jesus Critically Examined*, trans. George Eliot from fourth German edition (London: George Allen, 1848), 71–73, 365–86, and *passim*; Strauss, *A New Life of Jesus*, 2 vols. (London: Williams and Norgate, 1879), 1:33–36, 77–101. For some reason, Carson (*John*, 30) says that *The Life of Jesus Critically Examined* was not translated until 1973.

11. William Baird, *History of New Testament Research*, 3 vols. (Minneapolis: Fortress, 1992–2013), 1:246–58.

century, perhaps around AD 160–170, a point at which its developed theology was confirmed and any connection with apostolic authorship was completely severed.[12] This marked a major transformation in Johannine scholarship, in which a number of scholars then adopted late dates for John's gospel, with the concomitant conclusions that the gospel was written independent of apostolic tradition. This relatively late date fluctuated from around AD 110–170, and included such well-known scholars, among others, as the highly skeptical and arch-critical Bruno Bauer (1809–1882), who followed Baur's date; Eduard Zeller (1814–1908), Baur's student, who argued for around AD 150; and the French polymath Ernest Renan (1823–1892), who argued for the gospel being written by a later follower who constructed the gospel around fictitious discourses; among numerous others.

The highly skeptical view of the Johannine writings, including John's gospel, became the mainstream of much critical scholarship, certainly in Germany, but increasingly elsewhere in western scholarship in the latter part of the mid-to-late nineteenth century. We do not include any contributor to our volume who has addressed the work of any of these important early critical scholars. However, in the essays we do make clear that many of them are responding, in some cases directly, to the views first propounded by Strauss and Baur, and promoted by many since.

TRADITIONAL REACTION

It would be unfair to say, however, that historical-critical skepticism swept all of scholarship away before its mighty brush. Almost from the outset, there were those scholars who disputed such findings. They were not as skeptical about any of the major issues regarding John's gospel. Hence, many of them reaffirmed traditional authorship or at least authorship by a close associate of John the son of Zebedee, did not doubt the fundamental historical reliability of the gospel even if

---

12. F. C. Baur, *Kritische Untersuchungen über die kanonischen Evangelien, ihr Verhältnis zueinander, ihren Character und Ursprung* (Tübingen, 1847), *passim*, according to Werner Georg Kümmel, *The New Testament: The History of the Investigation of Its Problems*, trans. S. MacLean Gilmour and Howard Clark Kee (Nashville: Abingdon, 1972), 137, 428, an opinion Baur apparently came to in 1838 and published by 1844. See also Baur, *The Church History of the First Three Centuries*, trans. Allan Menzies, 3rd ed., 2 vols. (London: Williams and Norgate, 1878–1879), 1:177–81. See Hughson T. Ong, "Ferdinand Christian Baur's Historical Criticism and *Tendenzkritik*," in *Pillars in the History of Biblical Interpretation*, 1:118–38.

they recognized its differing orientation and more theological stance (than the Synoptics), and did not place its date of composition so late as to sever the tie to apostolic tradition.[13] Some of the scholars who held to this traditional position (usually including a date of around AD 80–100) but who preceded Strauss and Baur were such scholars as Johann Albrecht Bengel (1687–1752), Johann David Michaelis (1717–1791), who argued for an early date around AD 70, and Johann Gottfried Herder (1744–1803). Concurrent with or after Baur, others who held to similar traditional views, usually including a date of composition of around AD 80–100, were such noteworthy scholars as Henrich Eberhard Gottlob Paulus (1761–1851), one of the major scholars against whom Strauss argued, Wilhelm Leberecht de Wette (1780–1849), Eduard Reuss (1804–1891), and Carl Weizsäcker (1822–1899). Friedrich Schleiermacher (1768–1834) not only considered John's gospel more reliable than the Synoptics but thought that it was written earliest of the Gospels.[14]

The publications of Strauss and Baur, as mentioned above, led to a seismic shift in Johannine studies so that many scholars began to assert a later date and a less reliable gospel disconnected from apostolic tradition. In light of this movement, there were two major lines of reaction. The first major response was that there were many scholars who continued to argue for the middle date of around AD 80–100, the connection of John's gospel with the Synoptics and apostolic tradition, and usually historical reliability. These Johannine scholars included such well-known authors as some of the early major commentators, the German Heinrich August Wilhelm Meyer (1800–1873) and the Frenchman Frédéric Louis Godet (1821–1900), along with Constantine Tischendorf (1815–1874), Brooke Foss Westcott (1825–1901), Bernhard Weiss (1827–1918), Joseph Barber Lightfoot (1828–1889), Fenton John Anthony Hort (1828–1892), Theodor Zahn (1838–1933), William Sanday (1943–1920), Adolf Harnack (1851–1930), Adolf Schlatter (1852–1938), and the important Roman Catholic scholar Marie-Joseph Lagrange (1855–1938), among others.[15] Tischendorf published

---

13. For this section, see Porter, "Date of John's Gospel," 13–16. See also Baird, *History of New Testament Research*, vols. 1 and 2, for more detailed treatment of the scholars mentioned.

14. See Baird, *History of New Testament Research*, 1:208–20; and Jan H. Nylund, "Friedrich Schleiermacher: His Contribution to New Testament Studies," in *Pillars in the History of Biblical Interpretation*, 1:91–117.

15. See Porter, "Date of John's Gospel," 14. See also Baird, *History of New Testament Research*, vols. 1 and 2, for more detailed treatment of the scholars mentioned.

a popular booklet or pamphlet in 1865, entitled *When Were the Gospels Written?*, in which he disputes the findings of Renan and Strauss, and probably Baur, regarding the date and reliability of John's gospel. Tischendorf places high credibility in the testimony of Irenaeus as a student of Polycarp to have known the authenticity of John's gospel. Tischendorf believes that this testimony indicates that John's gospel was written by an eyewitness to the events it reports, by a close acquaintance of Jesus, and independent of the other gospels.[16] One would not normally mention a popular level book as significant in this discussion, except that Tischendorf's aroused the ire of some of those scholars who were arguing for a later date. Edward Zeller refers to Tischendorf's booklet in a footnote to his book on the findings of the time, where he calls it a "pretentious and superficial pamphlet." He claims that his own view regarding the external evidence of John's gospel is not "in any way shaken." The reason is that "The most in this pamphlet is nothing more than a repetition," in a very confident tone, of apologetic observations long since controverted; while what the composer has lately added is so untenable, that it cannot cause any serious difficulties whatever to any one who has surveyed this department with a critical eye."[17] Lightfoot wrote three essays or lectures on what he called the "authenticity and genuineness" of John's gospel.[18] The first essay, which was delivered in 1871 and then published in 1890, discusses the internal evidence.[19] The second essay, which consists of

---

16. Stanley E. Porter, *Constantine Tischendorf: The Life and Work of a 19th-Century Bible Hunter. Including Constantine Tischendorf's* When Were Our Gospels Written? (London: Bloomsbury, 2015), 137–39, for the pages in *When Were Our Gospels Written?*, summarized on 96–97. See also Baird, *History of New Testament Research*, 1:322–28.

17. Eduard Zeller, *Strauss and Renan: An Essay* (London: Trübner, 1866), 38.

18. Joseph Barber Lightfoot, *Biblical Essays* (London: Macmillan, 1893), 1–44, 45–122, 123–93, and additional notes 194–98. On Lightfoot, see Baird, *History of New Testament Research*, 2:66–73; Ronald Dean Peters, "Brooke Foss Westcott, Fenton John Anthony Hort, and Joseph Barber Lightfoot," in *Pillars in the History of Biblical Interpretation*, 1:139–62, esp. 147–49. All three of Lightfoot's essays are reprinted, along with the notes for Lightfoot's commentary on John's gospel (previously unpublished), in J. B. Lightfoot, *The Gospel of St. John: A Newly Discovered Commentary*, The Lightfoot Legacy Set 2, eds. Ben Witherington III and Todd D. Still (Downers Grove, IL: InterVarsity Press, 2015), 41–78, 205–327. However, the first essay has had an inexplicable change in title, as well as having headings added presumably so that it serves as the introduction to the commentary. Similarly, a comparison of the photographs of the Lightfoot manuscript (between pp. 48 and 49) shows that at least in transcribing this particular portion of text the editors have not created a verbatim transcription of the manuscript but have taken large interpretive liberties, nowhere explained in the edition so far as we can tell.

19. This essay was also republished in Ezra Abbot, Andrew P. Peabody, and J. B. Lightfoot, *The Fourth Gospel: Evidences External and Internal of Its Johannean Authorship* (London: Hodder and Stoughton, 1892), 131–71, along with an essay by Abbot, "The Authorship of the Fourth Gospel: External Evidences," 3–108, that is also a major and enduring essay on the topic.

lecture notes from 1867–1872, discusses the external evidence. The third and final essay (1867–1868) also discusses internal evidence. In print form, these essays total nearly two hundred pages, and provide one of the most thorough examinations of authorship of John's gospel, certainly to that point but also since. In the first of his essays, Lightfoot states that, until within a generation of his writing (clearly referring to the historical-critics mentioned above), there had been only one exception (the Alogi) to the universal attestation of John's gospel being written by John the son of Zebedee, a position he himself then argues for at length. Although late in his life he claims that he was wrong on John's gospel, earlier in his career Sanday wrote two books in which he argued for a more traditional view.[20] In the first book on John's gospel, Sanday takes an inductive approach that leads him to the conclusion that the work was by an eyewitness who was familiar with Palestine and who had seen the events recorded, and that the author was the beloved disciple, John the son of Zebedee.[21] Sanday later returned to John's gospel, where he presents a similar view, even if perhaps slightly tempered in light of German criticism, of John's gospel, but where he continues to endorse its reliability and use of the Synoptics.[22]

A few scholars of this time even argued for an early date for John's gospel (pre-AD 70), and thus for a more intrinsic connection to apostolic tradition. The number arguing for this position remains relatively small, as the early date, apart from perhaps Schleiermacher, has remained outside of the major debate over the traditional or later date. Of these scholars, perhaps the best known during this period is Alfred Resch (1835–1912), the German theologian known for his several volumes on the words of Jesus and extracanonical texts, who argues for a date of around AD 70.[23] One of the possible reasons that such an early date is often dismissed is that it is usually argued on the basis of the supposed use of a present-tense-form verb in John 5:2 with regard to the pool of Bethesda still being in existence at the time of writing, an argument no longer supportable.[24]

---

20. See Baird, *History of New Testament Research*, 2:263–64, esp. 264.

21. William Sanday, *The Authorship and Historical Character of the Fourth Gospel Considered in Reference to the Contents of the Gospel Itself: A Critical Essay* (London: Macmillan, 1872).

22. William Sanday, *The Criticism of the Fourth Gospel: Eight Lectures on the Morse Foundation, Delivered in the Union Seminary, New York in October and November, 1904* (Oxford: Clarendon, 1905).

23. See James Moffatt, *An Introduction to the Literature of the New Testament*, 3rd ed. (Edinburgh: T&T Clark, 1918), 581–82, for others. Most of them apparently were pastors writing more popular works.

24. This argument relies upon treating the Greek verbal tense-forms as time-based, as well as analyzing

Despite the onslaught of continental, and especially German, historical criticism, there were those, especially but not entirely in the English-speaking world, who resisted its allures. This does not mean that they did not benefit from the rigors of German scholarship. Nevertheless, a number of scholars continued to argue for the traditional or even early date of John's gospel. This volume presents the work of two of those who responded to the developments within especially German historical criticism, Westcott and Schlatter. Westcott, the close friend of both Lightfoot and Hort, was an English scholar who not only held to similar positions as his Cambridge colleagues, but did so on the basis of his own prolonged study of John's gospel. He too wrote one of the enduring arguments regarding authorship of John's gospel by John the son of Zebedee.[25] Schlatter, who wrote a wide variety of volumes on various areas of the New Testament, was well known in German scholarship of the time for his traditional and conservative critical opinions. He is perhaps less well known in English-speaking scholarship especially on John, because his major commentary has never been translated from German into English. This volume hopes to help redress the imbalance in our knowledge of Schlatter.[26]

THE HISTORY OF RELIGION MOVEMENT

The history of religion movement had a significant influence upon Johannine scholarship. As William Baird states, the history of religion school "was a school without a teacher and without pupils."[27] The history of religion school is, therefore, an informal conglomeration of scholars with varying yet compatible beliefs about the development of early Christianity, comprising scholars associated in various ways with the

---

the verb εἰμί, "be," as a tensed rather than aspectually vague verb. Neither of these suppositions is necessarily true.

25. Brooke Foss Westcott, *The Gospel According to St. John: The Authorized Version with Introduction and Notes* (London: John Murray, 1881), v–xxxii. See Baird, *History of New Testament Research*, 2:73–82; Peters, "Brooke Foss Westcott," 140–44.

26. Adolf Schlatter, *Der Evangelist Johannes: Wie er spricht, denkt und glaubt: Ein Kommentar zum vierten Evangelium* (Stuttgart: Calwer, 1975), originally published in 1930; Schlatter, *Das Evangelium nach Johannes ausgelegt für Bibelleser* (Stuttgart: Calwer, 1899). See Werner Neuer, *Adolf Schlatter: A Biography of Germany's Premier Biblical Theologian*, trans. Robert W. Yarbrough (Grand Rapids: Baker, 1995); and Andreas J. Köstenberger, "Theodor Zahn, Adolf Harnack, and Adolf Schlatter," in *Pillars in the History of Biblical Interpretation*, 1:163–88, esp. 174–80.

27. Baird, *History of New Testament Research*, 2:222; cf. Porter, "History of Biblical Interpretation," 20–21.

university at Göttingen at the end of the nineteenth century. Some of the most important biblical scholars associated with the history of religion movement are William Wrede (1859–1906), Johannes Weiss (1863–1914), Hermann Gunkel (1862–1932), Albert Eichhorn (1856–1926), Wilhelm Heitmüller (1869–1926), Wilhelm Bousset (1865–1920), and Rudolf Bultmann (1884–1976). Non biblical scholars associated with the movement included Franz Cumont (1868–1947), an expert in oriental religions; and Richard Reitzenstein (1861–1931), an expert in mystery religions and other ancient religions; and the classicist Eduard Norden (1868–1941). The essential unifying factor for the school, such as it was, was their common approach to the study of religion. The history of religion school made a clear distinction between theology, which they associated with systematic theology, and religion, and they sought to study Christianity as an example within the larger notion of the history of religion. As a result, Christianity was viewed from the standpoint of the development of its traditions, rather than the literary relationships among its sources, and lines of connection and influence were often drawn to other religions, especially Greco-Roman religion and other oriental religions (such as Egyptian), to the point (in some extreme versions) of Christianity being seen as a syncretistic religion.[28]

In many ways, the history of religion movement was a result of the naturalism and rationalism of the Enlightenment regarding Christianity, especially in its rejection of traditional dogmatic or systematic theological categories. Wrede is best known for his work on the so-called Messianic Secret in Mark and on Paul as the second founder of Christianity, both of which have had a tremendous influence upon New Testament studies. Wrede, however, also wrote a significant work on John's gospel during the course of his abbreviated career. Wrede thinks that no book in the New Testament is so popular yet so misunderstood as John's gospel, which introduces a foreign world to the reader. For him, John's gospel is not a depiction of the historical Jesus in his humanity but an apologetic work in defense of Jesus as a divine character.[29] Weiss was ambivalent regarding his relationship

---

28. Baird, *History of New Testament Research*, 2:222–23; cf. 2:223–29, 238–53.
29. W. Wrede, *Charakter und Tendenz des Johannesevangeliums*, 2nd ed. (Tübingen: Mohr Siebeck, 1933), originally published in 1903. On Wrede, see Baird, *History of New Testament Research*, 2:144–51; Stanley E. Porter, *When Paul Met Jesus: How an Idea Got Lost in History* (Cambridge: Cambridge University Press, 2016), 51–56; and Dieter T. Roth, "William Wrede and Julius Wellhausen," in *Pillars in the History of Biblical Interpretation*, 1:189–98.

to the history of religion school, in that he wished to study Christianity and its beliefs in relationship to previous Jewish and Greek thought, but he did not wish to see it merely as the product of these other forms of religion.[30] Weiss is perhaps best known today as arguing for Jesus's realized or thoroughgoing eschatology (or apocalyptic view of Jesus), developed more fully in the thought of Albert Schweitzer (1875–1965).[31] More important here, however, is the fact that he was the teacher of Bultmann when Bultmann was a student at Marburg, where Weiss taught before leaving for Heidelberg. Bultmann wrote his initial doctoral dissertation on cynic-stoic diatribe and Paul's preaching style under the initial supervision of Weiss (though it was completed under Heitmüller).[32] Gunkel began as a New Testament scholar under the influence of the history of religion approach before becoming an Old Testament scholar, and was arguably the person who drew the group or movement together through his influential book, *Creation and Chaos*. This book argues that the creation account in Genesis 1 is dependent upon ancient Babylonian creation myths, and that this explains Revelation 12.[33] This approach clearly demonstrates the history of religion method. Gunkel's development of form criticism, in which language is varied in its use depending upon circumstance (or *Sitz im Leben*), was also a contribution from the history of religion. The best known of all members of the history of religion school, however, was Bousset. Bousset wrote many books that reflect the history of religion approach, but the best known today is his *Kyrios Christos: A History of the Belief in Christ from the Beginnings of Christianity to Irenaeus*. Bousset takes an evolutionary approach to religion, in which Christianity, even if it was the highest form of religion, was nevertheless the result of a developmental process. In *Kyrios Christos*, he traces how the complex religious environment of the first century developed into the worship of Jesus as the Christ, and then how it

---

30. Baird, *History of New Testament Research*, 2:223, 229.
31. Ibid., 2:229–37; and Andrew W. Pitts, "Albert Schweitzer: A Jewish-Apocalyptic Approach to Christian Origins," in *Pillars in the History of Biblical Interpretation*, 1:211–38.
32. See Rudolf Bultmann, *Der Stil der paulinischen Predigt und die kynisch-stoische Diatribe* (Göttingen: Vandenhoeck & Ruprecht, 1910); cf. Porter, *When Paul Met Jesus*, 57–58; Stanley E. Porter and Jason C. Robinson, *Hermeneutics: An Introduction to Interpretive Theory* (Grand Rapids: Eerdmans, 2011), 226–37; and James D. Dvorak, "Martin Dibelius and Rudolf Bultmann," in *Pillars in the History of Biblical Interpretation*, 1:257–77.
33. Hermann Gunkel, *Creation and Chaos in the Primeval Era and the Eschaton: A Religio-Historical Study of Genesis 1 and Revelation 12*, trans. K. William Whitney Jr. (repr., Grand Rapids: Eerdmans, 2006), originally published in 1895. See Baird, *History of New Testament Research*, 2:238–39.

developed further under the influence of Greek thought in the Pauline
churches, and then finally into the realized eschatology and deification
of believers in John's gospel.[34]

Bultmann is the only figure associated with the history of religion school that is included in our volume, and not necessarily
because of this association. There has been continuing question
whether Bultmann is even to be considered a member of the history
of religion school. Baird conveniently divides Bultmann's career
into two, with the first part acknowledged as having been strongly
influenced by the history of religion approach, and the second
part, under the later influence of Martin Heidegger (1889–1976),
given to his hermeneutical and theological period.[35] However, this
bifurcation may not be entirely accurate, as Bultmann evidenced
the influence of the history of religion approach throughout his
career.[36] The influence of the history of religion approach on Bultmann has been well-substantiated, and is especially true of its influence upon his approach to John's gospel. The initial influence of the
history of religion school is seen in Bultmann's doctoral dissertation
on cynic-stoic diatribe. This is a study of comparisons among various schools of religious thought based on their texts. This reflects
the influence of Weiss, even if Bultmann did not go as far as Weiss
wished that he had gone, and was useful in establishing the influences upon and style of Paul as author.[37] The second area of corre-
lation is seen in Bultmann's development of New Testament form
criticism. This reflects the influence of Gunkel upon his thought,
in which he seeks to define how the New Testament gospel
authors and the early Christian community shaped the discourse
of Jesus according to transmissional patterns that crossed religious

---

34. Wilhelm Bousset, *Kyrios Christos: A History of the Belief in Christ from the Beginnings of Christianity to Irenaeus*, trans. John E. Steely (Nashville: Abingdon, 1970; repr., Waco, TX: Baylor University Press, 2013), a translation of a work originally published in 1913. See Baird, *History of New Testament Research*, 2:243–51, esp. 249–51.

35. Baird, *History of New Testament Research*, 2:280 n. 221; cf. 2:280–86 and 3:85–117. On Heidegger, see Porter and Robinson, *Hermeneutics*, 57–69; and Edward Ho, "Martin Heidegger, Hans-Georg Gadamer, and Paul Ricoeur," in *Pillars in the History of Biblical Interpretation*, 2:96–118.

36. See Porter and Robinson, *Hermeneutics*, 233–35, depending upon the convincing arguments of Helmut Koester, "Early Christianity from the Perspective of the History of Religions: Rudolf Bultmann's Contribution," in Koester, *Paul and His World: Interpreting the New Testament in Its Context* (Minneapolis: Fortress, 2007), 267–78.

37. Konrad Hammann, *Rudolf Bultmann: A Biography*, trans. Philip E. Devenish (Salem, OR: Polebridge, 2013), 46–48.

boundaries.[38] The third is Bultmann's development of his view of demythologization.[39] His views of demythologization are both an acceptance of the need to demythologize and hence distance oneself from the mythology of the ancient world, but also an endorsement of the history of religion approach toward Christianity as a form of expression of ancient myth as also found in a variety of religions. The fourth area is Bultmann's broad conception of how Christianity fits with other ancient religions, seen in his 1949 publication of *Primitive Christianity*.[40] The fifth and final area of influence is in his approach to John's gospel. Bultmann wrote on John's gospel numerous times before he wrote his well-known commentary.[41] However, his commentary, despite being written relatively late in his career, still reflects the history of religion approach in a variety of ways.[42] This includes his claim that it is dependent upon Mandaean Gnostic thought. Even if Bultmann did not accept all the major tenets of history of religion methodology (such as the irrationality of religion), he did examine the New Testament from a mythological and eschatological viewpoint that minimized historicality and emphasized various types of religious syncretism.

NEW SOURCE-CRITICAL PROBLEMS

A revival of interest in various areas of Johannine studies occurred in the twentieth century. We are characterizing them here according to the development of new source-critical problems. We wish to identify

---

38. Rudolf Bultmann, *The History of the Synoptic Tradition*, trans. John Marsh (Oxford: Blackwell, 1963), originally published in 1921.

39. Rudolf Bultmann, "New Testament and Mythology," in *Kerygma and Myth: A Theological Debate*, ed. Hans Werner Bartsch, trans. Reginald H. Fuller (London: SPCK, 1953), 1–44, an essay originally published in 1941.

40. Rudolf Bultmann, *Primitive Christianity in Its Contemporary Setting*, trans. Reginald H. Fuller (Philadelphia: Fortress, 1956), originally published in 1949 with the title: *Das Urchristentum im Rahmen der antiken Religionen* (Zurich: Artemis, 1949) or "Early Christianity in the Setting of Ancient Religions."

41. Rudolf Bultmann, "Der religionsgeschichtliche Hintergrund des Prologs um Johannes-Evangelium," in *EUXARISTHRION: Hermann Gunkel zum 60. Geburtstag*, 2 vols., ed. Hans Schmidt, FRLANT 36 (Göttingen: Vandenhoeck & Ruprecht, 1923), 2:3–26 (in English as "The History of Religions Background of the Prologue to the Gospel of John," in *The Interpretation of John*, ed. and trans. John Ashton, 2nd ed. [London: T&T Clark, 1997], 27–46); and Bultmann, "Die Bedeutung der neuerschlossenen mandäischen und manichäischen Quellen für das Verständnis des Johannesevangeliums," *ZNW* 24 (1925), 100–46.

42. Rudolf Bultmann, *The Gospel of John: A Commentary*, trans. G. R. Beasley-Murray (Oxford: Blackwell, 1971), originally published in 1941.

several of these problems of particular value: synoptic relationships, other sources, and multiple communities.

The question of the relationship of John's gospel to the Synoptic Gospels has undergone significant change over the last one hundred or so years.[43] The nineteenth and early twentieth centuries in Johannine scholarship tended to argue for a dependent relationship between John's gospel and the Synoptics. As we have observed above, this relationship was virtually always seen as John's gospel being later, sometimes much later, and dependent upon the Synoptics in some form, whether one or more gospels. This conclusion is consonant with the view of John's gospel as historically unreliable due to its lack of relationship to apostolic tradition either through authorial or historical connection. There were exceptions to this perspective, especially among those who still argued for the moderate or even early date of composition of John's gospel; however, they were often considered, at least by many, as outside of the mainstream of critical scholarship.[44] The consensus in the early twentieth century was represented by B. H. Streeter (1874–1937), in his highly influential *The Four Gospels*, where he argued that John was dependent upon Mark and Luke.[45]

In 1938, the British scholar Percival Gardner-Smith (1888–1985) published a small book in which he argues, contrary to the consensus, that John's gospel is independent of the Synoptic Gospels. Gardner-Smith's approach is simply to acknowledge the consensus, but then go through John's gospel section by section to show what he considers a lack of dependence. His approach is forthright and straightforward, simply calling into question the assumed consensus.[46] The single most important scholar to accept Gardner-Smith's conclusions and develop his ideas further was C. H. Dodd (1884–1973). Dodd argued that

---

43. For various summaries and references to representative scholars in this section, see Smith, *Jesus among the Gospels*, passim; Robert Kysar, *The Fourth Evangelist and His Gospel: An Examination of Contemporary Scholarship* (Nashville: Abingdon, 1975), 54–67; Edwards, *Discovering John*, 14–15; and Stanley E. Porter, *John, His Gospel, and Jesus: In Pursuit of the Johannine Voice* (Grand Rapids: Eerdmans, 2015), 64–67.

44. An exception is Julius Schniewind (*Die Parallelperikopen bei Lukas und Johannes* [Leipzig: O. Brandstetter, 1914]). See Smith, *John among the Gospels*, 88–91.

45. Burnett Hillman Streeter, *The Four Gospels: A Study of Origins Treating of the Manuscript Tradition, Sources, Authorship, and Dates*, rev. ed. (London: Macmillan, 1930 [1924]), 393–426. On Streeter, see Paul Foster, "B. H. Streeter and the Synoptic Problem," in *Pillars in the History of Biblical Interpretation*, 1:278–301. Other scholars of the time who made convincing cases for this were Benjamin Bacon and V. H. Stanton.

46. P. Gardner-Smith, *Saint John and the Synoptic Gospels* (Cambridge: Cambridge University Press, 1938). See Smith, *John among the Gospels*, 37–43.

John's gospel made use of independent, previous oral tradition.[47] If Dodd is the single most important scholar to pursue this line, perhaps its most provocative is John A. T. Robinson (1919–1983). First in his *Redating the New Testament* and then in his *The Priority of John*, Robinson argues for John's gospel being independent of the Synoptics, which allows for a pre-AD 70 date for the composition of the gospel (as well as all of the books of the New Testament).[48] Robinson's notion of priority indicates that John had access to traditions at least as early as those available to the writers of the Synoptics.

As a result of this contrary view (found mostly in British scholarship), there are several streams of thought that have developed regarding John's relation to the Synoptics. The first stream is those who have continued to argue for a relatively direct relationship between John and the Synoptics. One of the key figures in this discussion is John Bailey (1929–1981). Although Bailey also thinks that John's gospel was dependent upon Mark, he argues strongly for its dependence upon Luke.[49] The position of Johannine dependence continues to be followed by C. K. Barrett (1917–2011) in his important and enduring commentary on John's gospel.[50] In this respect, even though he has written one of the most influential commentaries on John's gospel in the second half of the twentieth century, at the time of writing (certainly the second edition) Barrett's commentary was outside of the mainstream of critical thought regarding the relationship between John and the Synoptics. However, in some ways he foreshadowed further developments by maintaining his view of dependence.

The second stream regarding dependence is far more complex, in that it posits that John's gospel had a complex relationship with Synoptic material, possibly including the Synoptics themselves but

---

47. C. H. Dodd, *Historical Tradition in the Fourth Gospel* (Cambridge: Cambridge University Press, 1963), but also in his earlier *The Interpretation of the Fourth Gospel* (Cambridge: Cambridge University Press, 1953), especially his analysis in part III of the argument and structure of John's gospel. See Baird, *History of New Testament Research*, 2:265–66; Smith, *John among the Gospels*, 53–62; Beth M. Stovell, "C. H. Dodd as New Testament Interpreter and Theologian," in *Pillars in the History of Biblical Interpretation*, 1:341–66.

48. Robinson, *Redating*, 254–311; Robinson, *The Priority of John*, ed. J. F. Coakley (London: SCM, 1985; Oak Park, IL: Meyer Stone, 1987).

49. John A. Bailey, *The Tradition Common to the Gospels of Luke and John*, NovTSup 7 (Leiden: Brill, 1963). See Smith, *John among the Gospels*, 93–96.

50. C. K. Barrett, *The Gospel According to St. John*, 2nd ed. (Philadelphia: Westminster, 1978 [1955]), 42–54. See Baird, *History of New Testament Research*, 3:538–81.

not necessarily.[51] This broad category includes a wide range of proposals.[52] For example, Günter Reim argues for a two-stage compositional
process of John's gospel, with John's original framework being supplemented by material that is from a synoptic gospel now unknown to
us.[53] The French scholar Émile Boismard (1916–2004) argues that
John's gospel originated independent of the Synoptics but, through
a multi-stage developmental process, it utilized the Synoptic material and even the Gospels at various points along its way, until the
final gospel itself is dependent upon the Synoptics.[54] Frans Neirynck
(1927–2012) sees a similar complex relationship between John and
the Synoptics, but instead sees the Synoptic Gospels as fundamental sources for the gospel of John at the outset.[55] With these major
works of the 1970s, the consensus that had formed around Gardner-
Smith's proposal broke down, so that there were a number of proposals
that continued to develop regarding John and the Synoptics. One of
the most significant of these theories is that of interlocking tradition.
Rather than seeing the relationship between John and the Synoptics
as a developmental or chronologically linear one, even if complex in
nature, those arguing for interlocking or mutually informing tradition
see a shared tradition being utilized by both, so that in some instances
the Synoptics and in some instances John's gospel seems to assume
knowledge of the other. This view was first proposed by Leon Morris
(1914–2006), and has been followed by a number of more conservative scholars, such as the conservative Roman Catholic scholar Rudolf
Schnackenburg (1914–2002) (although without apparently knowing
Morris's position), D. A. Carson, and Craig Blomberg.[56] A somewhat

---

51.   There are more variations on these theories than we can discuss here. For example, F. Lamar Cribbs
      ("St Luke and the Johannine Tradition," *JBL* 90 [1971]: 422–50; "A Study of the Contacts That Exist
      between St. Luke and St. John," *SBL Seminar Papers 1973*, 2 vols. [Cambridge, MA: SBL, 1973],
      2:1–93) argues that Luke may have used John's gospel. See Smith, *John among the Gospels*, 99–103.

52.   See Smith, *John among the Gospels*, 141–58.

53.   Günter Reim, *Studien zum alttestamentlichen Hintergrund des Johannesevangeliums*, SNTSMS 22
      (Cambridge: Cambridge University Press, 1974); repr. with further essays as *Jochanan: Erweiterte
      Studien zum alttestamentlichen Hintergrund des Johannesevangeliums* (Erlangen: Verlag der Ev.-Luth.
      Mission, 1995).

54.   M. E. Boismard and A. Lamouille, with G. Rochais, *L'Évangile de Jean: Commentaire*, vol. 3 of
      Synopse des quatre Évangiles en français (Paris: Cerf, 1977).

55.   Frans Neirynck, "John and the Synoptics," in *L'Évangile de Jean: Sources, redaction, théologie*, ed.
      M. de Jonge, BETL 44 (Leuven: Leuven University Press, 1977), 73–106; and Neirynck with Joël
      Delobel, et al., *Jean et les synoptiques: Examen critique de l'exégèse de M.-E. Boismard*, BETL 49
      (Leuven: Leuven University Press, 1979).

56.   Rudolf Schnackenburg, *The Gospel According to St. John*, vol. 1, trans. Kevin Smyth (London: Burns

similar view, though not one that depends upon the interlocking of tradition, is proposed by Robinson, who argues that both the Synoptics and John's gospel make use of independent tradition, with Robinson arguing that John's gospel is also an early witness to this tradition.[57]

For those who treated the sources as independent of the Synoptics, alternative source theories were needed. Many of these have concentrated upon the supposed signs source, but have considered other sources as well (besides the Synoptic Gospels). Although he certainly was not the first to propose sources,[58] Bultmann in his commentary on John's gospel marks a turning point in source criticism of John's gospel, in his identification of three major sources: a signs source, the discourses, and the passion and resurrection accounts, along with some other minor sources. Bultmann was not the first to identify such sources, but was the first to argue as methodologically rigorously for such sources.[59] Source analysis has been continued by numerous Johannine scholars. Three important ones to note who have been formative of the discussion are Robert Fortna, W. Nicol, and Howard Teeple.[60] Fortna has authored two major books on the sources of John's gospel. The first one, concentrating on the signs source and the death and resurrection narratives, uses a variety of analytical stylistic criteria to establish and reconstruct the pre-gospel narrative signs source. In the appendix to his first volume, he provides his reconstructed text. He refines his analysis further in his second volume. In this volume, he builds upon his previous analysis but draws upon redaction criticism to provide a commentary on John's gospel. Nicol provides a more modest proposal than does Fortna (or Teeple; see below), and goes

& Oates, 1980 [1965]), 42; Leon Morris, *Studies in the Fourth Gospel* (Exeter: Paternoster, 1969), 15–63, esp. 40–63; Carson, *John*, 51–52; and Craig L. Blomberg, *The Historical Reliability of John's Gospel: Issues and Commentary* (Downers Grove, IL: InterVarsity, 2001), 53–54. On Schnackenburg, see Baird, *History of New Testament Research*, 3:396–407.

57. Robinson, *Priority of John*, passim. Robinson had a further formative influence on Johannine scholarship with his article, "The New Look on the Fourth Gospel," in *Studia Evangelica*, TU 73, ed. Kurt Aland (Berlin: Akademie, 1959), 338–50 (originally a paper given in Oxford in 1957), repr. in Robinson, *Twelve New Testament Studies*, SBT 34 (London: SCM, 1962), 94–106.

58. See Howard M. Teeple, *The Literary Origin of the Gospel of John* (Evanston, IL: Religion and Ethics Institute, 1974), 30–41, for predecessors.

59. Kysar, *Fourth Evangelist*, 14–16.

60. Robert Fortna, *The Gospel of Signs: A Reconstruction of the Narrative Source Underlying the Fourth Gospel*, SNTSMS 11 (Cambridge: Cambridge University Press, 1970); Fortna, *The Fourth Gospel and Its Predecessor: From Narrative Source to Present Gospel* (Philadelphia: Fortress, 1988); W. Nicol, *The Semeia in the Fourth Gospel: Tradition and Redaction*, NovTSup 32 (Leiden: Brill, 1972); Teeple, *Literary Origin*, part 2. See Kysar, *Fourth Evangelist*, 17–37, for presentation and analysis.

through a three-stage process of identifying or separating out the signs source. Finally, Teeple identifies four sources: a narrative source (he calls S), a Hellenistic mystical source (G), the work done by an editor (E), and the work of a redactor (R). Teeple then provides an analysis of the entire gospel differentiating these four sources, along with several other features. Arguably the most extensive effort to define Johannine sources is found in the relatively recent work of Urban C. von Wahlde, who argues for three editions of John's gospel.[61] In his first major book on the topic, he concentrates upon the Johannine gospel of signs as the original form of the gospel that was editorially expanded in subsequent editions. In his much larger and more developed commentary, he uses the aporiai and seams of John's gospel to analyze its three editions. There has been much critical response against these various source theories, with much of it focusing upon the ability of contemporary scholarship to identify stylistic features and various aporiai that might indicate sources, as well as the ability to reconstruct such a source without a means of verification.[62] Nevertheless, with current developments in Johannine studies (see below) such source theories seem to have decreased in significance.

The final source-oriented development to discuss here is various community theories. Community hypotheses regarding John's gospel are also forms of source theories, but they are less concerned with the positing of earlier documents then they are about reconstructing the early Johannine community that used these documents in the production of the Johannine literature. Although community theories of various sorts preceded him (often associated with sources),[63] Raymond Brown (1928–1998) was the first to offer the basis of a tentative community hypothesis regarding composition of John's gospel in five stages, from the traditional material through several editorial periods.[64] His community hypothesis emerged fully in his later work devoted specifically to the Johannine community. He there argues for

---

61. Urban C. von Wahlde, *The Earliest Version of John's Gospel: Recovering the Gospel of Signs* (Wilmington, DE: Michael Glazier, 1989); von Wahlde, *The Gospel and Letters of John*, ECC, 3 vols. (Grand Rapids: Eerdmans, 2010).

62. For a recent example, see David I. Yoon, "The Question of Aporiai or Cohesion in the Fourth Gospel: A Response to Urban C. von Wahlde," in *The Origins of John's Gospel*, 219–38.

63. E.g. Streeter, *Four Gospels*, whose theory is based upon geographical locations.

64. Raymond E. Brown, *The Gospel according to John*, AB 29, 29A (Garden City, NY: Doubleday, 1966, 1970), 1:xxxiv–xxxix. See also Brown, *The Epistles of John*, AB 30 (Garden City, NY: Doubleday, 1982). See Kysar, *Fourth Evangelist*, 39–42.

four phases of community development, within which John's gospel and the epistles are placed.[65]

However, the major figure responsible for the community hypothesis is J. Louis Martyn (1925–2015), who published his monograph on it in 1968. In fact, the community hypothesis is often identified with him. The community hypothesis posits a two-level narrative in John's gospel. The prelude to Martyn's analysis is that every telling of the story of Jesus has both a tradition and the unique character of the retelling that accompanies it. Martyn assumes that John's gospel originated with an earlier form of the account, something perhaps like the kind of narrative source that Fortna posits (Fortna was Martyn's doctoral student, when he was working on his narrative signs source). Fortna does not believe that John's gospel used the Synoptic Gospels. The source used was the form of their gospel used by the Johannine community when they were part of the synagogue. However, during their time in the synagogue the group grew in size and significance, to the point where they were expelled from the synagogue. Martyn examines several Johannine episodes that have similarities to the Synoptic accounts and finds that they are told differently in John's gospel, a process that he characterizes as a dramatization. Martyn examines the healing story in John 9 and finds the story and its dramatic development, which culminates in synagogue expulsion, as a template for the construction of the gospel. He then examines other synagogue expulsion accounts and differentiates material that comes from the time of Jesus (around AD 30), the first level of the account, and material that is part of the dramatic retelling that dates to around AD 90, the second level of the drama. Martyn finds similar patterns of dramatic retelling in other accounts, such as miracle stories (John 5 and 7), and likewise concludes in establishing a two-level dramatic narrative.[66] Whereas the Johannine community hypothesis came to dominate much of mainstream Johannine scholarship for a considerable amount of time (approaching forty years), the theory has

---

65. Raymond E. Brown, *The Community of the Beloved Disciple: The Life, Loves, and Hates of an Individual Church in New Testament Times* (New York: Paulist, 1979). See Baird, *History of New Testament Research*, 3:407–23.

66. J. Louis Martyn, *History and Theology in the Fourth Gospel*, 3rd ed. (Louisville: Westminster John Knox, 2003 [1968]). See Baird, *History of New Testament Research*, 3:604–22. For a different hypothesis regarding a Johannine circle, this one in opposition to one that produced the Synoptic Gospels, see Oscar Cullmann, *The Johannine Circle: Its Place in Judaism, among the Disciples of Jesus and in Early Christianity. A Study in the Origin of the Gospel of John*, trans. John Bowden, NTL (London: SCM, 1976 [1975]).

recently been called into serious question. One of the first to question the notion of John's gospel as a community product produced over time was Richard Bauckham in his attack on the notion of gospels as written for particular Christian communities, rather than for Christians more universally.[67] His view has been accepted and expanded upon by his student Edward Klink, who questions the idealized view of community and uses in its place a relational view of community that attempts to speak to a wide and varied audience.[68]

In this volume, we discuss several of those many scholars mentioned in this section, in particular Dodd, Morris, Brown, and Robinson. Whereas Dodd is indeed a well-known Johannine scholar, he was also a very diverse scholar who tackled numerous other issues in New Testament studies, such as form criticism, which further links him to the work of Bultmann. Morris, as will be mentioned below in discussing the conservative resurgence, has been part of a wider movement endorsing the historical reliability of John's gospel, and that emerges in his views of source relationships. Brown, though also with other interests, will always be known as a major Johannine scholar, with his commentaries remaining some of the major commentaries written in the twentieth century on John's gospel and the epistles. Although Robinson wrote on a variety of subjects, his work on John's gospel has continued to challenge scholars, not least because, despite his theologically liberal ideas, he advocated a variety of arguably conservative critical positions.

LITERARY AND SOCIAL-SCIENTIFIC THEORIES

There have been two major recent turns that have occurred in New Testament studies as a whole that have affected study of the Johannine literature in particular. The first is the rise of literary criticism and the second is the rise of social-scientific criticism. Although at some points, especially in the critical past, these two fields have had lines of convergence and confluence, in their present manifestations within Johannine studies they represent distinct approaches to the Johannine writings.

---

67.   Richard Bauckham, ed., *The Gospels for All Christians: Rethinking the Gospel Audiences* (Grand Rapids: Eerdmans, 1998), esp. Bauckham's "For Whom Were Gospels Written?," 9–48.

68.   Edward W. Klink III, *The Sheep of the Fold: The Audience and Origin of the Gospel of John*, SNTSMS 14 (Cambridge: Cambridge University Press, 2007). An apparent revival of at least a form of Martyn's view, but from a viewpoint that wishes to give more credit to the historicity of the first level, is Paul N. Anderson's so-called bi-optic view in *The Christology of the Fourth Gospel: Its Unity and Disunity in the Light of John 6*, WUNT 2.78 (Tübingen: Mohr Siebeck, 1996).

In the 1980s, there was a literary turn in New Testament studies that affected studies of John's gospel as well. These developments in other areas of New Testament studies, perhaps combined with general exhaustion over current debates, led to some new directions in Johannine studies that departed from traditional debates over authorship, sources, and history, and introduced new literary interpretive frameworks.[69]

Alan Culpepper was not the first to introduce literary interpretation to gospel studies. That honor probably belongs to David Rhoads.[70] However, Culpepper was arguably the first to do so for Johannine studies, where his work has had enduring significance. Culpepper's *Anatomy of the Fourth Gospel* is an exercise in what has come to be widely known as "narrative criticism," but was at its outset an attempt to bring the findings of recent literary theory to bear on interpretation of John's gospel.[71] As a result, Culpepper introduces the new terminology and interpretive categories to Johannine scholarship. Rather than talking about sources, forms, and redactions, Culpepper instructs readers in narrator and point of view, narrative time, plot, characters, implicit commentary, and the implied reader (his chapter headings). His reading of John's gospel directly employs the terminology gleaned from literary theory—narratology, the New Criticism, and the like—but is applied not to works of fiction or poetry but to John's gospel. The categories may not be new, but some of the insights have helped to avoid some of the previous problems of Johannine scholarship, especially as narrative art distances the text from supposed historical problems. The literary approach has had a huge impact on Johannine studies, and has resulted in a quantity of work being produced, even if not all of it has lived up to the promise of Culpepper's initial venture.[72] Some of the important work to note is Mark Stibbe's *John as Storyteller*, which treats John 18–19 from four different perspectives: practical criticism, genre criticism,

---

69. See Porter, "History of Biblical Interpretation," 23–32.

70. David Rhoads and Donald Michie, *Mark as Story: An Introduction to the Narrative of a Gospel* (Philadelphia: Fortress, 1982) with Joanna Dewey being added as one of the writers for the second (1999) and third (2012) editions. See Sean A. Adams, "Loveday Alexander, David Rhoads, and Literary Criticism of the New Testament," in *Pillars in the History of Biblical Interpretation*, 2:441–57, esp. 441–46.

71. R. Alan Culpepper, *Anatomy of the Fourth Gospel: A Study in Literary Design*, FF (Philadelphia: Fortress, 1983). See Porter and Robinson, *Hermeneutics*, 275–85.

72. See Stanley E. Porter, *Linguistic Analysis of the Greek New Testament: Studies in Tools, Methods, and Practice* (Grand Rapids: Baker, 2016), 278–92, for a summary of Johannine literary scholarship.

social function, and narrative-historical approach.[73] Few works have been as methodologically clear or as insightful into a passage as Stibbe's. Helen Orchard in her *Courting Betrayal*[74] recognizes the potential static element in Culpepper's approach—after all, it tends to be a summary of the previous thoughts of a variety of literary theorists, as good as they are—and attempts to introduce a more dynamic element into literary analysis by emphasizing social function. The introduction of social function opens up a new area of potential Johannine scholarship that we will return to below. The final work to note is the ambitious sequential reading of Peter Phillips.[75] In some ways, Phillips's work represents the apex of literary criticism by his bringing together an intriguing and apparently disharmonious group of theoretical orientations but it also represents the catastrophe of creating a complex brew of various theoretical pullings and pushings. This tends to represent much of what has happened to recent attempts at literary readings of John's gospel. They may avail themselves of various literary-theoretical approaches, but they do not always result in insightful and dynamic readings.

One of the insights of some literary readings of John's gospel is that the social function of the text is an important factor for gaining insight into how to interpret the gospel. The notion of social function fits squarely within the realm of social-scientific approaches to John's gospel.[76] There have been several attempts to approach the gospel from such a perspective, some of them influenced by literary and linguistic methods and others by historical concerns. One of the earliest social-scientific approaches to John was an essay by Wayne Meeks, entitled "The Man from Heaven in Johannine Sectarianism."[77] This article has had a lasting effect on a variety of Johannine studies. However, one of the first monographs to reflect the influence of the social sciences was Jerome Neyrey's *An Ideology of Revolt*.[78] In this

---

73. Mark W. G. Stibbe, *John as Storyteller: Narrative Criticism and the Fourth Gospel*, SNTSMS 73 (Cambridge: Cambridge University Press, 1992).

74. Helen C. Orchard, *Courting Betrayal: Jesus as Victim in the Gospel of John*, JSNTSup 161 (Sheffield: Sheffield Academic, 1998).

75. Peter M. Phillips, *The Prologue of the Fourth Gospel: A Sequential Reading*, LNTS 254 (London: T&T Clark, 2006).

76. See Porter, "History of Biblical Interpretation," 48–55.

77. Wayne A. Meeks, "The Man from Heaven in Johannine Sectarianism," *JBL* 91 (1972): 44–72. See James D. Dvorak, "Edwin Judge, Wayne Meeks, and Social-Scientific Criticism," in *Pillars in the History of Biblical Interpretation*, 2:179–203, esp. 189–98.

78. Jerome Neyrey, *An Ideology of Revolt: John's Christology in Social-Science Perspective* (Minneapolis: Fortress, 1988).

book, Neyrey examines the notion of the Johannine community—
and in that sense, this is part of the community discussion above—
from the standpoint of the sociology of knowledge of Peter Berger
and Thomas Luckmann (1927–2016),[79] but in a more specified form
used by sociologist Mary Douglas (1921–2007).[80] Neyrey is therefore interested in the intersection of the historical issues regarding
the early Johannine community and a sociology of knowledge that
sees Johannine Christology as reflecting the estranged social location
of the community. Also reflecting Berger and Luckmann, Norman
Petersen has written a small and intriguing book that draws upon
the work of Bruce Malina and his interpretation of Michael Halliday's view of anti-language.[81] Petersen argues that the Johannine
community redefines its language into an anti-language, so that the
terms have special meaning for the community. The social-scientific
trend in recent Johannine scholarship has become more focused in
some recent work on questions of empire. In such treatments, John's
gospel is seen as providing a counterargument to the language of
empire promoted by the Romans.[82]

The only scholar from this section discussed in our volume is
Culpepper. Nevertheless, Culpepper's work has not only stimulated
much further research into John's gospel, but his pursuit of literary analysis as opposed to (or in addition to?) the historical criticism in which
he was educated marks a significant move in New Testament studies.

CONSERVATIVE RESURGENCE

We conclude with a final section on authors who have been part of what
might best be called a conservative resurgence in Johannine studies. The

---

79. Peter L. Berger and Thomas Luckmann, *The Social Construction of Reality: A Treatise in the Sociology of Knowledge* (New York: Doubleday, 1966).

80. Mary Douglas, *Essays in the Sociology of Perception* (London: Routledge & Kegan Paul, 1982), esp. 1–30. See Dustin J. Boreland, "Mary Douglas: Living in Literature," in *Pillars in the History of Biblical Interpretation*, 2:204–29.

81. Norman Petersen, *The Gospel of John and the Sociology of Light: Language and Characterization in the Fourth Gospel* (Valley Forge, PA: Trinity Press International, 1993), referring to Bruce Malina, "The Gospel of John in Sociolinguistic Perspective," *Center for Hermeneutics Studies*, Colloquy 48 (Berkeley: Center for Hermeneutical Studies, 1985); and Michael A. K. Halliday, *Language as Social Semiotic: The Social Interpretation of Language and Meaning* (London: Arnold, 1978).

82. See, for example, Lance Byron Richey, *Roman Imperial Ideology and the Gospel of John*, CBQMS 43 (Washington, DC: Catholic Biblical Association, 2007) and Tom Thatcher, *Greater Than Caesar: Christology and Empire in the Fourth Gospel* (Minneapolis: Fortress, 2009).

twentieth century came to be dominated in many ways by discussion
of questions of authorship, sources, and, as a result, historicity, whether
implicitly or explicitly. These were often tied to the date of composition
of the gospel. However, while this discussion was continuing, there were
a number of authors who seriously departed in one or more ways from
the traditional view, not in literary-theoretical ways, but in their rejection of the dominant hypotheses of Johannine scholarship. This usually
meant departure from one or more of either a late or even a middle date,
the two-level hypothesis, source dependence, non-apostolic authorship, and the like. For example, even though he attributes the gospel
to four sources (Jesus, the Paraclete, the disciples including especially
the Beloved Disciple, and the narrator), Paul Minear (1906–2007)
believes that John's gospel is a martyrology testifying to the victory of
the martyrs, and was written pre-AD 70.[83] One of the most important evangelical Johannine scholars of this resurgence was Leon Morris
(1914–2006). Morris wrote widely on many areas of New Testament
study but is perhaps best remembered for his work on John's gospel. His
massive commentary on John's gospel was revised in a second edition,
and his Johannine scholarship was also reflected in several important
collections of essays.[84] Some of the other scholars who have followed in
Morris's steps include D. A. Carson, who has written several volumes
on the Johannine literature, including a commentary on John's gospel.
Even though Carson accepts the middle date for composition of John's
gospel, he widely disputes the various source hypotheses and gives high
credibility to the historical reliability of the gospel.[85] Craig Blomberg
has gone so far as to write a commentary on John's gospel in defense of
its historical reliability.[86] As already mentioned above, the scholar who
is perhaps most often and clearly associated with an early date for John's

---

83. Paul S. Minear, *John: The Martyr's Gospel* (Cleveland, OH: Pilgrim, 1984). See Baird, *History of New
    Testament Research*, 3:500–13, esp. 505.
84. Leon Morris, *The Gospel according to John*, NICNT (Grand Rapids: Eerdmans, 1971; rev. ed.,
    1995); Morris, *Studies in the Fourth Gospel*; and Morris, *Jesus is the Christ: Studies in the Theology of
    John* (Grand Rapids: Eerdmans, 1989).
85. Carson, *John*.
86. Blomberg, *Historical Reliability*. Although not all the contributors or editors are part of the
    conservative resurgence, the three (to date) volumes in the John, Jesus, and History project
    organized by Paul N. Anderson, Felix Just, and Tom Thatcher (as editors of the volumes), provide
    the opportunity for a wide range of scholars to participate. These volumes include: *John, Jesus, and
    History*, Volume 1: *Critical Appraisals of Critical Views* (Atlanta: SBL, 2007); Volume 2: *Aspects of
    Historicity in the Fourth Gospel* (Atlanta: SBL, 2009); and Volume 3: *Glimpses of Jesus through the
    Johannine Lens* (Atlanta: SBL, 2006). This work was preceded by Paul N. Anderson, *The Fourth
    Gospel and the Quest for Jesus: Modern Foundations Reconsidered* (London: T&T Clark, 2006).

gospel is Robinson. First in his book on redating the New Testament and then in more detail in his book on the priority of John, he argues that John's gospel, independent of the Synoptic Gospels but sharing their early date of composition, reflects an early, independent, and reliable witness in its account of Jesus.[87]

The arguably most significant of those who represent the conservative resurgence is Richard Bauckham. An historian by education, Bauckham has throughout his career engaged in rethinking the historical foundations of various areas of New Testament scholarship. We mentioned him above for his view on the gospels being for all Christians, a proposal that he applies to John's gospel as well as the Synoptics. Bauckham has throughout his scholarly career written numerous other works on the Johannine literature. A number of these essays have been gathered together into a single volume as a testament to disputing what he calls the "dominant approach" in Johannine scholarship.[88] He characterizes this dominant approach as minimalistic regarding traditions and reliability, but emphasizing a complex compositional history involving a staged process invoking the so-called Johannine community, especially Martyn's involving two levels. Bauckham argues against the entirety of the various features of this dominant approach. Rather than seeing a complex and involved process developing over time and involving a range of documents, with the result being an unreliable community product distant from its traditions, Bauckham instead argues for the Beloved Disciple—not one of the twelve disciples but a close follower of Jesus—as the source of John's gospel. This eyewitness testimony of the Beloved Disciple, supplemented by accounts from others of Jesus's closest followers, forms the basis of John's account, which was carefully nurtured until it was released for the benefit of all Christians. The result is that John's gospel, like the Synoptics, is an ancient biography about Jesus, not an apologetic or means of reconstruction of a Johannine community. This eyewitness testimony hypothesis has been extended by Bauckham to the other gospels as well.[89]

A second trend within the conservative resurgence worth mentioning briefly is a revisitation of the theological dimension of

---

87. Robinson, *Redating*; Robinson, *Priority of John*.
88. Richard Bauckham, *The Testimony of the Beloved Disciple: Narrative, History, and Theology in the Gospel of John* (Grand Rapids: Eerdmans, 2007), esp. 9–31.
89. Richard Bauckham, *Jesus and the Eyewitnesses: The Gospels as Eyewitness Testimony* (Grand Rapids: Eerdmans, 2006), esp. 358–471.

John's gospel. In contemporary scholarship, there had been a recognition of the humanness of Jesus even in John's gospel. In reaction to Bultmann, who saw this human dimension even though he believed that the gospel was written within the purview of gnostic influence, his student Ernst Käsemann (1906–1998) had departed from his teacher in emphasizing the divine depiction of Jesus, verging on Docetism. Käsemann's study, *The Testament of Jesus*, aroused critical response, some of it positive and other of it negative.[90] The result was an increase of interest in the theology, and in particular the Christology, of John's gospel. Marianne Meye Thompson has been one of the important conservative respondents in this field. In her first book, *The Humanity of Jesus*, she responds directly to Käsemann by establishing the basis of seeing the humanity of Jesus in John's gospel.[91] This has led her, among others, to a revival of discussion of the theological dimension of John's gospel. However, whereas much previous research has been concerned primarily with Christology, the new emphasis, at least according to Thompson, is upon the theocentric character of John's gospel, in which there is a pervasive influence of God the father upon the entirety of the gospel, including especially the relationship between God and Jesus.[92]

This collection of essays features two of those featured in the conservative resurgence, Morris and Robinson, both already mentioned above. Morris is tried and true in his evangelical credentials, having displayed them on various occasions whether he is dealing with matters of history or theology. Robinson finds common cause with evangelicals in his argument for an early date and independent character of John's gospel, giving it equal priority with the Synoptics. However, for all his conservative historical findings, Robinson was known, through his varied theological writings, to represent a liberal perspective on most matters. Nevertheless, he has raised important questions through the course of his research that merit further discussion.

---

90. Ernst Käsemann, *The Testament of Jesus: A Study of the Gospel of John in the Light of Chapter 17*, trans. Gerhard Krodel (Philadelphia: Fortress, 1968).

91. Marianne Meye Thompson, *The Humanity of Jesus in the Fourth Gospel* (Philadelphia: Fortress, 1988).

92. Marianne Meye Thompson, *The God of the Gospel of John* (Grand Rapids: Eerdmans, 2001); cf. Thompson, *The Promise of the Father: Jesus and God in the New Testament* (Louisville: Westminster John Knox, 2000). Her view is, by her own admission (*God*, 46–47), similar to that of Richard Bauckham, *God Crucified: Monotheism and Christology in the New Testament* (Grand Rapids: Eerdmans, 1998).

CONCLUSION

These are certainly not the only trends and developments that have occurred in Johannine scholarship over the last several centuries. There are no doubt many other areas, as well as individual scholars, that would warrant mention in the summary above, and other scholars will no doubt retell this narrative with other participants as their featured contributors. However, the history of Johannine scholarship as we are treating it in this volume revolves around various milestones in its scholarship that are represented in the essays included.

What we have attempted to provide in this summary of the course of Johannine scholarship is an overview of some of the major trends in especially its last two centuries. The framework that we offer has provided enough distinctions so as to illustrate the representative roles played by the eight scholars treated in more detail within this volume as evidencing milestones in modern Johannine scholarship. We have not tried to balance the categories or provide equal numbers in each of the major developments that we have identified. To the contrary, we have written this history independent of the choices made of participants, as a convenient way of interweaving the complex matrix of what comprises Johannine scholarship so as to help establish further connections among those represented.

BROOKE FOSS WESTCOTT: JOHANNINE SCHOLAR EXTRAORDINAIRE

Stanley E. Porter

INTRODUCTION

B rooke Foss Westcott (1825–1901) was one of what has often been called the Cambridge triumvirate.[1] This triumvirate consisted of Joseph Barber Lightfoot (1828–1889), Fenton John Anthony Hort (1828–1892), and Westcott. [2] All three of them were educated at Cambridge, became Cambridge dons and then professors, participated

---

1. For information on Westcott, I have found extremely helpful: Graham A. Patrick, *The Miners' Bishop: Brooke Foss Westcott*, 2nd ed. (London: Epworth, 2004), esp. 1–16 for his life, which I follow in the recounting below; Arthur Westcott, *The Life and Letters of Brooke Foss Westcott*, 2 vols. (London: Macmillan, 1903); V. H. S., "Westcott, Brooke Foss," in *The Dictionary of National Biography*, Supplement, III (Oxford: Oxford University Press, 1912), 635–41, which appears to provide the framework for Patrick; F. H. Chase, "Bishop Brooke Foss Westcott," *The Biblical World* 20.1 (1902): 9–24; Wilbert Francis Howard, *The Romance of New Testament Scholarship* (London: Epworth, 1949), 55–83; Howard Tillman Kuist, "Brooke Foss Westcott (1825–1901)," *Int* 7 (1953): 442–52; Stephen Neill and Tom Wright, *The Interpretation of the New Testament 1861-1986*, 2nd ed. (Oxford: Oxford University Press, 1988), 35–38, 74–81, 92–116; C. L. Church, "Westcott, B(rooke) F(oss) (1825–1901), and F(enton) J(ohn) A(nthony) Hort (1828–1892)," in *Dictionary of Major Biblical Interpreters*, ed. Donald K. McKim (Downers Grove, IL: IVP, 2007), 1038–43; and William Baird, *History of New Testament Research*, 3 vols. (Minneapolis: Fortress, 1995–2013), 2:60–82, esp. 73–82.
2. On the triumvirate, see the above, but especially Baird, *History*, 2:60–82.

---

in the first major English-language translation of the Bible since the King James Version, and faithfully served the Anglican church, with both Lightfoot and then Westcott becoming influential and effective bishops of Durham. In scholarship today, Lightfoot is probably the best known and best remembered, not least because of recent publication of some of his previously unknown and unpublished scholarship, but also because of his enduring legacy as a commentary writer and staunch adversary of German nineteenth-century liberal biblical criticism as fomented especially by Ferdinand Christian Baur.[3] Hort is occasionally mentioned, but usually for his part in the production of the Westcott-Hort hand edition of the New Testament, the first eclectic text using the earliest manuscripts and produced for widespread use in scholarship—especially for formulating the text-critical principles contained within the second volume. If Hort is remembered as a commentator, he is usually known for having started several and finished none. He also wrote a number of other works that are now usually forgotten (unjustifiably so, I might add).[4] Westcott is probably even less well-known for his accomplishments than is Hort, even if his name is more readily identified. He was the other half of the Westcott-Hort edition, produced several Bible commentaries—none of them very widely used today, by my estimation—and a host of other volumes usually overlooked and often difficult to find, perhaps because many were collections of sermons and addressed to issues of his contemporary church.

At one time, however, Westcott was one of the most famous and influential scholars in the English-speaking world, but today he is, even for most scholars, a recognized name to which a few general ideas may be attached, but no large ideas attributed. In this chapter, I wish first to trace briefly the life and work (apart from Johannine studies) of Westcott, and then turn to his signal contribution to Johannine

---

3. On Baur, see Horton Harris, *The Tübingen School: A Historical and Theological Investigation of the School of F. C. Baur* (repr., Leicester: Apollos, 1990), esp. 11–54; cf. Baird, *History*, 1:258–69; Neill and Wright, *Interpretation*, 20–30. Lightfoot's most important work in opposition to Baur was contained in his *The Apostolic Fathers*, 2 parts, 5 vols. (London: Macmillan, 1869–1885).

4. These include: Fenton John Anthony Hort, *The Way the Truth the Life: The Hulsean Lectures for 1871* (London: Macmillan, 1893); *Judaistic Christianity: A Course of Lectures* (Cambridge: Macmillan, 1894); *Prolegomena to St Paul's Epistles to the Romans and the Ephesians* (London: Macmillan, 1895); *The Christian Ecclesia: A Course of Lectures on the Early History and Early Conceptions of the Ecclesia and Four Sermons* (London: Macmillan, 1897); *Notes Introductory to the Study of the Clementine Recognitions: A Course of Lectures* (London: Macmillan, 1901), none of which were published in his lifetime, though several were published from his prepared papers.

scholarship, before offering an evaluation of the enduring legacy of his contribution. In the end, I believe that I will show that Westcott merits much more significant attention than he often attracts in the current scholarly climate.

LIFE AND WORK OF BROOKE FOSS WESTCOTT

Brooke Foss Westcott was the first of the Cambridge triumvirate born and the last to die. He was born three years before either Lightfoot or Hort, and lived twelve years longer than Lightfoot and nine years longer than Hort. He is the only one of the three to live into the twentieth century. Westcott was a Brummy—a person born in Birmingham in the midlands of England. He was from a relatively well-established family, with his father a successful college lecturer and his mother from a business family. Westcott was born twelve years before his only sister, so he grew up independently in a family that was typical of nineteenth-century England in its relatively straight-laced and nominally Christian environment. Westcott was precocious, and involved himself in a number of pursuits beyond simple academics. Some of these, such as his interest in painting and art, he would pursue for his entire life. For his secondary school education, he went to the famous King Edward VI School, known as King Teddy. He advanced quickly so that by the age of fourteen he was in the sixth or highest form, and as a result was given special tutoring by the headmaster of the school, James Prince Lee, who was known to be an excellent teacher (at least for the nineteenth century) and later became bishop of Manchester. Lee was the one who both introduced Westcott to serious scholarship and provided a model of piety and religious seriousness that had a strong influence upon him for the rest of his life. Westcott's interest in New Testament Greek apparently originated with Lee. Even though Westcott was characterized as "a small, shy, intense boy, who had a quick and eager walk, was devoted to work, and rarely joined in games,"[5] he was also recognized to have excellent intellectual prospects.

In 1844, Westcott went to Trinity College, Cambridge, generally regarded at the time as the most prestigious of the Cambridge colleges. There he read for both the classical and the mathematical tripos (or degree; the name "tripos" comes from the three-legged stool

---

5. Patrick, *Miners' Bishiop*, 2.

upon which candidates used to sit to take their final examinations for the degree). He established at this time a pattern of behavior that he followed throughout his life of rising early, eating little, and working late, as well as reading widely in a variety of subjects outside of those he was studying. During this time, his religious consciousness grew, in conjunction with his pious lifestyle. He became particularly concerned with issues of social justice, as well as with the diversity and even division within the Anglican Church. As Patrick states, Westcott longed "for the recovery of the apostolic simplicity of the Church."[6] Westcott at this time also recognized a call to vocational ministry. Westcott fulfilled his academic promise at Cambridge by winning various prizes in Greek and Latin during the course of his studies, and in 1848 he gained first class degrees in both mathematics and classics.

As a result of his superior academic performance, Westcott was able to secure a fellowship at Trinity College, so that he could support himself by taking students. Two of his students, Lightfoot (a fellow King Edward VI student) and Hort (from Rugby School), were later to become some of his closest collaborators, and another, E. W. Benson (another from King Teddy), would become Archbishop of Canterbury. The following year, at the age of twenty-five, Westcott won the Norrisian Prize for an essay entitled, "On the Alleged Historical Contradictions of the Gospels."[7] This essay was then expanded into his first book and published a year later with the title *The Elements of the Gospel Harmony* (1851), which took a *via media* in explaining difficulties in the gospel accounts by taking neither the highly skeptical approach represented in German higher criticism nor a naïve view that simply accepted everything as it presented itself. As Patrick notes, this book anticipated some of the controversies that were to erupt in a fuller form with publication of *Essays and Reviews* and the response to them.[8] This book regarding the gospels was later revised and further expanded to become his first major publication, *An Introduction to the Study of the Gospels* (1860),

---

6. Patrick, *Miners' Bishop*, 3.
7. See C. D., "The Harmony of the Gospels," *The Journal of Sacred Literature* 3 (1853): 600–86, here 665.
8. Patrick, *Miners' Bishop*, 4. See *Essays and Reviews* (London: Longman, Green, Longman, and Roberts, 1860), responded to in particular by *Replies to "Essays and Reviews"* (Oxford: John Henry and James Parker, 1862). Westcott, Lightfoot, and Hort took an intermediate position in the controversy. See Neill and Wright, *Interpretation*, 36 and note 2; C. K. Barrett, "Westcott as Commentator," in *Jesus and the Word and Other Essays* (Allison Park, PA: Pickwick, 1995), 1–14, esp. 4–6.

which went through eight editions (1896).[9] This volume consists of an introduction and eight chapters. The introduction sets the philosophical and religious foundation for his treatment, as well as offering a lengthy treatment of inspiration, which, for Scripture, includes both literal and spiritual dimensions to produce Inspired History. Chapter one concerns the historical background for the gospels; chapter two a study of the Jewish beliefs regarding Messiah, from the Old Testament to the later Jewish writings; chapter three the origin of the gospels, in which he defends oral tradition reflecting apostolic preaching as the basis of the written gospels; chapter four the general characteristics of the gospels; chapter five John's gospel in relation to the Synoptics; chapter six the differences in the Synoptic Gospels; chapter seven the matter of arrangement in the Synoptics; and chapter eight difficulties in the gospels. These chapters are followed by appendixes on quotations, inspiration, apocryphal traditions regarding Jesus, apocryphal gospels, miracles, and parables.

Also in 1851, Westcott was ordained as a deacon in the Anglican Church, and then six months later was ordained as a priest. Because of his decision to marry, he was compelled to leave Cambridge as dons could not be married, and eventually ended up as Assistant Master at Harrow School in 1852 and married near the end of that year a woman who was a strong Wesleyan Methodist. He remained at Harrow until 1869. The influence of his wife, Louisa Mary Whithard, was great upon Westcott, both theologically and especially personally, and he came to value family life in all of its dimensions and implications, as well as appreciating other Christian traditions. The master of Harrow at the time was C. J. Vaughan, a scholar of significance who was the first to use the work of Westcott and Hort on the Greek New Testament for his commentary on Romans.[10] Westcott benefited from his time at Harrow in terms of his scholarship, as it gave him impetus to retain his classical scholarship while also expanding his range of interests into the Greek fathers, where he identified with their incarnational theology.[11] West-

---

9. Brooke Foss Westcott, *An Introduction to the Study of the Gospels* (London: Macmillan, 1860). See Baird, *History*, 2:74–77; cf. Stanley E. Porter, "The Legacy of B. F. Westcott and Oral Gospel Tradition," in *Earliest Christianity within the Boundaries of Judaism: Essays in Honor of Bruce Chilton*, eds. Alan J. Avery-Peck, Craig A. Evans, and Jacob Neusner (Leiden: Brill, 2016), 326–45, for discussion of Westcott's legacy regarding oral tradition.

10. C. J. Vaughan, *St Paul's Epistle to the Romans* (London: Macmillan, 1859; 5th ed., 1880).

11. Incarnational theology seems to have been a feature of all three of the triumvirate. See Neill and Wright, *Interpretation*, 35.

cott's incarnational theology, grounded in the church fathers, became the basis for his social theory and the development of his later social thought.[12] It is fair to say, however, that Westcott was not well suited to the life of a school master, especially in nineteenth-century Britain. Westcott was more oriented to the disciplined life that he followed, rather than the boisterous adolescent lives of his students (an exception to this pattern was Charles Gore, one of his students, who founded the Community of the Resurrection, an ascetic Anglican religious order).

Nevertheless, it was during this time that Westcott and his former student and continuing friend Hort began their hand edition of the Greek New Testament. This project began in 1853 but was not published until 1881 for the text and 1882 for the text-critical volume, a project of twenty-eight years' duration. However, before returning to this project, note that there were six major publishing projects that Westcott undertook during his time at Harrow.[13] The first was his major work on the formation of the New Testament canon, entitled *A General Survey of the History of the Canon of the New Testament*.[14] Westcott divided canon formation into three periods. The first, from AD 70–170, included discussion of the apostolic fathers, the Greek apologists (e.g., Justin Martyr), the early versions of the New Testament, such as the Peshitta and the Old Latin, and the early heretics (e.g., Marcion). The second period, from AD 170–303, treated the canon of recognized books by such people as Irenaeus, Clement and Tertullian, the testimony regarding the disputed books, and the testimony of various heretical and apocryphal writings. The third and final period, from AD 303–397, included Eusebius, the councils, and, somewhat surprisingly, the sixteenth century and the editions and translations. Westcott clearly endorsed an early emergence of the New Testament canon. The second publishing project was his work in response to German higher criticism of the Baur sort, *Characteristics of the Gospel*

12. See Louis J. Voskuil, "The Idea of Cooperation: The Social Thought of Brooke Foss Westcott," *Fides et Historia* 16 (1983): 68–81.

13. During this time, Westcott also wrote a number of articles—"Alexandria," "Philo," "Monasticism," "Canon," "Herod," "New Testament," "Philosophy," and "Vulgate"—for *A Dictionary of the Bible: Comprising Its Antiquities, Biography, Geography, and Natural History*, ed. William Smith, 3 vols. (London: John Murray, 1863).

14. Brooke Foss Westcott, *A General Survey of the History of the Canon of the New Testament* (London: Macmillan, 1855; 7th ed., 1896); cf. his *The Bible in the Church: A Popular Account of the Collection and Reception of the Holy Scriptures in the Christian Churches* (London: Macmillan, 1864).

Miracles.[15] This volume included chapters on the miracles of nature, man, the spirit world, and conversion of Paul. The third publishing project was the institution of the well-known yet unfinished commentary series with his former students and colleagues, Lightfoot and Hort.[16] Under the influence of the publisher Daniel Macmillan, the three friends planned to write a set of commentaries on the entire New Testament. These commentaries reflected Westcott's *via media* in the critical debate, as they were both to utilize the finest in historical criticism and to recognize the character of the New Testament documents.[17] Westcott's assignment was to write commentaries on John's gospel, the epistles of John, Revelation, and (eventually) the epistle to the Hebrews, a task that he and he alone came close to accomplishing in the 1880s, even though the commentary on John's gospel as it would have been presented in the series was not finalized until after his death. (None of his collaborators came close to finishing their assigned tasks, although Lightfoot finished four of the commentaries and started at least five others, and Hort began three and finished none.)[18] The fourth project was a series of articles that he wrote on a range of ancient and modern authors, first published in the popular magazine *Contemporary Review,* several of which were later gathered together in *Essays in the History of Religious Thought in the West.*[19] This volume

---

15. Brooke Foss Westcott, *Characteristics of the Gospel Miracles: Sermons Preached Before the University of Cambridge with Notes* (Cambridge: Macmillan, 1859).

16. There was also a second commentary project involving the Old Testament. See Barrett, "Westcott as Commentator," 2–4, for fuller details on both projects.

17. According to Neil and Wright (*Interpretation,* 93–94) there were four criteria for the commentaries: critical, linguistic, historical, and exegetical, as well as being done "from faith to faith."

18. Lightfoot was to write on Paul's letters and Acts. He finished the following commentaries: J. B. Lightfoot, *Saint Paul's Epistle to the Galatians* (London: Macmillan, 1865); *Saint Paul's Epistle to the Philippians* (London: Macmillan, 1868); *St. Paul's Epistle to the Colossians and to Philemon* (London: Macmillan, 1875). We also have portions of similar commentaries (published posthumously) on Romans, 1 Corinthians, Ephesians, and 1 and 2 Thessalonians in *Notes on Epistles of St. Paul from Unpublished Commentaries* (London: Macmillan, 1895), on Acts in *The Acts of the Apostles: A Newly Discovered Commentary,* eds. Ben Witherington III and Todd D. Still (Downers Grove, IL: InterVarsity Press, 2014), and on 2 Corinthians in *The Epistles of 2 Corinthians and 1 Peter: Newly Discovered Commentaries,* eds. Ben Witherington III and Todd D. Still (Downers Grove, IL: InterVarsity Press, 2016). Hort was to write on the Synoptic Gospels and Catholic letters. After his death, the following incomplete commentaries were published: F. J. A. Hort, *The First Epistle of St Peter I. I–II. 17: The Greek Text with Introductory Lecture, Commentary, and Additional Notes* (London: Macmillan, 1898); *The Apocalypse of St John I–III: The Greek Text with Introduction, Commentary, and Additional Notes* (London: Macmillan, 1908); *The Epistle of St James: The Greek Text with Introduction, Commentary as far as Chapter IV, Verse 7, and Additional Notes* (London: Macmillan, 1909).

19. Brooke Foss Westcott, *Essays in the History of Religious Thought in the West* (London: Macmillan, 1891). See also Brooke Foss Westcott, "Comte on the Philosophy of the History of Christianity,"

contained individual essays on topics such as the myths of Plato (from *Contemporary Review*), Aeschylus (from *Contemporary Review*), Euripides (from *Contemporary Review*), Dionysius the Areopagite, Origen, Robert Browning, the relation of Christianity to art (a chapter later included in his commentary on the Johannine epistles; see below), and Christianity as the absolute religion. The fifth project from his time at Harrow was a work of theology, entitled *The Gospel of the Resurrection*.[20] This too is a work of apologetic value. Westcott begins with resurrection as the central tenet of Christianity, considering it both revelation and fact. After a chapter on various ideas regarding God, nature, and miracles, he discusses the resurrection and history, including the evidence for the resurrection in both testimony and the nature of the event itself; the resurrection and man, in which the resurrection has a key role to play in the relation of sinful humanity to God; and the resurrection and the church, in which the resurrection is central to the unity of the church. The sixth and final project was his publication of a history of the English Bible.[21] Westcott originally wrote this before becoming involved in the revision of the Authorized Version, so this volume is based upon recounting how English translations developed into the Authorized Version and its characteristics. He divides his treatment into what he calls "external" and "internal" history of the Bible. The external history includes Wycliffe's version, Tyndale, Coverdale, Matthew (Rogers), the Great Bible, Taverner, the Geneva Bible, The Bishops' Bible, the Rheims and Douay Version, and the Authorized Version as printed editions. Then he discusses the internal history, that is, the means by which these respective Bibles came about. Westcott's distinction of the history of the printed Bible and its translational principles is a useful one, not often differentiated by subsequent histories of the Bible.

As one might imagine, Westcott's scholarship was becoming widely recognized, so that in 1869 he became a canon of Peterborough cathedral, and the next year became Regius Professor of Divinity at Cambridge University (Lightfoot refused to be considered for this

The Contemporary Review 6 (1867): 399–421; "Aspects of Positivism in Relation to Christianity," *The Contemporary Review* 8 (1868): 371–86.

20. Brooke Foss Westcott, *The Gospel of the Resurrection: Thoughts on Its Relation to Reason and History* (London: Macmillan, 1866; 7th ed., 1891). The appendix on positivism and Christianity was previously published in *Contemporary Review*.

21. Brooke Foss Westcott, *A General View of the History of the English Bible* (London: Macmillan, 1868).

position, so that his friend could receive the appointment). He was relieved to be returning to Cambridge (where a married don could now have a position), as he believed that he could fully participate in the education of the new generation of clergy in an effort to bring vitality to the Anglican Church, although he retained his position as canon and spent three months in Peterborough during the year. Westcott took his church commitments very seriously, to the point of writing on the relevance of the cathedral in contemporary church life and on church architecture.[22] He believed that the cathedral should form a central position in church life, and so he did all he could to create such a vibrant and central atmosphere. As a result, he rewrote the organization of the psalms so that they could be sung more intelligibly.[23] He delivered numerous sermons while canon of Peterborough, many of which were published in several different volumes.[24] He also began at this time to lecture regularly on John's gospel, a book to which he would return many times. However, during the first ten years of his being professor, Westcott published very little serious scholarship, with his time taken up with his preparation of the edition of the Greek New Testament with Hort (Westcott was a full contributor to this project in every way) and with church and other matters.

During his time as Regius Professor in Cambridge, Westcott was reunited with both Lightfoot and Hort. Lightfoot was already the Hulsean Professor (a position he held from 1861 to 1875, then Lady Margaret's Professor until 1879, when he became Bishop of Durham, for which Westcott preached the sermon at Lightfoot's consecration at Westminster Abbey)[25] and Hort returned to Cambridge in

---

22. Patrick, *Miners' Bishop*, 7–8. See Brooke Foss Westcott, "Cathedral Foundations in Relation to Religious Thought," in *Essays on Cathedrals*, ed. J. S. Howson (London: John Murray, 1872).

23. Brooke Foss Westcott, *Paragraph Psalter Arranged for the Use of Choirs* (Cambridge: Cambridge University Press, 1879).

24. Brooke Foss Westcott, *The Christian Life, Manifold and One: Six Sermons Preached in Peterborough Cathedral* (London: Macmillan, 1869), on a range of topics, including the ascension, the Spirit, the resurrection, the sufficiency of God, actions and faith, and confession of God; *The Revelation of the Risen Lord* (London: Macmillan, 1881), with treatment of the character of revelation, revelation through love, revelation through thought, faith, the Great commission, spiritual sight, revelation in the work of life, revelation through active work, revelation through patient waiting, revelation of the kingdom, revelation in blessing, and revelation from heaven and on earth; and *The Historic Faith: Short Lectures on the Apostles' Creed* (London: Macmillan, 1883), with chapters on faith, creeds, nine chapters on the major sections of the creed, and nine notes on various related topics, such as religion, faith, divine fatherhood, christology, the blood of Christ, and the communion of saints, among others.

25. Brooke Foss Westcott, *From Strength to Strength: A Sermon Preached at Westminster Abbey on St. Mark's Day, at the Consecration of J. B. Lightfoot, to the See of Durham* (London: Macmillan, 1879);

1872 (and was then appointed Hulsean Professor in 1878 and Lady Margaret's Professor in 1887). In 1870, all three became members of a committee to revise the Authorized Version. The committee was called the New Testament Revision Company. The revision of the New Testament is symptomatic of a number of changes that were taking place in academic and church life within England at the time. Cambridge and Oxford Universities both abolished religious tests for entrance in 1871, so that those from churches other than the Anglican could be admitted. As a result, there was also a reconceptualizing of the relationship between the church and the university. Westcott delivered a number of sermons on this topic, later published as *On Some Points in the Religious Office of the Universities*.[26] The function of the university was not to be doctrinaire but to provide a broad knowledge that brought the Christian faith and modern knowledge together. As a further result, there was the need to revise the curriculum for the study of divinity, including the institution of a new BA degree that was broader than the BD. Westcott was a part of this process, especially as it had direct implications for those preparing for ordination. He helped to institute a preliminary examination for those entering training for the Anglican ministry, he was the head of the Clergy Training School in Cambridge, which eventually led to purchasing a building and becoming (after his death) Westcott House, and he served as a parish priest, which went with his Regius professorship. Some of his sermons delivered in his local parish were published as *Village Sermons*.[27] For his teaching, Westcott began as a church historian (there was no church history professor at Cambridge at this time), lecturing in particular on the creeds of the church, and a theologian. He published *The Gospel of Life* in 1892, his only book of what might be called systematic theology.[28] When Lightfoot left Cambridge in 1879 for Durham, to become bishop, Westcott then assumed a greater role in lecturing on the New Testament, to the point that he became a very popular lecturer with up to three

reprinted in *From Strength to Strength: Three Sermons on Stages in a Consecrated Life* (London: Macmillan, 1890), with two other sermons.

26. Brooke Foss Westcott, *On Some Points in the Religious Office of the Universities* (London: Macmillan, 1873).

27. Brooke Foss Westcott, *Village Sermons* (London: Macmillan, 1906).

28. Brooke Foss Westcott, *The Gospel of Life: Thoughts Introductory to the Study of Christian Doctrine* (London: Macmillan, 1892). See Baird, *History*, 2:73–74, who notes Westcott's incarnational theology in which the resurrection plays a central role.

hundred students in a class at a time. This was perhaps surprising for a man who had a high, thin voice and small stature—although he worked to make it possible to give such lectures. Perhaps most indicative of Westcott's shift to New Testament was the completion and publication in 1880 of his English language commentary on John's gospel, later revised and published on the Greek text (see below for more detailed discussion).[29]

In 1881, Westcott and Hort published the text of their Greek New Testament and the following year their Introduction and Appendix in a second volume—mostly the work of Hort, although the principles were agreed upon by both scholars.[30] This project represented the culmination of nearly thirty years of work. Also in 1881, and based upon the Greek text of Westcott and Hort, the Revised Version of the New Testament was published. Not only did Westcott (and Hort) provide their text for the Revised Version, but Westcott, along with Hort and Lightfoot, was involved in the translation itself,[31] and later published in 1897 a book with articles that he had written about this version previously published in the *Expositor* of 1887. The book was entitled *Some Lessons of the Revised Version of the New Testament*.[32] In his introduction, Westcott outlines what the revisers of the Bible had intended and their general procedure regarding various features of translation (e.g., synonyms, tenses, the article, pronouns, etc.). Then he treats topics such as exactness in grammar, how the Revised Version restored uniformities of language, how it marked differences of language, the conveyance of details, renderings regarding what he calls the Christian life, matters of

---

29. Brooke Foss Westcott, "The Gospel According to St. John," in *The Speaker's Bible Commentary*, ed. F. C. Cook, 6 vols. (London: John Murray, 1880), volume 5; republished as a separate volume, *The Gospel according to St. John: The Authorized Version with Introduction and Notes* (London: John Murray, 1881) (which I use below); *The Gospel according to St. John: The Greek Text with Introduction and Notes*, 2 vols. (London: John Murray, 1908). Westcott followed this with *The Revelation of the Father: Short Lectures on the Titles of the Lord in the Gospel of St. John* (London: Macmillan, 1884).

30. Brooke Foss Westcott and Fenton John Anthony Hort, *The New Testament in the Original Greek*, 2 vols. (Cambridge: Macmillan, 1881–1882). See Neill and Wright, *Interpretation*, 74–75; V. H. S., "Westcott," 641. There are many accounts of this edition. See Stanley E. Porter, *How We Got the New Testament: Text, Transmission, Translation* (Grand Rapids: Baker, 2013), 64–65. This is the only major accomplishment that is recognized for Westcott in Werner Georg Kümmel, *The New Testament: The History of the Investigation of its Problems*, trans. S. MacLean Gilmour and Howard Clark Kee (Nashville: Abingdon, 1972), 185–86.

31. For an account of their involvement, see Owen Chadwick, *The Victorian Church*, 2 vols. (London: A&C Black, 1966–1970), 2:45–56. He notes that the Westcott-Hort edition's readings were only accepted in sixty-four places (p. 48). See also Patrick, *Miners' Bishop*, 25–30.

32. Brooke Foss Westcott, *Some Lessons of the Revised Version of the New Testament* (London: Hodder and Stoughton, 1897).

creation, providence, and the person of the Lord, and then changes that were made to the changed text. This volume provides a model treatment of the kinds of issues raised by Bible translation, written by one who had dealt closely with both the Greek text and the translation itself. Westcott was also one of those involved in translating Wisdom and 2 Maccabees for the Revised Version of the Apocrypha.

Westcott and Hort's new edition of the Greek New Testament, along with the Revised Version, became centers of controversy for a number of reasons. These include the general strain on church relations that came about with the rise of modernism and the changes and innovations that were occurring in the nineteenth century. A second was the departure from the Textus Receptus that had formed the basis of the Authorized Version, as well as other versions of the translated Bible. There were those who thought that the implications of a new Greek text were that the text that had been the basis of the church for so long was now being undermined by new discoveries that were the product of modernism. The translation suffered a similar condemnation, as it marked the first major translation effort to secure such widespread endorsement and approval since the Authorized Version. On several different fronts there were those who thought that their Bible was being tampered with, and Westcott was accused of being one of the tamperers. Less controversial, but perhaps almost as important, was Westcott's publication in 1883 of his commentary on the Johannine letters.[33] I discuss this commentary more fully below.

Even though Westcott continued to grow in stature as a major scholar in Britain, his interests in the church also continued to expand. At this time, Westcott developed an interest in the modern missions movement, in particular missions in India. As a result of his interest, he studied other religions and developed his own theology of missions. Four of his sons ended up serving in India as a direct result of Westcott's efforts. Westcott also became chaplain to the Queen and was chosen as Select Preacher at Oxford two times. He also received an honorary doctorate from Oxford University in 1881 (DCL), followed by Edinburgh (DD) and Dublin (DD) in 1884 and 1888, as well as being made a fellow of King's College, Cambridge (1882). Even though Westcott was dismissed from his position in Peterborough, he then became examining chaplain to the Archbishop of Canter-

---

33. Brooke Foss Westcott, *The Epistles of St John* (London: Macmillan, 1883).

bury, and then was appointed in 1884 to be a canon of Westminster Abbey. Westcott maintained his position as professor at Cambridge, while spending time also preaching at Westminster and in residence in London in the abbey close to three months of the year. It was during this time that Westcott developed his strong and arguably progressive social concerns, even though he remained opposed to women being admitted to the university and opposed the elimination of Greek as a requirement for students of divinity. He became focused upon how his Christian faith could speak to the serious social and political concerns of late Victorian England. These concerns are reflected in two sets of sermons that he later published, entitled *Christus Cosummator*, published in 1886, and *Social Aspects of Christianity*, published in 1887.[34] He later became the first president of one of the most important Christian socialist groups, the Christian Social Union. He even purportedly contemplated resigning from his position at Cambridge so that he could devote himself exclusively to social concerns and causes. Despite offers to become dean of Lincoln and of Norwich, Westcott remained at Westminster, probably thinking that this would be his final ecclesial position. The year 1889, however, was a turning point in Westcott's life. In this year, he published his commentary on the epistle to the Hebrews, in partial fulfillment of his commitment to the commentary series that he had pledged to write with Lightfoot and Hort.[35] This commentary follows the same pattern that we will observe when we discuss his commentaries on John's gospel and the Johannine letters below. This means that he begins with an introduction, treating such topics as the text, title, position of the book within various canonical groupings, original language, destination, date, place of writing, style and language, outline, characteristics, history and authority, and relation of Hebrews to the *Epistle of Barnabas*. Westcott

---

34. Brooke Foss Westcott, *Christus Consummator: Some Aspects of the Work and Person of Christ in Relation to Modern Thought* (London: Macmillan, 1886); *Social Aspects of Christianity* (London: Macmillan, 1887). The former includes sermons on the destiny of humankind as fulfilled by Christ through suffering, Christ as the king priest, the universal society brought about by Christ, the new covenant, and several on the incarnation. The latter includes sermons on the family, the nation, the human race, the church, the kingdom of God, and the Quakers, among others. During this time, Westcott also wrote a number of articles—"Ambrosius," "Clement of Alexandria," "Demetrius," "Dionysius," and "Origenes"—for *A Dictionary of Christian Biography, Literature, Sects, and Doctrines: Being a Continuation of 'The Dictionary of the Bible,'* eds. William Smith and Henry Wace, 4 vols. (London: John Murray, 1877–1887).

35. Brooke Foss Westcott, *The Epistle to the Hebrews* (London: Macmillan, 1889). See Baird, *History*, 2:80–82.

concludes that Hebrews was written by one of a number of different people (but not Paul), sometime around AD 64 to 67. He then
offers a commentary on the Greek text, which is printed above the
double column commentary, along with forty-two additional notes
and an appendix on the use of the Old Testament in Hebrews. This
commentary is considered by some to be the finest commentary that
Westcott wrote.[36] However, in December of 1889, his longtime friend
Lightfoot died, and the last service that he performed in Westminster
Abbey was to preside over the funeral service of the great Victorian
British poet, Robert Browning.

With the death of Lightfoot, Westcott was appointed to succeed
him as the Bishop of Durham. There were those of the time who
thought that, despite all of his activism during the preceding years
(or perhaps because of it), he was unsuited to being the bishop of
such an important and ancient diocese. After some wrangling and
arm-twisting (of course of a political and ecclesial sort), Westcott
was appointed and persuaded to accept the position, in part because
of the opportunity to continue the legacy begun by his predecessor and friend Lightfoot. When he was consecrated as bishop in
1890 at Westminster Abbey, his other friend Hort preached the
sermon. Westcott was enthroned in Durham Cathedral on May 15,
1890, as well as receiving an honorary DD from the University of
Durham. Whereas Lightfoot had devoted his efforts to organiza-
tional issues in the diocese, as well as writing a number of important
works of scholarship, Westcott determined to apply the principles
of Christianity to the major social and political issues that society
was confronting. The major event that both illustrates Westcott's
concerns to integrate faith and practice and defines his tenure as
Bishop was the coal miners' strike of 1892. Coal had long been
important for the north of England, and the major issues were
not finally settled until nearly a hundred years later in the 1980s.
However, the relations between the coal owners and the pit workers
(this was the day before the coal industry had been nationalized)
had reached a particularly low level, and resulted in a three-month
strike in 1892. Westcott convened a meeting of both sides at the
Bishop's residence, Auckland Castle, on May 1, 1892, and mediated
a solution to the strike. Although the lasting benefits of the resolu-

---

36. Patrick, *Miners' Bishop*, 32.

tion were not what one might have imagined or perhaps even hoped (both sides thought the other unduly benefited), Westcott emerged from this major incident as ingratiated to those of Durham and an example of how a bishop with minimal practical experience could in fact solve a major social problem by drawing upon the strength of his Christian convictions. This is a pattern that he repeated several other times during his tenure as Bishop of Durham. He would convene various groups of representatives, some of them opposed to the others, to discuss major social and political issues of the day, whether these involved such topics as national insurance, housing, and other subjects. His beneficence extended throughout his sphere of influence to encompass the clergymen within his diocese. He allowed a diversity of theological thought although was more rigid on preservation of ritual within the church. He took a special interest in the younger clergy and continued to meet with groups of them in an organization begun by Lightfoot called the Auckland Brotherhood. He also endorsed a greater role for the laity in the activities of the church, as well as supporting foreign missions. No doubt in part because his wife had been brought up in the Methodist church, Westcott was amenable to nonconformists, in particular the Primitive Methodists. Soon after the resolution of the miners' strike, Hort died, leaving Westcott as not only the first born but the last to die of the three Cambridge companions.

In the closing years of Westcott's bishopric and his life, he was well-known throughout Britain. He spoke and preached widely, attended the House of Lords (as Bishop of Durham he was automatically a member of the House of Lords) as he was able, continued his activities with the Christian Social Union, and worked on various publications as he was able. Some of these publications were based on lectures that he had given through the years in Cambridge, such as his material on John's gospel, and others on more recent work such as his commentary on Ephesians.[37] He also published a number of volumes of sermons delivered during his time at Durham. These are found in *The Incarnation and Common Life*, published in 1893, *Christian Aspects of Life*, published in 1897, and *Lessons from Work*, published in 1901.[38] All

37. Brooke Foss Westcott, *Saint Paul's Epistle to the Ephesians* (London: Macmillan, 1906). This edition was prepared by J. M. Schulhof.

38. Brooke Foss Westcott, *The Incarnation and Common Life* (London: Macmillan, 1893); *Christian Aspects of Life* (London: Macmillan, 1897); and *Lessons from Work* (London: Macmillan, 1901).

of these sermons and the resulting books embody what Patrick refers to as his application of "his incarnational theology to the social questions of the day." These problems included "[p]overty, unemployment, class conflict, gambling, drink, the pressures of family life," in which Westcott addresses them both realistically and optimistically from his Christian standpoint.[39] By 1897, Westcott was showing the effects of his work and age, and his health began to deteriorate. Several tragedies also struck him. One of his sons died in Delhi in August of 1900, and then his wife of over fifty years herself died in May of 1901. He preached a sermon at the annual miners' gala in Durham Cathedral on July 20 of that year, the third time that he had preached at such an event, and died a week later on July 27, 1901.

Thus the reign of the Cambridge triumvirate, and in particular the work of B. F. Westcott, came to a close. He had been born three years before the other two, had been their teacher, and had outlived both of them by at least nine years. He was a devoted clergyman, a leader in church reform, a caring and effective bishop, but most of all he was one of the great New Testament scholars of his generation, and perhaps of any generation. He published twenty works of scholarship, along with another nineteen minor works, often of lectures or sermons or other short studies. He only published a few articles and chapters in other books. However, today Westcott is probably known for two things: as the coeditor with Hort of the Greek New Testament, and as a commentator on the gospel of John—if he is recognized at all as anything other than an antiquary of a bygone age.

WESTCOTT AS JOHANNINE INTERPRETER

At this point, I wish to turn to Westcott as a Johannine interpreter. As I have mentioned above, Westcott is often known, if he is known at all, as the coeditor with Hort of the Greek New Testament, and as a commentator on John's gospel. Westcott himself never saw published the commentary on the Greek text of John that he had envisioned. He published a commentary on the English text of the Authorized Version, but the commentary on the Greek version was prepared from the English version with some notes that Westcott prepared on some but not all of the chapters. This does not appear to be promising

---

39. Patrick, *Miners' Bishop*, 16.

regarding Westcott as a Johannine scholar. Nevertheless, once we have examined his two major works in Johannine scholarship, I think that it will become more evident why he should still be regarded as one of the major Johannine interpreters of his or of any generation. In fact, whereas Lightfoot was the historian and Hort the philosopher, Westcott was probably the best exegete among the three, perhaps one of the best exegetes of the modern era.[40]

Commentary on John

Westcott's commentary on John's gospel has an intriguing and protracted history (not unlike the protracted history of his edition of the Greek New Testament with Hort). As mentioned above, around 1859–1860, Westcott, Lightfoot, and Hort—under the influence of Daniel Macmillan—began their plans to write commentaries on the entire New Testament. Westcott apparently was already working on the commentary on John's gospel. However, as noted above, Westcott was also readily involving himself in other projects, until in 1869, rather than seeing his way clear to finish his commentary on the Greek text, he agreed to prepare the commentary on John for the *Speaker's Bible Commentary* on the Authorized Version. This was published in 1880. Westcott then published his commentary on the Johannine letters in 1883 (see below). From 1883–1887, Westcott continued to prepare comments for the Greek commentary on John's gospel, continuing to lecture on John's gospel at Cambridge in 1885 and at Westminster Abbey in 1887. However, along the way, there was a disagreement over which publisher would get this commentary, and it ended up with John Murray rather than with Macmillan. In the end, Westcott appears to have made notational changes to all of chapters 3, 4, 6, 7, 8, 9, 10, 11 and 12, as well as portions of chapters 1, 16, and 20, although in most instances these changes are relatively minor. There are other additions as well, including material from the patristic writers. His son, Arthur Westcott, who prepared the Greek text for publication, used Westcott and Hort's Greek text for the commentary, indicating some text-critical issues, along with the Revised Version as a translation since Westcott had worked on this translation.[41]

---

40. Neill and Wright, *Interpretation*, 36. For the fullest study of Westcott as commentator, see Barrett, "Westcott as Commentator," 1–14, although he concentrates upon the commentary on Hebrews.
41. Arthur Westcott, "Prefatory Note," to Westcott, *John*, 1:v-viii.

The task of reviewing the commentaries of Westcott is a large one, since his English language John commentary contains an introduction of ninety-seven pages, followed by 307 pages of commentary, and the Greek language one 195 pages of introduction and 670 pages of commentary along with the Greek text and translation.[42]

Introduction

Westcott's English and Greek commentaries have virtually the same introduction, except that the Greek commentary introduction uses Greek throughout. The introduction provides one of the fullest and most complete discussions of the range of Johannine scholarship in defense of the apostolic authorship of the gospel that has ever been written. The introduction begins with a discussion of the internal evidence regarding authorship. Westcott believes that there is indirect internal evidence from the gospel that the author was a Jew from Palestine, an eyewitness, an apostle, and in fact John the younger son of Zebedee (whose mother was Salome, sister of Mary).[43] He cites as direct evidence three passages: John 1:14, regarding the author seeing the incarnate logos; 19:35, regarding the author bearing witness to what he has seen as a true witness; and 21:24, regarding the witness and the writer being the same one. Westcott also surveys the external evidence. Then, on this basis, he speaks in more detail regarding the composition of the gospel in relation to a number of factors:[44] the author both within and outside of the gospel as John the son of Zebedee; the occasion and date of the gospel as being written from Ephesus in the last decade of the first century, that is, by someone who had seen the temple standing; the object of the gospel to elicit a response of belief in its hearers (John 20:30–31, with the present subjunctive, even though he refers to those who are coming to faith, contrary to many more recent commentators); the organization of the gospel, in which John 21 as an epilogue was written by John but appended later; the direct, coordinated and sometimes repetitious style; its historical

---

42.   For another summary, see Baird, *History*, 2:77–80; Tord Larsson, *God in the Fourth Gospel: A Hermeneutical Study of the History of Interpretations*, CBNT 35 (Stockholm: Almqvist & Wiksell International, 2001), 101–106. For evaluation, see Neill and Wright, *Interpretation*, 99–101, 158–59.

43.   See Baird, *History*, 2:78.

44.   See Edwyn Clement Hoskyns, *The Fourth Gospel*, ed. Francis Noel Davey, 2nd ed. (London: Faber and Faber, 1947), 41–44, esp. 42, where he notes that the section on composition is where Westcott's account becomes particularly interesting. He calls Westcott's commentary the classic Johannine commentary.

exactness, including the verbal parallels with the Johannine epistles; and the peculiar problems of the last discourses, with their interesting mix of authorial and dominical wording. In the next section, Westcott defines the characteristics of the gospel in relation to four factors: the Old Testament, which is fulfilled in Christ; the Messianic idea, which is unfolded throughout the gospel; the dramatically developed characters depicted in the gospel; and the widespread and unifying symbolism found throughout the gospel. After considering the gospel itself in detail, Westcott turns to the relation of John's gospel to other important writings. These include: the Synoptic Gospels, in relation to which John's gospel, with its own limited scope, nevertheless evidences overlap with similar tradition as is found with the Synoptics; the book of Revelation, which forms the element that doctrinally unites John's gospel with the Synoptics; and the Johannine epistles, which serve as a type of commentary or form of application of the history found in the gospel. In the final section, Westcott discusses the history of John's gospel in relation to both its text, where he cites the important evidence found in the early majuscule texts, and the interpretation of it, beginning with Heracleon's commentary and continuing through Origen, Augustine, and others.

When Westcott's introduction is compared to other introductory statements regarding John's gospel, we note a number of important differences. One is the sheer breadth and depth of his knowledge. Whereas Bultmann considered it unnecessary to provide an introduction to his commentary on John (one was later added by Walter Schmithals, because, after all, a commentary cannot not have an introduction!), and others have been content with short introductions, Westcott provides a thorough introduction that deals with a wide range of topics, from authorship and date to history of reception (a hundred years before history of reception became important for New Testament studies), and from textual criticism to Synoptic relations. He does not merely introduce the topics or simply provide his answers, but he provides discussion of the evidence and the options to consider. A second is the boldness of his statement regarding authorship. We must remember that earlier in the nineteenth century (when this introduction was first published), David Friedrich Strauss and F. C. Baur had both contended that John's gospel was a second-generation Christian work, written in the middle of the second century. For both Strauss and especially Baur, this temporal placement of John's gospel fit well their reconstructions of early Christianity.[45] Westcott responds directly to this position on most if not all fronts. He first offers a reasoned defense of traditional authorship, citing both direct and indirect internal evidence, along with the support from the external evidence. He then offers a chronological reconstruction that addresses most of the issues raised by the Tübingen school, apparently consciously placing the gospel within a different framework. For Westcott, the gospel is an eyewitness account by someone who both saw Jesus along with the temple standing, and wrote from that framework. The third difference is the conservative nature of Westcott's conclusions. Westcott not only accepts traditional Johannine authorship, but he argues for both the historicity and the valid theology of the gospel. However, he is also not simply one to repeat uncritically views that he holds. He claims that John 21 is a Johannine epilogue, he appreciates the symbolism throughout the gospel, and he sees its purpose as addressing the issue of true testimony for the purpose of leading to faith (even though he goes against the usual equation of the present subjunctive with Christian address).

English and Greek Commentaries on John

I now turn to the commentary (or commentaries) itself. I will treat both the English and Greek-based commentaries at the same time (giving priority to the Greek commentary), because there is significant overlap between the two, only addressing the matter of where they depart from each other where such comments reflect an important change in Westcott's thought. I am brief and selective in my comments, and of course other passages might just as easily be selected. I have selected passages that are important in the commentary tradition on John and that offer insight into the approach of Westcott, realizing that others may well choose other passages.

1:1–18: Prologue. Westcott takes the length of the Prologue as extending from John 1:1 to 18. Westcott's distinctive regarding the prologue is that he believes that John 1:1 stands on its own as a kind of title of the gospel. His heading for this section is: "The Word in His

---

45. For discussion, see Stanley E. Porter, "The Date of John's Gospel and Its Origins," in *The Origins of John's Gospel*, eds. Stanley E. Porter and Hughson T. Ong, JOST 2 (Leiden: Brill, 2016), 11–29.

Absolute, eternal Being."[46] John 1:2–18 forms the rest of the prologue, entitled: "The Word in Relation to Creation."[47] Regarding the body of the prologue, Westcott sees it as reflecting the thought of Genesis 1, with the logos terminology found in Jewish *memra*, rather than Hellenistic Judaism's understanding of *logos*. He believes that "word" should be retained in translations. He takes the final clause in John 1:3 with verse 4, rather than with verse 3: "what came about in him was life, and the life. . . ." In verse 6 he takes the two verbs, "become" and "sent," not as periphrastic but as indicating the person (coming into being) and mission (being sent) of John the Baptist. In verse 14, which he sees as an unusually constructed verse, Westcott finds not only the incarnation clearly expressed, but the "miraculous Conception" as well.[48] Becoming flesh describes the incarnation as "complete," "real," "permanent," "universal," and "united in one Person."[49]

2:13–22: Cleansing of the Temple. Westcott argues that there were two temple cleansings, and John records the first. Westcott recognizes the difficulties in relation to the Synoptic Gospels, and that the two events are equated. He disagrees with this analysis for a number of reasons. These include the contextual connections of the accounts to their respective situations, the different justifications for the actions (Mark 11:17; John 2:16), the different nature of the cleansing itself, the single, unified act of John's account versus the protracted nature of the Synoptic account (Mark 11:16), the different atmosphere of the accounts, and the lack of improbability in there being two cleansings. John's cleansing also fits well within the flow of John's argument.[50]

3:3: "from above" or "again." Westcott includes an additional note on the use of the word variously translated "from above" or "again" in the Nicodemus episode. Whereas the tendency among interpreters is to play the meanings off of each other, and to maintain that there may be ambiguity in the usage, Westcott takes a different approach. In fact, in an interesting coincidence and anticipation of later lexical developments, he notes that the word has a fundamental sense that is used

---

46. Westcott, *John*, Greek 1:2; English 1.
47. Ibid., Greek 1:3; English 1.
48. Ibid., Greek 1:19; English 10.
49. Ibid., Greek 1:20; English 11.
50. See Ibid., Greek 1:96–97; English 44.

throughout the gospels, but that it has two different interpretations in this context that both derive from the common meaning. The first interpretation is "from the beginning," "over again," and "anew," and the second is "from above," "from heaven." Westcott himself notes the variation among translators (although he notes that Tyndale rendered it "anew"). Westcott cites but dismisses the major arguments for "from above," noting that parallels use different wordings and the lack of contextual support for this rendering. He instead notes that Nicodemus uses the term to mean not born from God but reborn. Thus, the best rendering is "again" or "anew."[51]

4:1–41: Samaritan Woman. Westcott treats Jesus's meeting and conversation with the Samaritan woman as having elements of being the reporting of an eyewitness, even though it is found only in John's gospel. To be more specific, the account of Jesus's conversation with the Samaritan woman in verses 4–26 is ordered in such a way as to be "perfectly natural." By this, he means that Jesus's "simple request" elicits the entire conversation, which ranges over a number of topics that emerge from the question, such as the differences between the Jews and Samaritans, and all that follows from it.[52]

7:53–8:11: Woman Caught in Adultery. Westcott comments on these verses in his English commentary, because they are included in the Authorized Version. He introduces the section by noting that this is what he calls "a most characteristic incident in the Lord's life," but he also says that it "is certainly not a part of St John's narrative."[53] He includes an additional note in which he examines the external and internal evidence, the best of which, he believes, indicates that it is not to be included.[54] Nevertheless, because the verses do appear in the translation upon which he is commentating, he includes a commentary upon them. However, in the Greek commentary, Westcott does not comment upon the verses. In fact, he does not include them at all in his volume. Volume one ends at 7:52 and volume two begins at 8:12, with no comment regarding the text in question.

---

51. Ibid., Greek 1:136–37; English 63.
52. Ibid., Greek 1:142, 144; English 66, 67.
53. Ibid., English 125.
54. Ibid., English 140–41.

8:58: Abraham and Jesus. Westcott has an extended discussion of John 8:48–59. When he arrives at 8:58, he is clear in his results. Regarding the reference to Abraham in verse 58, he states: "There can be no doubt as to the meaning of the final answer which follows as a natural climax to what had been said before. Abraham died: Christ was the giver of life. Abraham was the father of the Jews: Christ was the centre of Abraham's hope. Abraham came into being as a man: Christ is essentially as God."[55] Then regarding the use of the "I am" terminology, he concludes: "The phrase marks a timeless existence. In this connexion 'I was' would have expressed simple priority. Thus there is in the phrase the contrast between the created and the uncreated, and the temporal and the eternal."[56]

9:22: Expulsion from the Synagogue. This verse has been at the heart of much scholarly discussion, and forms one of the central passages for development of the two-level or multi-stage view of John's gospel, promoted by such scholars as J. Louis Martyn and Raymond Brown, along with many who have followed them.[57] There has been a recent reaction against such an analysis, in which the gospel is said to function on two levels, that of the narrative and that of the historical context of those to whom it was addressed. However, Westcott's comments on this verse are intriguing, as well as being cryptic. Here is what he says on the "synagogue expulsion" part of verse 22: "This excommunication appears to have been exclusion from all religious fellowship (comp. Matt. xviii. 17) from 'the congregation of Israel.' In later times there were different degrees of excommunication, the Curse (חרם), and the Isolation (שמתא)."[58] In other words, Westcott reads this passage as directly related to the historical circumstances of the narrative, with the later exclusions not those of the recipients of the gospel but of a different time.

Chapter 11: Raising of Lazarus. Westcott recognizes both the unique elements of the raising of Lazarus and the historical nature of this miracle and its plausibility within its Johannine context. He in fact

---

55. Ibid., Greek 2:28; English 140.
56. Ibid., Greek 2:28; English 140.
57. See, in particular, J. Louis Martyn, *History and Theology in the Fourth Gospel*, 3rd ed., NTL (Louisville: Westminster John Knox, 2003); and Raymond E. Brown, *The Community of the Beloved Disciple* (New York: Paulist, 1979).
58. Westcott, *John*, Greek 2:39–40; English 147.

refers to the account as "history." He states: "The history [of Lazarus's raising] is more complete than that in ch. ix. [healing of the blind man; see above] because the persons stand in closer connexion with the lord than the blind man, and the event itself had in many ways a ruling influence on the end of His ministry."[59] Westcott also recognizes that the Synoptics and John differ as to the miracles that they include: "The omission of the raising of Lazarus by the Synoptists is no more remarkable in principle than the omission of these raisings by St. John," referring to Mark 5:22ff. and parallels; and Luke 7:11ff. "In each case the selection of facts was determined by the purpose of the record." In this regard, "There is no difference between the Synoptists and St. John as to the 'supernatural' character of the Lord's life."[60] Instead, "Numerous minute touches mark the fullness of personal knowledge, or the impression of an eye-witness," at which point he lists a number of examples.[61] Rather than simply leaving the account as concerned with history, however, Westcott puts this in its literary perspective: "That, however, which is most impressive in the narrative, as a history, is its dramatic vividness. . . . There is a clear individuality in the persons," such as Thomas, Martha, and Mary.[62] Westcott recognizes that such an opinion flies in the face of much critical scholarship. He is not troubled by this fact: "Apart from the antecedent assumption that a miracle is impossible, and that the record of a miracle must therefore be explained away, it is not easy to see any ground for questioning the literal exactness of the history. No explanation of the origin of the narrative on the supposition that it is unhistorical, has even a show of plausibility. Those who deny the fact are sooner or later brought to maintain either that the scene was an imposture, or that the record is a fiction. Both of these hypotheses involve a moral miracle."[63]

Chapter 13: Jesus Washes the Disciples' Feet. One of the major issues for Westcott to consider regarding this episode is how the washing of the disciples' feet relates to the Lord's Supper. He accounts for this by saying that its omission by John "belongs to the plan of the Gospel. It is impossible on any theory to suppose that the author was

---

59. Ibid., Greek 2:77; English 163.
60. Ibid., Greek 2:77; English 163.
61. Ibid., Greek 2:77–78; English 163.
62. Ibid., Greek 2:78; English 163.
63. Ibid., Greek 2:78; English 164.

unacquainted with the facts."[64] So far as Westcott is concerned, both the washing of the disciples' feet and the Lord's Supper occurred. However, the question is when the Lord's Supper occurred in relation to the washing according to John. Westcott dismisses the idea that the supper occurred on a different day than the washing (even though his friend Lightfoot held to this view), but attempts to reconcile the two accounts, to the point that he assumes that "the meal described in [John 13] is identical with that described in the Synoptists, as including the Institution of the Lord's Supper."[65] He concludes that the distribution of the bread occurred after 13:2 and the cup after 13:32.[66]

Chapter 18: The Trials of Jesus. Westcott differentiates the two trials of Jesus as a "double trial." The first consists of the "ecclesiastical trial" and the second the "civil trial." He recognizes that "The record of the examination before Annas is peculiar to the narrative of St. John." However, this does not deter Westcott from believing that "the Evangelist appears to have been present at the inquiry."[67] This accounts for his being able to report on the details of the appearance of Jesus before Annas and the Sanhedrin. The trial before Pilate is similar. Westcott recognizes that the "detailed account of the private examinations before Pilate" is "peculiar to St. John." He accounts for this as he does for the first trial: "St. John probably went within the palace. He would not be deterred by the scruple of the Jews (*v.* 28) under such circumstances, and there does not appear to have been any other obstacle to entrance. The apostle who had followed the Lord to the presence of the high-priest would not shrink from following Him to the presence of the governor."[68] This perspective of Westcott accounts not only for the historical details within John's gospel but for its relationship to the Synoptics. "St. John's narrative explains the language of Pilate to the Jews and to the Lord, which is abrupt and unprepared in the Synoptic narratives." Thus in this instance, inferring from Westcott, John's gospel provides a more detailed historical account than do the Synoptics because of its eyewitness testimony from the author, John.

---

64. Ibid., Greek 2:143; English 188.
65. Ibid., Greek 2:143; English 188.
66. Ibid., Greek 2:144; English 188.
67. Ibid., Greek 2:271; English 254.
68. Ibid., Greek 2:279; English 258.

21:15–19: Jesus and Peter. In this episode, there has been much discussion of the difference between the two words for love used. Jesus asks Peter if he loves him, using ἀγαπάω. Peter answers with φιλέω. Jesus asks him a second time with ἀγαπάω, and Peter answers again with φιλέω. The third time Jesus asks with φιλέω, and Peter answers with the same verb. Westcott distinguishes between the senses of these two words, both here and elsewhere. In his treatment of John 5:20, he defines them in this way. "The word φιλεῖν marks personal affection, based upon a special relation . . . and not the general feeling of regard, esteem, consideration (ἀγαπᾶν) which comes from reflection and knowledge: the former feeling answers to nature, the latter to experience and judgement . . . and so is specially appropriate to spiritual relations. This love expresses (so to speak) the moral side of the essential relation of the Father to the Son. And so it is through the Son that the personal love of God is extended to believers."[69] In 21:15–19, Westcott notes that Peter is only able to assent to "the feeling of natural love (φιλῶ σε, amo te v.), of which he could be sure. He does not venture to say that he has attained to that higher love (ἀγαπᾶν) which was to be the spring of the Christian life."[70] Thus, in the third question, Jesus gives up on the "loftiest" kind of love.[71]

The Letters of John

I turn now to Westcott's commentary on the Johannine epistles.[72] In this commentary, as Westcott notes at the outset, we see a work that resembles in many ways his earlier *Speaker's Bible Commentary* on John's gospel, in which he does not concentrate upon offering a compendium of the opinions of other scholars on various issues and passages, but instead offers his conclusions on the text so as to aid students of the books concerned. We also note that the format of the commentary is like that of his Greek commentary on John's gospel, with the Greek text given at the top of the page (but no English translation provided) and commentary in two columns on each page. The commentary is divided into three sections. The introduction, which I will examine below, consists of the first sixty-five pages. The commentary proper is 245 pages. Then there is a third section of three appendixes totaling 125 pages.

---

69. Ibid., Greek 1:190; English 85.
70. Ibid., Greek 2:367; English 302–303.
71. Ibid., Greek 2:368; English, 303.
72. For a summary, see Baird, *History*, 2:80.

The unusual and noteworthy feature of this commentary is the three appendixes, which constitute almost one third of the entire volume. These appendixes are on "The Two Empires: The Church and the World" (later published as its own book),[73] "The Gospel of Creation," and "The Relation of Christianity to Art."[74] These have struck later readers as perhaps not germane to his purposes in this commentary, as Westcott himself acknowledged in the "Notice to the Second Edition," where he offers his defense of their integrity to his task—especially as the commentary was written with practical application in mind, which the appended essays address.[75] However, I think that it is also worth noting that all three of them very much reflect strong interests of Westcott throughout his life. As a strong socialist, Westcott was very much interested in the relationship between the church and the world in which it functioned. As we noted above, throughout much of his career, Westcott was concerned to bring renewal to the church through his work with both lay and ordained people. In this first appendix, anticipating much recent discussion regarding empire, Westcott addresses the two empires as the kingdom of God and the Roman Empire, and discusses their relationship during the first two centuries, including the role played by emperor worship. Westcott also had a scientific bent that he developed early on and that continued throughout his life (he earned a degree in mathematics). This clearly accounts for his interest in the relationship of the gospel of creation. In this second appendix, he treats how the incarnation reveals God's view of creation and how humanity is to be seen as created in the image of God and as representative of his creation. The third appendix is probably the most intriguing. This one also reflects longstanding interests of Westcott. From early on, he was interested in art, and continued to paint and draw throughout his adult life. Therefore, it is natural that he would be concerned with Christianity and art. Westcott believed that the human was created to seek beauty and that nature, through art, needed to be interpreted. Though art was not acknowledged in the New Testament, and Christian antipathy to art was against it as idolatry, Westcott believed that there was a role for what he called Christian art. This was to be seen in a variety of artistic expressions in

---

73. Brooke Foss Westcott, *Two Empires: The Church and the World* (London: Macmillan, 1909).
74. Westcott, *Epistles*, 249–82, 283–328, 329–75.
75. Ibid., x.

the early church, such as painting and architecture. He concludes that Christian art, in its examination of nature as part of the revelation of God, used the contemplation of the temporal and ephemeral as pointing to contemplation of that which is eternal. In that sense, there is a place for Christian art.[76] Even though the lines of connection between these appendixes and the rest of the commentary might seem tenuous, I think that we can see that there are some clear interconnections for Westcott, especially as he contemplates books that are concerned with how Christians reflect upon what they have seen and heard. In any case, I know of no equivalent commentary today that has such a provocative appendix as the relation of Christianity to art.

Introductions. The introduction to John's epistles is divided into two parts, one for 1 John and the second for 2 and 3 John. The introduction to 1 John is divided into ten sections. These include: text, where he notes the manuscript evidence for the letter and the preferability of the oldest manuscripts; the title of the book, as a catholic epistle; the form, which is without the kinds of personal features of other letters, but still has a personal character to it; authorship, date, place of writing, where he believes that the closeness to John's gospel indicates common authorship, probably in the last decade of the first century from Ephesus; destination, as addressed to churches in Asia Minor; character, in which it addresses a new church situation with established churches, where the main issue concerns the "Person and Work of the Lord" against various views that have developed in the early church;[77] object, in harmony with John's gospel to indicate that Jesus is the Christ; style and language, in which it closely resembles John's gospel, to the point of verbal parallels; the epistles and the gospel, in which there are common ideas, developed differently according to whether the book is an epistle or a history.

The introductions to 2 and 3 John discusses three topics. These include: the text, in which there is similar manuscript evidence for 2 and 3 John as there is for 1 John; authorship, in which Westcott recognizes that Eusebius placed them in the "disputed" letters, a fact

---

76. As mentioned above in several places, Westcott appreciated the work of Robert Browning. See also Brooke Foss Westcott, *On Some Points in Browning's View of Life: A Paper Read before the Cambridge Browning Society, November, 1882* (Cambridge: Browning Society, 1883), repr. in *Essays in the History of Religious Thought*, 253–76.

77. Westcott, *Epistles*, xxxiv.

that he explains according to their limited circulation and the fact that the author refers to himself as "the elder," who Westcott thinks is best explained as the John of 1 John and the gospel; character, in which specifics of writing are few but nevertheless an indication of developments within the early church.

Commentary. There are a number of important passages in the Johannine epistles worth examining in relation to Westcott's comments. I use the same criteria as above, selecting significant verses in the epistolary commentary tradition that illustrate Westcott's approach.

1 John 1:1–4: Letter Opening. This passage is both literarily and theologically important for understanding 1 John. Westcott sees striking correspondences between the opening of 1 John and John's gospel. He seems them as "complementary" but "not parallel." Whereas the gospel introduces the "personal Word," leading to the incarnation, 1 John begins with the "revelation of life" leading to the life of the Christian.[78] Westcott also sees these introductory verses as imbued with Old Testament images, especially from Genesis, even though there is no explicit quotation within the book. The use of the Greek tense-forms marks three divisions of the opening verse: *"that which was* (ἦν) *. . . that which we have heard* (ἀκηκόαμεν) *. . . that which we beheld* (ἐθεασάμεθα)."[79] He interprets these uses as follows: as for the first, "That which we understand by the eternal purpose of God . . . the relation of the Father to the Son . . . the acceptance of man in the Beloved . . . *was* already, and entered as a factor into the development of finite being, when the succession of life began (ἦν ἀπ᾽ ἀρχῆς, *was from the beginning*)";[80] as for the second, "these truths were gradually realised in the course of ages, through the teaching of patriarchs, lawgivers, and prophets, and lastly of the Son Himself, Whose words are still pregnant with instruction (ὃ ἀκηκόαμεν, *which we have heard*)";[81] and as for the third, "this Presence of Christ itself, as a historic fact, was the presence of One truly man. The perfection of His manhood was attested by the direct witness of those who were sensibly convinced of it (ὃ ἐθεασάμεθα, κ.τ.λ., *which we beheld and*

---

78. Ibid., 3.
79. Ibid., 4.
80. Ibid., 4.
81. Ibid., 4–5. He later says (p. 6) that "The perfect in every case preserves its full force."

our hands handled)."[82] As Westcott concludes regarding this introductory verse, "All the elements which may be described as the eternal, the historical, the personal, belong to the one subject, to the fullness of which they contribute, even *'the word of life.'*"[83]

1 John 1:8–10; 3:6, 8–9; 5:18: Sin. These verses have posed numerous problems for interpreters, because of the appearance of stating that Christians do not sin, but then that there is remedy for them when they do sin. Westcott provides an additional note on "The idea of sin in St John."[84] In that note he equates sin with lawlessness, especially in its self-oriented nature. However, he also notes that the language used of "sin," whether in the noun or verb form, can mean both individual acts of sin or a sinful character. Sin is recognized as a universal fact, and it brings the human into a sinful condition. This sinful condition can only be remedied through "forgiveness, redemption, reconciliation."[85]

1 John 2:12–14: Writing. Westcott recognizes the issues involved in interpreting these verses: "The exact relation of γράφω to ἔγραψα has been variously explained."[86] He then lists four options: reference to another writing or John's gospel, a suggestion he dismisses on the basis of use of the aorist elsewhere (e.g. 1 John 2:21, 26); reference to this part of the letter and a former part; a change in the author's "mental position," in which he changes his relationship to his readers, from present to past; a change in orientation to the letter, from the process of being written to being complete. Westcott seems to endorse the second viewpoint, although this is not entirely clear. He states in his comment on verse 14: "Looking back on the record of his purpose the apostle appears to resume the thread of his argument: 'I write, yea I have written, because you have had experience of the Faith.'"[87]

---

82. Ibid., 5. On the change from perfect to aorist, Westcott states (p. 6), "The change of tense marks the difference between that which was permanent in the lessons of the manifestation of the Lord, and that which was once shewn to special witnesses." He also notes that the change of lexeme "is significant."
83. Ibid., 5; cf. Baird, *History*, 2:80.
84. Westcott, *Epistles*, 37–40.
85. Ibid., 39.
86. Ibid., 57.
87. Ibid., 60.

1 John 2:1, 22; 4:3: The Antichrist.[88] For Westcott, "the antichrist" "expresses the embodiment of a principle, and is not to be confined to one person. The character of 'the antichrist' is described in the words which follow [2:22]."[89] These words that follow are that it is the one who denies the Father and the Son. This is then further explicated in 2:23.

1 John 5:16: The Sin unto Death. Westcott includes an additional note on this verse, and lists four different interpretations of this concept: "a sin requiring the punishment of natural death"; "an offence which was reckoned by moral judgment to belong to the same class"; "a sin which in its very nature excludes from fellowship with Christians"; "tending to death," as "its natural consequence, if it continue."[90] West-cott interprets it "not of specific acts as such, but of acts which have a certain character: 'There is that which must be described as sin unto death, there is that which wholly separates from Christ.'"[91]

2 John 7: Deceivers Going Out into the World. Westcott sees the deceivers of 2 John as a particular group of people. As he states, "The tense [of the verb: an aorist] . . . appears to mark a particular crisis. They went out from the bosom of the Christian society to fulfill their work."[92]

3 John 7: The Name. Reference to "the name" is not frequent in the New Testament, only being used absolutely in Acts 5:41 (though note the preceding "name of Jesus" in verse 40). It is used more in later church writers. Westcott states that "From the contexts it is evident that 'the Name' is 'Jesus Christ' ('the Lord Jesus's'), or, as it is written at length, 'Jesus Christ, the Son of God' (John xx. 31; I John iv. 15). This 'Name' is in essence the sum of the Christian Creed (comp. I Cor. xii. 3; Rom. x. 9)."[93]

There are, of course, many other passages that could be cited throughout his commentary, but these offer a representative selection.

---

88. Ibid., 70, 92–93, with an additional note on Antichrist. This is one of the words for which Barrett ("Westcott as Commentator," 9) says that Westcott provides word studies that anticipate Kittel. The example that he cites as emblematic is ἱλασμός (Westcott, *Epistles*, 85–87). However, whereas Kittel attempts a word-theology, most of Westcott's study is simply of usage, with relatively little overt theologizing.

89. Westcott, *Epistles*, 75.

90. Ibid., 209–10.

91. Ibid., 192.

92. Ibid., 228.

93. Ibid., 238–39. Westcott also provides an additional note on the divine name, 243–45.

EVALUATION OF WESTCOTT'S CONTRIBUTION TO JOHANNINE SCHOLARSHIP

On the basis of this work, I wish to offer a brief evaluation of Westcott's Johannine scholarship. The strength of his commentary writing makes it difficult to understand how it is that he has become so neglected. A few thoughts come to mind. These might include the constant publication of new commentaries by publishers that creates a (false) environment that the newer commentaries are necessarily better, the general thought that only those who have access to all of the latest exegetical, historical, and other discoveries can provide adequate commentary, and general disregard for older generations of scholars. In this day and age, when there are many commentaries on the market, how do we evaluate Westcott's contribution to Johannine interpretation? On the basis of reviewing his two major Johannine commentaries, I think that there are many positive comments to make regarding his Johannine scholarship, as well as some negative ones.

Positive Accomplishments

The positive comments regarding Westcott's scholarship on the Johannine writings are numerous. Westcott offers a nuanced and attentive close reading of the text. Whether the text is English or Greek (and it is clear that the Greek text underlies his comments on the English translation), Westcott offers an exemplary commentary that reads easily and well, without being verbose. Westcott offers overview statements of major units, then shorter comments to introduce subunits, and then the commentary statements themselves. The result is that the reader is always aware of how the particular comments fit within their immediate and larger context. The kind of commentary that Westcott offers is reminiscent of the better of the so-called literary or even linguistic commentaries, rather than the word for word commentaries of so many recent technical works. This means that, although Westcott does comment on individual words and constructions, these comments are often embedded within discussion of the larger clause or sentence, and this discussion occurs within the larger unit being considered. However, Westcott's comments are made within the context of a technical commentary on the Greek text, so that there is information upon the individual words and constructions. In both his commentary on the Greek text of John's gospel and on the Johannine epistles, Westcott often offers the Latin rendering of the text under consideration, followed by his English comments. Despite this, the commentary flows smoothly from section to section. His writing is fluid and not overburdened with references to other biblical literature and certainly not to other secondary literature. This helps him to streamline his writing and keep his focus upon the text. He sometimes is able to handle a single verse in a matter of lines. Westcott seems to prioritize his references to other biblical literature by focusing first upon the cross-references within the book itself, then on the Johannine corpus, and then beyond it on the rest of the New Testament and finally the early church writers. This approach does not mean that Westcott is not aware of critical discussion. At points, he shows his knowledge of secondary literature either by citing it (he notes at the outset the works that he has found most helpful as discussion partners) or offering a list of the range of opinions on such a passage, even if he does not cite all of the scholars who hold to such a position (as noted above). In many ways, modern commentary writers could learn much from Westcott in his focus upon the text, his resistance to getting mired in extraneous discussion of any type, and his continuing attention to the larger argument of the text. Westcott, along with Lightfoot, helped to develop a particular type of commentary that has come to distinguish the best in the English-language (in particularly British) commentary tradition. Its close attention to the text and emphasis upon language provide a model for emulation. However, if recent commentaries in English, including many from Britain, are any indication, the English commentary tradition is in danger of being lost, being replaced by commentaries that do not share the virtues of Westcott and Lightfoot's writing.[94]

As far as knowledge of the Johannine literature itself is concerned, and the light that is shed upon the text, Westcott excels. Westcott spent nearly thirty years on each of his commentaries on the Johannine writings, during which time he lectured on the material numerous times in a variety of venues. Some of these venues were academic ones and others were pastoral ones. The result is obvious in his commentary itself. Westcott is completely at home in the Johannine writings. The evidence of this is found in several regards. One of these is the kind of comments that he makes that link the various ideas and themes of

---

94. See Stanley E. Porter, "The Linguistic Competence of New Testament Commentaries" and "Commentaries on the Book of Romans," in *On the Writing of New Testament Commentaries: Festschrift for Grant R. Osborne on the Occasion of His 70th Birthday*, eds. Stanley E. Porter and Eckhard J. Schnabel, TENT 8 (Leiden: Brill, 2013), 33–56, 365–404.

the book together. Westcott approaches the Johannine writings with a broad and complete perspective on the major topics that are discussed in these books, and how they are discussed. In his treatment of John's gospel, while he recognizes the deep theology that is found within the book, he offers his interpretation of it from the standpoint of a historical account of the life and teaching of Jesus. This is not a popular viewpoint today, but Westcott provides a plausible account of how to read John's gospel as one written by an eyewitness who was recounting his own experience. When he turns to the Johannine epistles, however, Westcott takes into account that John is now writing letters, letters to actual recipients and churches. This results in differences in approach because of the kinds of issues raised and addressed, particularly as they affect developments in the early church in the late first century. A second way that Westcott shows his attention to detail is his use of additional notes. He includes twenty-eight such notes in his commentary on the Johannine epistles, and twenty-nine additional notes in his commentary on John's gospel, along with a number of extra notes on readings in the gospel. Rather than overburden his individual notes on particular verses, Westcott provides these additional notes on topics that demand further insight and develops important ideas within the books in more detail.

Westcott wrote his commentaries with students of the text primarily in mind. I take it that he means all of those who wish to study the text, including both teachers and what we would call students today. As noted above, Westcott throughout his career was interested in how those interested in the Bible, including those training for ministry, would understand the Bible. There is much pressure today in commentary writing to get away from close attention to the text and to engage in theologizing. In fact, many commentaries today appear to be little more than (or perhaps nothing less than) theologies of the particular book under discussion. The extreme form of this is found in various types of practical or applied commentaries that even do the applicational thinking for the interpreter. Westcott does not appear to have had this perspective in mind when he wrote his commentaries—and is to be commended for it. There are certainly theological comments made along the way in his commentaries, but these are guided by what is suggested by the text, not imposed upon it, so as to make the biblical text a type of systematic theology. Westcott clearly had theological ideas that he wished to develop, but he seems to have commented most readily upon those that emerged from the text. For wider discussions he often used his additional notes.

Negative Features

There are no doubt many places where other commentators on John's gospel may wish to criticize Westcott's individual comments, his choices among options, or his interpretations of various verses. This is to be expected in a commentary. There is also the fact that he does not refer to the wealth of Jewish literature now available—if for no other reason than much of it was not available at the time.[95] This can hardly be considered his fault. However, the major issue that I wish to raise as a negative comment is one that is, when viewed from a different perspective, a positive one. At numerous places in his commentary—in fact, the comments are very frequent, perhaps averaging close to one every two pages, if not more (I have not been able to count them all)—Westcott makes reference to the meanings of the Greek tenses.[96] In his comments, he reflects a traditional view of their meanings, in which the aorist tense-form refers to past time, present tense-form refers to present time, and perfect tense-form to past action with abiding results. He also takes the aorist as indicating a form of, if not specifically punctiliar, at least "decisive" or singular action (particular action). So, his view seems to reflect the kind of view found in a grammar such as that of Winer, although with a hint at developments in comparative philology that led to the development of *Aktionsart*-theory.[97] There are two major comments to make about this. First, his level of comments on the importance of the verbs for interpreting the Greek of the New Testament probably (I cannot say for certain as I have not investigated all others) reflects a greater attention to the meaning of the verb-tenses for interpretation than most other interpreters. There are some who think that comments upon the tense-forms are often overdrawn; however, I think that Westcott is totally appropriate in his comments that draw attention to matters in the text, especially when he cites them at decisive points of interpretation. The second comment is that Westcott is no doubt wrong in his interpretation of some of these uses of the tense-forms, such as when he looks to the temporal characteristics of the aorist and present, and the perfect as having past reference and abiding results. However, we must take into account that Westcott wrote his

---

95. See Barrett, "Westcott as Commentator," 10–12.

96. One of the oft-repeated criticisms of Westcott as an interpreter is his oversubtlety. See V. H. S., "Westcott," 641; Neill and Wright, *Interpretation*, 99–100; and Patrick, *Miners' Bishop*, 37.

97. For the history of such developments, see Stanley E. Porter, *Verbal Aspect in the Greek of the New Testament, with Reference to Tense and Mood*, SBG 1 (New York: Peter Lang, 1989), 22–65, *passim*.

English commentary on John's gospel before 1880 (when it was first published) and his commentary on the Johannine epistles before 1883 (when it was published). In other words, Westcott was writing within the language framework of his time (*Aktionsart* theory was not developed and published in a Greek grammar until 1885, and of course did not change the world over night). Since then, not only has the rationalist, time-bound conception given way to *Aktionsart* theory, but *Aktionsart* theory has given way to aspect theory—or at least it should have for those who are concerned to continue to develop in their understanding of Greek. In other words, whereas Westcott is now out of date on his comments regarding Greek, he was working within the current framework of his day and age, something to be commended to other commentators today, and even intimating some of the developments of his time within larger linguistic thought.

CONCLUSION

There is much more that could and should be said about Westcott. He was undoubtedly a significant figure in the nineteenth century for his scholarship, church work, and general humanitarian work. He was also a man of multiple talents, who was willing to use them in a variety of ways, serving the church, academy, and society. However, it is as a New Testament scholar that Westcott is still best remembered. He is remembered for his important work with Hort on the Greek text of the New Testament, work that began a new movement toward readily accessible hand editions of the Greek New Testament that transformed the critical consensus regarding the use of the earliest and best manuscripts of the Greek New Testament. It is as a commentator on the Greek New Testament that Westcott, though now not often remembered, should perhaps be re-remembered as a major contributor. In many ways, his commentaries read as fresh and acutely observant treatments of the Greek text—what a commentary should primarily be focused upon, whether written one hundred years ago or today. By focusing upon the text, Westcott continues to call his readers back to the primary focus of commentary writing: the text of John's gospel and his epistles.

ADOLF SCHLATTER'S CONTRIBUTION TO INTERPRETATION OF THE FOURTH GOSPEL

Robert Yarbrough

T his essay will focus chiefly on a stock-taking of the scholarship by Adolf Schlatter (1852–1938) relating to John's gospel. Not all relevant works can be factored in; I will pass over, for example, Schlatter's well-known essay translated by Robert Morgan as "The Theology of the New Testament and Dogmatics."[1] Nor will I draw to any great extent on a book by Schlatter published in 2013 from newly edited manuscript sources and containing hermeneutical insights germane to his fourth gospel (FG) labors,[2] nor a yet more recent book relevant to his epistemology and ultimately hermeneutics.[3] Fresh insights are also available

---

1. In Robert Morgan, ed., *The Nature of New Testament Theology*, SBT 2/25 (London: SCM, 1973), 117–66, 194.
2. Adolf Schlatter, *Einführung in die Theologie* (Stuttgart: Calwer, 2013).
3. Schlatter, *Das Verhältnis von Theologie und Philosophie I. Die Berner Vorlesung (1884): Einführung in die Theologie Franz von Baaders*, ed. Harald Seubert with Werner Neuer (Stuttgart: Calwer, 2016). At the end of this volume of previously unpublished material is an appendix "Was ist Wahrheit? Johannes 18,37.38" (175–76). For a translation see Robert Yarbrough, "Critical Note: A New Schlatter Publication and Rumination on Truth," *Presbyterion* 42:1–2 (December 2016): 76–77.

in a recent groundbreaking foray into Schlatter's Christology, relevant hermeneutically to his FG researches and expositions.[4] Space does not permit investigation of all possible fruitful resources and angles.

Confining myself to what is feasible in this chapter, and after sizing up Schlatter's FG contributions, I will briefly characterize reception of that work by other scholars. It will be seen that there is some recognition of Schlatter's stature, but appropriation of his FG views is spotty apart from one seminal contribution. I will conclude with a comment on future prospects for the appropriation of Schlatter's contribution in Johannine studies, which may appear fairly meager, but may also hold noteworthy promise.

BIOGRAPHY[5]

Although the majority of Schlatter's professorial career unfolded in German universities (Greifswald 1888–1893; Berlin 1893–1898; Tübingen 1898–1922; active retirement in Tübingen until death), he was born in St. Gallen, Switzerland. Following schooling in Basel and Tübingen, he pastored several small Swiss state (Reformed) churches (1875–1880). At the urging of local conservatives alarmed by liberal dominance of the university theology faculties, Schlatter wrote a dissertation on John the Baptist, withstood stringent challenges from a hostile academic dean and faculty, and was appointed to an academic post at Bern where from 1881–1888 he lectured in New Testament, historical theology, and philosophy.

Schlatter was the seventh of nine children; he often noted his appreciation for a godly upbringing by parents graced with a healthy marriage. Both parents were dedicated Christians, although Schlatter's father worshipped in a small baptistic fellowship, while his mother remained in the Swiss state church, where Schlatter eventually took ordination. He traced his ecumenical instincts to growing up in a

---

4. Michael Bräutigam, *Union with Christ: Adolf Schlatter's Relational Christology* (Eugene, OR: Pickwick, 2015). This is reviewed by Robert Yarbrough in *Unio cum Christo* 2/2 (October 2016): 258–62.

5. See especially Werner Neuer, *Adolf Schlatter*, trans. Robert Yarbrough (Grand Rapids: Baker, 1995); idem, *Adolf Schlatter: Ein Leben für Theologie und Kirche* (Stuttgart: Calwer, 1996); idem, "Schlatter, Adolf (1852–1938)," in *Evangelisches Lexikon für Theologie und Gemeinde* 3, eds. Helmut Burkhardt and Otto Betz (Wuppertal: Brockhaus, 1994); Robert Yarbrough, "Schlatter, Adolf (1852–1938)," in *Dictionary of Major Biblical Interpreters*, ed. Donald K. McKim (Downers Grove, IL: IVP Academic/Nottingham, England: InterVarsity Press, 2007), 881–85.

household where faith in Jesus was the basis for unity, not denominations or other human institutions.

Theological scholars' families often take a back seat to the scholar's quest for productivity and renown. Schlatter treasured his wife and five children. His wife's sudden death after a medical procedure (1907) prompted a spate of writings from Schlatter's pen as he suddenly sensed his own mortality. The battlefield death of his older son Paul in October 1914 threw his father into a funk, from which it took years to recover. His younger son eventually entered the pastorate. Two of his daughters remained single their entire lives, in part to care for their widower father. A third daughter married a pastor.

Retirement was mandatory for Schlatter in 1922, but he continued to offer lectures and seminars for another eight years. Also in retirement, Schlatter published nine rigorous commentaries (on Matthew, Mark, Luke, John, Romans, 1–2 Corinthians, the Pastorals, James, and 1 Peter), augmenting an earlier series (*Erläuterungen zum Neuen Testament*) covering every New Testament book at a more non-academic level (which is not to say that the *Erläuterungen* volumes were uninformed by academic considerations—quite the contrary). His final publication was a historical, theological, expositional, but also devotional appeal to the German people to consider their relation to Jesus as the evils of Nazi leadership took shape. Its title, *Kennen wir Jesus?*[6] (*Do We Know Jesus?*[7]), expresses a significant undercurrent detectable in much of the Schlatter corpus.

SCHLATTER'S FG SCHOLARSHIP

An inventory of Schlatter's publications produced by the Adolf-Schlatter-Stiftung in Stuttgart contains 432 works.[8] More have appeared since the inventory was printed in the 1970s–1980s, but little of it is directly related to the FG. Of the 432 publications, more than forty would be relevant to a comprehensive assessment of Schlatter's work on John broadly conceived. Of these forty-plus works, however, a

---

6. Schlatter, *Kennen wir Jesus?* 2d ed. (Stuttgart: Calwer, 1938).

7. Idem, *Do We Know Jesus?*, trans. Andreas Köstenberger and Robert Yarbrough (Grand Rapids: Kregel, 2005).

8. *Das Schrifttum Adolf Schlatters.* This undated, 170-page typescript was printed and bound in house by the Adolf-Schlatter-Stiftung, presumably as an inventory and guide to researchers at this archive and study center. My thanks to Werner Neuer for providing me a copy.

number are sermons on Johannine texts, popular-level lectures, conference presentations, or journal articles. Some fifteen works are to varying extents academically grounded and directly germane to our subject. These will be examined below. In some cases I will cite a passage from these works to convey their flavor and tone. The listing is in chronological order, from Schlatter's earlier to his later publications. Each work will be listed under the rubric of the periods Schlatter spent at the respective universities of Bern, Greifswald, Berlin, and finally Tübingen.

Schlatter's Bern Years, 1881–1888

Schlatter's first major publication was *Der Glaube im Neuen Testament* (*Faith in the New Testament*), 1885, with four more editions through 1963.[9] Some forty pages are devoted expressly to the language and conception of faith in John's gospel.[10] Later in the volume, Schlatter deals with "faith" in John's epistles and in Revelation,[11] all of which, like the FG, Schlatter regarded as from John the son of Zebedee. Schlatter serves notice early in the book that he will not be bound by the methodological atheism that was widespread in German scholarship and is still normative for many today; he writes:

> When New Testament ideas are presented as merely the product of temporal-human factors, which is to say divine causality is barred from consideration—and it is well known that the ignoring of God is tantamount to negating him—then the investigation is forced from the onset into a dogmatic premise, since a negative dogmatics is still a dogmatics; the question is only whether it is valid.[12]

A result of this for his work on the FG is that πίστις (German *Glaube*; "faith") is permitted to have the object (God in the form of the Word made flesh; cf. John 1:1, 14) that New Testament writers claimed rather than what German idealist exegetes with a strictly Kantian God permitted.[13]

---

9. Schlatter, *Der Glaube im Neuen Testament*. References in this chapter are to the second edition (Calw and Stuttgart: Verlag des Vereinsbuchhandlung, 1896).
10. Ibid., 111–41.
11. Ibid., 317–26.
12. Ibid., 7.
13. On knowledge of God in Schlatter vis-à-vis knowledge of God in a (neo-)Kantian like Karl Barth, see Bräutigam, *Union with Christ*, 101–104.

Biographer Werner Neuer devotes a lengthy section to this book's conception, content, and reception.[14] Schlatter observed that at that time, "faith" was an omnibus term for "anything pious and religious."[15] He sought to arrive at a fairly comprehensive and integrated conception of what "faith" signified "from Abraham to the final epistles of the New Testament."[16] One of his main results is that "faith" in biblical usage can rightly be understood in a unified sense, not radically different in various biblical writers despite its obvious varied nuances evident in given passages found among those writers. Another result is that Schlatter found "faith" not to signify solely the passive connotation often accorded to it, in which "faith" means no more than acceptance of God's act on behalf of the believer. Rather, "faith" also includes the believer's "thinking, willing, and acting in love"[17] as an essential expression of the outcome of the trust in God that Scripture calls "faith." Schlatter holds that faith is a God-given gift, but that it is not merely a quiestistic posture but at the same time a transformative force.

Since the verb for "to believe, trust, have faith" is found some one hundred times in the FG, this seminal work by Schlatter is significant for grasping his view of John's language and theology of faith.

Schlatter's Greifswald Years, 1889–1893

During this period Schlatter brought out *Einleitung in die Bibel* (1st ed. 1889).[18] Some twenty-one pages deal with the FG,[19] much of it highly original. In the introduction to this work,[20] Schlatter writes of eight aspects of biblical introduction according to his conception. He speaks (1) of the need to go beyond the merely academic questions of authorship, date, purpose, and the like; (2) of the necessity of seeing Scripture as God's Word; (3) of the effect of seeing Scripture as God's Word; (4) of what happens with denial of Scripture as God's Word; (5) of the necessity of seeing God's Word in a "historical" context; (6) of the logic of a "historical" reading of Scripture; (7) of the mechanics of a free investigation of God's Word; and (8) of two false ways in

---

14. Neuer, *Schlatter: Ein Leben für Theologie und Kirche* (see n. 5 above), 184–95.
15. Ibid., 185.
16. Ibid., 186. This information was contained in a letter to his mother in 1882, when Schlatter was setting about composing the book.
17. Ibid. 191.
18. By 1933 it had appeared in its fifth edition.
19. Schlatter, *Einleitung in die Bibel*, 4th ed. (Stuttgart: Calwer Vereinsbuchhandlung, 1923), 319–339.
20. Ibid., 5–8.

approaching the Bible: rationalist autonomy and fideist paranoia. This statement is typical of what Schlatter says about the proper approach to Scripture including the FG:

> The honor that we must accord to the divine word consists in this: we relate to it as learners and receptors. For that word is ordained to be our leader, and to it we are submitted. Yet it does not lead us into immaturity and bondage; it rather bestows on us our own seeing, our own judgment, the free movement of the understanding that has been led to truth. Through this there is no rupture of the authority of Scripture and of our faith in it. Not until we attain understanding can we authentically bow beneath the word of Scripture without this becoming a burden and indolence. If we bow beneath Scripture, then we can make bold to carry out research and make judgments with respect to it, without that arrogance that disregarding God carries with it. The well-being, the peace, the inner harmony that exists between this dual relation to Scripture brings about the existence of a free science of God and his word in the community that believes in Jesus.[21]

The introduction devotes several pages to the FG in general (319–22), then offers a short exposition of individual sections (1:1–18; 1:19–4:54; chs. 5–6; chs. 7–12; chs. 13–17; chs. 18–21). Significantly, the longest of these expositions is devoted to John's prologue (1:1–18; see 322–25), an indicator of Schlatter's attention to the theological dimension of this gospel. Following this is discussion of similarities and differences between the FG and Matthew's gospel. Schlatter expands on this motif in a work cited below. Differences between Matthew's and John's respective gospels include chronological details, John's language, and his references to "the Jews." Yet far more unites Matthew and John than divides them.

Schlatter's Berlin Years, 1893–1898

The brief and busy years Schlatter spent in Berlin—called there expressly to offset the liberal influence of Adolf Harnack[22]—resulted in three more works on matters Johannine. First came *Die Parallelen in den Worten Jesu bei Johannes und Matthäus*. This seventy-two-page

---

21. Ibid., 7–8.
22. See Neuer, *Schlatter: Ein Leben für Theologie und Kirche*, 292–96.

study appeared in 1898 in the second volume of the academic monograph series *Beiträge zur Föderung christlicher Theologie*.[23] Expanding
on insights first mooted in his *Einleitung* (above), it shows how, in
what N. T. Wright might call a critical realist light,[24] Schlatter viewed
the author of the FG (John the son of Zebedee) alongside another
great apostolic figure, Matthew. While this book is mainly linguistic, it served as a basis for more historical and theological reflection
in Schlatter's later works. A shorter piece, "Der Bruch Jesu mit der
Judenschaft, Joh. 4 und 6," was a twenty-three-page book chapter that
appeared in 1898. Like the earlier *Der Glaube im Neuen Testament*, it
confirmed Schlatter's command of the history, literature, and theologies of Second Temple Judaism and their relevance to the interpretation of the FG. In an era where German scholarship was enamored of
the presumed Hellenistic background of the FG, Schlatter's insistence
on the relevance of Jewish backgrounds was prescient.

As Schlatter's time in Berlin was ending, he was completing *Das
Evangelium des Johannes* (1899, 2nd ed. 1902). This 370-page commentary appears in Schlatter's *Erläuterungen zum Neuen Testament*, a series
covering every book of the New Testament and containing primarily exposition along with some historical and theological reflection.[25]
Schlatter states his approach in these volumes as follows:

> The goal of the interpretation was to direct attention, not away from the
> text, be that around it, behind it, or beyond it, but rather with firm resolve
> to pay attention and then direct attention to *what the text itself says*. Then
> we may truly apprehend what Jesus's messengers said to Christianity.[26]

The conclusion to the lengthy section "Jesus reveals the divine
grace (1:19–4:54)" gives the flavor of Schlatter's reading of the FG:

> So John furnishes us with a very complete presentation of the circle
> of people Jesus served. We saw Jesus in the circle of his disciples and
> with his mother. Then the highly placed priests appeared before him,

---

23. For details of this series' founding see ibid., 335–41.
24. See Wright, *The New Testament and the People of God*, Christian Origins and the People of God 1 (Minneapolis: Fortress, 1992), 32–46 and *passim*.
25. For analysis of the rise and completion of *Erläuterungen*, a process that lasted some twenty-five years, see Neuer, *Schlatter: Ein Leben für Theologie und Kirche*, 213–17, 508–11.
26. Ibid., 510.

followed by the teacher Nicodemus, then the Baptizer with his band of followers, then the first fruits of the Samaritan believers. Finally came the Galileans with their excitement over Jesus's miracles and their support for him that still needed to be elevated to the level of faith. Each of these circles has its distinctive form of regarding Jesus and approaching him. On every hand arise those difficulties present in the human heart which did not make it easy for Jesus to render his service to people. Jesus engages all persons with the same inexhaustible grace: he gives his mother the wine, the teacher the truth, the Samaritan women the living water, the Galilean the rescue of his child from the danger of death. In this manner he steadfastly directs people's gaze to the Father and exalts the desire of man for fellowship with him.[27]

It is worth observing that precisely in the years that Schlatter was pitted against Harnack institutionally (personally the men enjoyed a friendly rapport[28]), part of his writing regimen involved classic Christian exposition of the FG. Perhaps this lent him resources and stability in his scholarly direction in contrast to that of Harnack: "While Harnack's critique of the Hellenization of dogma led factually to 'alienation from the New Testament,' Schlatter remained intent on 'liberation from the Greek heritage' for the sake of 'agreement' [*Einigung*] with the New Testament message."[29]

Schlatter's Tübingen Years, 1898–1938

During this lengthiest span of Schlatter's career, the Tübingen years, he produced the most publications on virtually all of the many fronts on which he wrote. His work on the FG from this period is rich, varied, and extensive. First was *Die Sprache und Heimat des vierten Evangelisten*. This is one of two scholarly tomes arguing for the FG's Jewish milieu, at a time in Germany where virtually all John scholars read it in a Hellenistic and even syncretistic light. Schlatter's dense 180-page study was volume six in the *Beiträge* series (see above) and appeared in 1902. He would expand this material in his critical FG commentary to appear nearly three decades later. That commentary and this work are the two most frequently cited Schlatter volumes on

---

27. Schlatter, *Das Evangelium nach Johannes,* Erläuterungen zum Neuen Testament 3 (Stuttgart: Calwer, 1947), 86.
28. Neuer, *Schlatter: Ein Leben für Theologie und Kirche,* 301–308.
29. Ibid., 308, citing one of Schlatter's autobiographical reminiscences.

the FG by later commentators. When first published, however, this work met with widespread collegial indifference and negative reviews.

Drawing deeply on the FG, and arising in the early years of Schlatter's Tübingen sojourn, was *Die Theologie des Neuen Testaments*, 1909–1910, second edition 1923 (*Die Geschichte des Christus*) and 1922 (*Die Lehre der Apostel*). Volume one contains some twenty specific references to John and/or the FG and alludes to or quotes about one hundred passages from the FG. Volume two contains some two dozen references to the FG and references close to two hundred FG passages. It is here that much of the FG's theology is detailed, as theology is not the focus of his mainly linguistic critical commentary, mentioned below. The theological-historical sections of volume 2, which serve to explicate the FG and so are integral to understanding of Schlatter's John scholarship, are thirteen in number:

1. The establishment of faith through the portrayal of Jesus
2. New christological elements
3. New anthropological elements
4. The interpretation of Jesus's cross
5. Statements regarding the Spirit
6. The evangelist's hope
7. The unity of the gospel and the epistle [i.e., 1 John]
8. The prophet and the evangelist
9. The Greek element in John
10. The Hebrew element in John
11. John and Matthew
12. John and Paul
13. John and Jesus

These thirteen sections are contained in more than sixty pages of Andreas Köstenberger's excellent translation of volume 2 of Schlatter's New Testament theology, *The Theology of the Apostles*. Here, from that volume, is a characteristic sample of Schlatter's assessment of John as author of Revelation, the FG, and 1 John:

> Since [Revelation] serves the substantiation of hope with the same resolve by which the [FG] requires faith and [1 John] requires ethical industry, the three writings preserved by the church because it considered them to come from John jointly stress the three constituent activi-

ties of the community's piety: faith, love, and hope. This "systematic" approach does not provide occasion for deriving it from a particular plan, say, that of a literary artist who spins reality out of his pen. It rather resulted from the fact that John in his dealings with the community was continually led to strengthen its hope, faith, and love. His apostolic commission required that he give it whatever it needed, and for this reason he served it as evangelist [the FG], teacher [1 John], and prophet [Revelation]. The church's conviction that John combined the hope proclaimed by his prophecy with faith as established by the Gospel and love as revealed by the epistle is confirmed by the fact that the same motifs, which are decidedly characteristic of a given individual, represent the constituent elements of all three documents.[30]

Johannine claims and insights are likewise present in Schlatter's *Das christliche Dogma* (1911, 2nd ed. 1923). This 667-page work makes explicit reference to the apostle John's doctrine of the cross, manner of presentation of Jesus's teaching, Christology, doctrine of justification, view of the Antichrist, and chiliasm. Aspects of Johannine theology or outlook can be detected more or less throughout the book. Bräutigam's concluding assessments of Schlatter reflect the effect of Schlatter's high regard for FG Christology (which Schlatter saw present also in the Synoptics). Here Schlatter was more than traditional, as Bräutigam notes:

> Ascribing only limited explanatory power to the classic two-natures exposition, Schlatter moves—on the basis of his New Testament seeing-act—towards a relational understanding of Jesus Christ which allows him to make inferences concerning Christ's essence from his relations. While subscribing to the Symbol of Chalcedon, Schlatter offers new avenues of thinking about the unity of the divine and the human in Jesus Christ.[31]

Schlatter's book on dogmatics did not signal abandonment of close textual study. His *Das Alte Testament in der johanneischen Apokalypse* (1912) was a 108-page linguistic study, volume 16 in the *Beiträge*

---

30. Schlatter, *The Theology of the Apostles*, trans. Andreas Köstenberger (Grand Rapids: Baker, 1998), 150.
31. Bräutigam, *Union with Christ*, 197.

series. It displays the same close and intense comparative linguistics work that one finds in *Der Glaube im Neuen Testament* as well as in Schlatter's two main FG studies, including his critical commentary (below). Such works explain why Schlatter was awarded a doctorate *honoris causis* by the University of Berlin in recognition of his achievement in philology.[32]

The First World War and the battlefield death of Schlatter's older son would dampen the volume of works flowing from Schlatter's pen. But before that pall descended, he brought out *Die christliche Ethik* (1914, 4th ed. 1961). The Scripture index of this 450-page tome contains about three dozen references to the FG. In a section on love for God, Schlatter cites John 1:16 in support of the idea of "the inexhaustibility of the divine fullness, from which we receive grace upon grace [*Gnade um Gnade*]."[33] In the same section he notes that "the knowledge of God is without end," i.e., infinite, citing John 17:3, in which Jesus's prayer teaches that to know God is eternal, i.e., infinite, life.[34] Schlatter draws on 1 John 5:4 for grounding of his comment that the struggle believers experience in this world will end in the victory of faith, through which "love will not end but rather be perfected" [*die Liebe nicht beendet, sondern vollendet sein wird*]. An enterprising student of Schlatter's FG scholarship would find close attention to Schlatter's *Ethik*, as well as to his *Dogmatik*, rich in yield.

Die Geschichte der ersten Christenheit (1926, 5th ed. 1971)[35] is one of Schlatter's few works to be translated. It appeared in 1955 as *The Church in the New Testament Period*.[36] It is, essentially, that relatively rare breed of work called a New Testament history. Out of thirty-three chapters, five deal with John or the FG or both. Chapter 5, "The Ministry and Effect of John," is rich with insight into John's place in the apostolic circle, his motives for following Jesus, his understanding of Judaism and its sects vis-à -vis Jesus's message, and his function alongside Peter. The chapter ends with these words:

---

32. Neuer, *Schlatter: Ein Leben für Theologie und Kirche*, 724. This honor was accorded by the philosophy faculty, not the theology.
33. Schlatter, *Die christliche Ethik*, 5th ed. (Stuttgart: Calwer, 1986), 122.
34. Ibid., 120 with n. 3.
35. Schlatter, *Die Geschichte der ersten Christenheit* (Gütersloh: C. Bertelsmann, 1926).
36. Idem, *The Church in the New Testament Period*, trans. Paul Levertoff (London: SPCK, 1955). Translations in this section are mine and not Levertoff's.

For John there was just one way to God, only one person who afforded access to God, and that was Jesus. Relationship with Jesus was by faith, a faith certain of his heavenly origin and confessing his name. In this certainty John together with Peter formed the unity of the church.[37]

Chapter 28 is called "John's Move to the Church in Asia." Schlatter describes here John's knowledge and assessment of Judaism and Jerusalem. There is also focus on what Paul had established in the Roman province of Asia and how John assumed leadership there and what the results of that were. Schlatter notes two reasons for continuity between the Pauline and the Johannine periods: first, John and Paul agreed in their assessment of Jesus; and second, they were united in how they viewed and appropriated the heritage of the Old Testament people of God in an area of primarily Gentile identity.[38]

Chapter 29 is called "John's Proclamation of the Imminence of Christ's Return." It deals with the puzzles of the historical setting of John's apocalypse as well as its message and reception. Chapter 30 is "John's Struggle against Gnosticism." Schlatter shared in the scholarly consensus of that time that gnosticism, at least in incipient form, was a factor from early in the church's rise. He writes, "Defense against gnosticism was one of John's concerns during the entire time he served in Ephesus. This struggle went all the way back to when he with Peter ejected Simon the Magician out of the Samaritan church." Chapter 31 is called "The New Gospel." It begins, "The greatest work of John was the issuance of his Gospel."[39] He sees the FG arising around AD 80, by which time John was sixty or older. But Schlatter states, "To portray him as a worn-out old geezer is ruled out by the efficacy of his narrative."[40] He comments:

> For John the basis for faith lay solely in Jesus. [The FG shows how] Jesus becomes that basis through his history, not through a Christology that spirals up into infinity, not through a doctrine of the Trinity that describes God before the creation of the world, not through a presentation of his heavenly transcendence that now unites him with the Father.[41]

---

37. *Die Geschichte der ersten Christenheit*, 66.
38. Ibid., 332.
39. Ibid., 353.
40. Ibid.
41. Ibid. 354.

This is not to say Schlatter denied any of those doctrinal verities; it is to delimit what he views as the focus of the FG: the here and now—or rather, the there and then, as best we can reconstruct it in today's here and now. John was a concrete observer and describer, he stressed, not a dreamer or poet. Schlatter believed that by the time John wrote, the Synoptic Gospels were in circulation, and that the FG

> strengthened this older tradition by not letting the church move away from Jesus. The FG rather bound the church to Jesus's history [*die Geschichte Jesu*], so that its faith would have its basis in that history. For the church to have that certainty, it must be stated clearly what gives Jesus's history its never-ending force, and how it is that his activity in Jerusalem and his crucifixion still touch the Greeks [i.e., the Gentile believers in Asia], even as John wrote.[42]

The final chapter of this important book touches significantly on John, author of five New Testament books in Schlatter's view, as Schlatter discusses processes that led to the canon, to early church practice, and to formation of portions of the Apostles' Creed. Most of all, the chapter puts finishing touches on this book's thesis that the greatest apostolic achievement, John's included, lies in the fact that the history of the early church led to the slow, often lurching, but inexorable ascent to affirmation of the New Testament.[43]

Just as above we noted that during Schlatter's heady Berlin years he was producing a lay-level exposition of the FG, so in the same years that he was producing a rigorous New Testament history (above) he was writing a much different book entitled *Andachten*.[44] This daily devotional guide went through four editions by 1967 and contains dozens of reflections on Johannine passages. From the foreword,[45] it is clear that Schlatter is writing with his fellow jaded-and-work-weary Germans in mind during the desperate and tumultuous mid-1920s in postwar Germany. Schlatter never wrote on John without textual and historical focus, but here he shows how he views application of John's message in that socially and politically needy setting, the time when conditions for Hitler's rise were ripening. Reflecting on John 1:12,

---

42. Ibid., 355.
43. Ibid., 383 (book's final sentence).
44. Schlatter, *Andachten* (Stuttgart: Calwer, n.d. [1927]).
45. Ibid., 5.

"But to all who did receive him, who believed in his name, he gave the right to become children of God," Schlatter stated:

> The status of being God's child cannot be manufactured, demanded, or finagled. It takes authorization. The call of Jesus is to give this to us. Through it he reveals himself to us as our Lord in glory. Children come into being only through the Father. While Jesus leads us into childhood before God, he deals with us in God's might and grace. Perhaps doubt assails me—may I really let something this great be said of me and treasure what I am as God's gift? May I regard what I think as God's word and what I will as God's will? The name of Jesus furnishes an answer to my question. I not only may, I must, cling to God as my Father. The alternative would be to expunge the name of Jesus from my soul.[46]

A comparable work of over a decade later was Schlatter's 1938 publication *Kennen wir Jesus?*,[47] another volume that yields understanding of his FG outlook. It has been published in English translation.[48] Whereas *Andachten* is a daily devotional guide focusing on theological reflection for harried German citizens, *Kennen wir?* walks the reader through the life of Jesus in its chronological unfolding with an eye in part to debunking Nazi and German Christian perversion of biblical understanding, scoring multiple hits at Hitler's expense. Schlatter's high regard for the FG as a central source of knowledge for Jesus's history and teaching, and contemporary regard for him by his followers, is consistent with what one finds in earlier works.

In some ways the crowning tribute to the FG's legacy in Schlatter's writings is *Der Evangelist Johannes* (1930; four editions through 1975). The subtitle runs: *Wie er spricht, denkt und glaubt. Ein Kommentar zum 4. Evangelium.*[49] The foreword gives an important clue to the book. Schlatter had recently published a massive Matthew commentary, in which he sought to show that the language of the first gospel confirmed a Palestinian provenance. Schlatter next wanted to counter views of John he said were current in scholarship: John as Hellenist, as Paulinist, as religious philosopher, as poet, as mystic, or as gnostic.

---

46. Ibid., 13.
47. Schlatter, *Kennen wir Jesus?*
48. Idem, *Do We Know Jesus?*
49. Schlatter, *Der Evangelist Johannes* (Stuttgart: Calwer, 1930).

His John commentary's major distinction is, accordingly, its linguistic focus. Schlatter patiently cites a clause or phrase from the FG, then next to it arrays citations from contemporary or roughly contemporary Greek sources like Josephus or Philo or the LXX, or from a wide selection of rabbinic sources including the Mishna, Tosefta, the Jerusalem or Babylonian Talmuds, and rabbinic commentary on books of the Torah. Hundreds of times the sequence runs like this: FG quotation, Hebrew parallel, then Schlatter's translation of the Hebrew into Greek to make the parallel with the FG unmistakable.

Appendices in the back of the commentary characterize the results of Schlatter's historical linguistics focus. One finds thirteen long columns of references to Greek expressions in John that Schlatter shows are attested in Hebraic or otherwise Semitic form in John's putative first-century Palestinian milieu. Next are fifteen columns of parallels between the FG and Josephus's language. By this time Schlatter was a recognized authority not only on Second Temple Judaica but also on Josephus, in terms of both his language and his theological outlook. A shorter appendix of about one hundred words lists Johannine terms absent from Josephus, like ἀγάπη, γογγυσμός, διάβολος, λιθάζω, προσκυνητής, τεκνίον. The FG is not *just* a reflection of co-temporal linguistic deposits. John was a creative as well as conservative writer.

Schlatter lists more than five columns of words that are common to the FG and the Apocalypse. Finally, he lists just twenty words used in the FG that are lacking in the Apocalypse. This demonstration of FG and Revelation affinities prompted Schlatter to call the notion of a Johannine school a complete fantasy, a theory unnecessary in light of the much greater likelihood that one hand is behind all five canonical Johannine documents, as demonstrated in his vocabulary and usage comparison. In his Johannine school skepticism Schlatter anticipated the confession of Robert Kysar, who in an SBL session over a decade ago "chronicled the rise and fall of the Martyn/Brown-style 'Johannine community' hypothesis and expressed personal regret for ever having endorsed it."[50]

Schlatter's decades-long close interaction with John in historical-linguistic and philological perspective did not reduce his regard for the theological message it conveyed. His entire system of thought (of

---

50. Andreas Köstenberger, *John*, BECNT (Grand Rapids: Baker Academic, 2004), 3.

which we can speak, since he wrote a metaphysics[51] to complement his dogmatics [discussed above], along with a history of philosophy[52]) was characterized by affirmation of "the unity of reality," a reality which "admittedly requires God for its recognition" and which Schlatter grounded in passages like John 1:3, from which Schlatter inferred "the world [as] an entirety, although it is endless."[53]

SCHLATTER ON THE FG TODAY

To say that Schlatter's commentary does not major on theology or exposition is not to say there is no impetus to theological or expositional reflection in it. Frederick Dale Bruner is prominent among recent English-language commentators in drawing significant spiritual or dogmatic food for thought from it, with close to one hundred references to Schlatter's commentary in Bruner's commentary's index. For example, Bruner notes from Schlatter that when John the Baptist says, "I am not the Christ" (John 1:20), "John shows his eminence; for anyone else to say this would be laughable."[54] Bruner draws on Schlatter to confirm Old Testament and Second Temple messianic expectation.[55] He also draws on Schlatter to clarify the meaning of perishing or destruction in the well-known verse John 3:16; Schlatter comments, Bruner writes, that "with the use of this word 'one is to think not only of the natural end of life but of life's violent destruction, which occurs through the sentencing judgment of God.'"[56] Bruner's quotation of Schlatter's FG commentary continues: "This thought that the human being stands in danger of losing one's life is seen also in Matt. 7:13 [the narrow gate]; and was a thought well known to the rabbinate since it practiced its piety earnestly in order to escape the second death and Gehenna."[57]

Among other recent FG commentators it is primarily Andreas Köstenberger who has made ample use of Schlatter, citing him perhaps

---

51.   Schlatter, *Metaphysik*, ZThK Beiheft 7 (Tübingen: Mohr Siebeck, 1987).
52.   Schlatter, *Die philosophische Arbeit seit Cartesius nach ihrem ethischen und religiösen Ertrag*, 2nd ed. (Gütersloh: C. Bertelsmann, 1910).
53.   Harald Seubert, "Vorwort," in Schlatter, *Das Verhältnis von Theologie und Philosophie*, 19 (quoting Schlatter's *Der Evangelist Johannes*).
54.   Frederick Dale Bruner, *The Gospel of John* (Grand Rapids: Eerdmans, 2012), 61.
55.   Ibid., 75.
56.   Ibid., 211–12.
57.   Ibid., 212.

slightly more frequently than does Bruner. More typically, Schlatter is barely acknowledged. There is a single reference to him in Jo-Ann Brant's 2011 commentary.[58] There is likewise only one reference in J. Ramsey Michaels's massive work of more than one thousand pages.[59] An index of current German assessment is Jörg Frey's volume containing prolegomena to his upcoming FG commentary in the *Evangelisch-katholischer Kommentar* (EKK) series.[60] In more than eight hundred wide-ranging pages, Schlatter is cited some dozen times. The main and repeated point is that Schlatter was ahead of his time in recognizing the Jewish milieu of the FG. Apart from that, there is no interest in, and in fact a polemical dismissal of, the notion that the FG describes real events and discourses as remembered by an eyewitness and disciple of the Christ named Ἰωάννης. Whereas scholars like B. F. Westcott, Theodor Zahn, Leon Morris, Don Carson, Andreas Köstenberger, Craig Blomberg, Craig Keener, and others follow Schlatter in pursuing a primarily historical situating of the Johannine narrative, and Schlatter in turn shared historiographical convictions often comparable to those of Martin Kähler,[61] Frey typifies today's scholarly consensus that the page has forever turned on such a naive, fearful, popularly motivated understanding, which was ruled out with the rise of the Enlightenment and which Frey in his book does not even deign to interact with apart from denouncing its viability. Frey even expresses suspicion of the SBL section that was called "John, Jesus, and History."[62]

Schlatter's historic Christian reading of the FG, for all its undergirding erudition, attracts little interest and less respect in most current mainstream FG scholarship. Hartwig Thyen's nearly fifty learned essays on the Johannine corpus that he composed over some four decades reflect this status quo: He cites Schlatter on two of his book's seven hundred pages.[63] There is more enthusiasm, it seems, for a scholar (F. C. Baur) whose historical hypotheses (1) fascinate despite their frequent erroneousness, and (2) call for a demolition of historic Christian understanding of Jesus and the rise of early Christianity,[64]

---

58.   Jo-Ann A. Brant, *John,* Paideia (Grand Rapids: Baker Academic, 2011), 61.
59.   J. Ramsey Michaels, *The Gospel of John,* NICNT (Grand Rapids: Eerdmans, 2010), 226.
60.   Jörg Frey, *Die Herrlichkeit des Gekreuzigten,* WUNT 307 (Tübingen: Mohr Siebeck, 2013).
61.   See Johannes Heinrich Schmid, *Erkenntnis des geschichtlichen Christus bei Martin Kähler und bei Adolf Schlatter,* Theologische Zeitschrift Sondband 5 (Basel: Friedrich Reinhardt, 1978).
62.   Frey, *Herrlichkeit des Gekreuzigten,* 12.
63.   Hartwig Thyen, *Studien zum Corpus Iohanneum,* WUNT 214 (Tübingen: Mohr Siebeck, 2007).
64.   For essays often strongly supportive of Baur see Martin Bauspieß, Christof Landmesser, and David

an understanding many would base largely on the apostolic witness
epitomized by the FG.

SCHLATTER AND FUTURE PROSPECTS
FOR FG UNDERSTANDING

Schlatter's high view of the truth of the FG, historically and theologically, is not without its supporters today.[65] Moreover, the year
2016 witnessed a burst of volumes arguing for the veracity not just of
John's writings but of the whole of Scripture.[66] There has been a parallel explosion in full-scale commentaries on Romans, with about one
per year appearing in this young century: N. T. Wright (2002), Grant
Osborne (2004), Ben Witherington III (2004), Leander Keck (2005),
Robert Jewett (2007), Craig Keener (2009), Arland Hultgren (2011),
Herman Waetjen (2011), Colin Kruse (2012), Richard Longenecker
(2015), Stanley Porter (2015), Michael Bird (2016), and Eckhard
Schnabel (2 volumes; 2015–2016). In 2018 Thomas Schreiner's 1997
commentary in the Baker Exegetical series will appear in an exten-
sively reworked second edition. New Romans commentaries by David
Peterson and Frank Thielman are also in press.

Fresh interest in the truth and authority of Scripture, along with
fresh articulations of the language and message of Romans, could
translate into a climate propitious for fresh exploration and affirmation of the FG witness.

Yet future prospects for reception of the Johannine corpus may be
determined even more by what lies beyond current scholarship's focus.
Around the world today, the old-time religion of a crucified and risen
incarnate Word (see John 1) has released new spiritual life on a scale,
missiologists tell us, never before seen in church history. The Bible's
historic message to a world argued by Westerners not long ago to be

---

Lincicum, eds., *Ferdinand Christian Baur und die Geschichte des frühen Christentums*, WUNT 333
(Tübingen: Mohr Siebeck, 2014).

65. See, e.g., Cornelius Bennema, "The Historical Reliability of the Gospel of John," *Foundations*
     67 (November 2014): 4–25; Craig L. Blomberg, *The Historical Reliability of the New Testament*
     (Nashville: B&H Academic, 2016), chs. 5–6.

66. John Piper, *A Peculiar Glory: How the Christian Scriptures Reveal Their Complete Truthfulness*
     (Wheaton, IL: Crossway, 2016); D. A. Carson, ed., *The Enduring Authority of the Christian Scriptures*
     (Grand Rapids: Eerdmans, 2016); Kevin Vanhoozer, *Biblical Authority after Babel: Retrieving the
     Solas in the Spirit of Mere Protestant Christianity* (Grand Rapids: Brazos, 2016); Matthew Barrett,
     God's Word Alone: The Authority of Scripture. What the Reformers Taught and Why It Still Matters
     (Grand Rapids: Zondervan, 2016).

turning away from religion has found dazzling reception, as seen in a recent analysis[67] that yields this information: In 1900, African Protestants were 1.7% of the world Protestant population. By 2000 it was 33.5%. In mid-2017 the projection is 40.8%. By 2050, 53.1% of Protestants in the world will be in Africa. This does not count African Protestants on other continents.

By comparison, today just sixteen percent of Protestants in the world are found in Europe, and only eleven percent in North America. Asia has more than either at this time: eighteen percent. By 2050, Europe will have just ten percent of the world's Protestants, North America will shrink to eight percent, and Asia hold about steady at seventeen percent.

Whether or not Adolf Schlatter's lifetime interaction with the FG (and other Johannine writings) receives explicit notice in the burgeoning Christian confession seen in much of the world today, the works he produced provide empirical grounding for the often Johannine character of faith in Jesus, human and divine, that prevails, and that is absent mainly in areas that beg to differ (as most of Schlatter's colleagues did) with the FG's witness to the truth.

---

67. Todd M. Johnson, Gina A. Zurlo, Albert W. Hickman, and Peter Crossing, "Christianity 2017: Five Hundred Years of Protestant Christianity," *International Bulletin of Missionary Research* 41/1 (January 2017) 41–52.

C. H. DODD
AND JOHANNINE SCHOLARSHIP

Beth M. Stovell

INTRODUCTION

C. H. Dodd has been recognized by many as one of the great scholars of the twentieth century in biblical studies. In a prolific, fifty-year writing career (1920–1970), Dodd wrote an abundance of small books on a wide variety of topics as well as several longer works. Dodd's contribution to biblical studies was predominantly in the study of the background of the New Testament and in the area of eschatology.[1] He has impacted fields as diverse as Synoptic problem and parable studies in the Synoptic Gospels, New Testament eschatology, backgrounds and origins of the New Testament, and developments within the fourth gospel. Dodd's work in Johannine literature also has impacted various methodological approaches to the discipline including narrative criticism, symbolism, and character studies.[2] In their 2013 edited work, *Engaging with C. H. Dodd on the*

---

1. Dodd's Festschrift notes Dodd's contribution in these two fields by its two main divisions. See the introduction of W. D. Davies and David Daube, eds., *Background of the New Testament and Its Eschatology: Studies in Honour of C. H. Dodd* (Cambridge: Cambridge University Press, 1956).
2. See R. Alan Culpepper, "C. H. Dodd as a Precursor to Narrative Criticism," in *Engaging with C.*

Gospel of John: Sixty Years of Tradition and Interpretation, Tom Thatcher and Catrin Williams highlight many of the ways that C. H. Dodd has impacted the face of Johannine studies over the past sixty years. The scholars in this volume highlight Dodd's contributions to context and method as well as Dodd's contributions to the history and tradition found in the fourth gospel.[3]

Extending the research of Thatcher and Williams, their contributors, and others who have examined the impact of Dodd on the face of Johannine studies, the goal of this chapter is to examine C. H. Dodd's scholarship in Johannine studies by focusing on the impact of Dodd's work on studies of intertextuality and the use of the Old Testament in Johannine studies. Towards this end, this chapter begins by examining Dodd as a Johannine scholar by reviewing the place of John's gospel in Dodd's work. Next, it explores how Dodd's work in John's gospel functioned within its academic context as response to Rudolf Bultmann and as a synthetic development of scholarships within its time. This leads to an extended section exploring how Dodd's use of the Old Testament and other sources within Hellenistic Judaism provided the foundations for modern studies of intertextuality in John's gospel. Finally, this essay ends with an overall survey of Dodd's major contributions to the study of John's gospel, demonstrating Dodd's continuing legacy in modern and postmodern Johannine studies.

THE PLACE OF JOHN'S GOSPEL AND
THE OLD TESTAMENT IN DODD'S WORK

In order to explore Dodd's impact on Johannine studies in terms of the use of the Old Testament and other sources in Hellenistic Judaism, it is first helpful to outline Dodd's chief works on these subjects and some of their key attributes as they relate to his other scholarship. This section provides an overview of Dodd's major works highlighting their

---

H. Dodd on the Gospel of John: Sixty Years of Tradition and Interpretation, eds. Tom Thatcher and Catrin H. Williams (Cambridge: Cambridge University Press, 2013), 31–48; J. G. Van der Watt, "Symbolism in John's Gospel: An Evaluation of Dodd's Contribution," in *Engaging with C. H. Dodd,* 66–85; Jaime Clark-Soles, "Characters Who Count: The Case of Nicodemus," in *Engaging with C. H. Dodd,* 126–45.

3. We see these two foci in the two major sections of this volume. See Tom Thatcher and Catrin H. Williams, eds., *Engaging with C. H. Dodd.*

development in terms of the role of the Old Testament in the New Testament and their relation to Dodd's work in Johannine studies.[4]

1. Pauline Writings

Several of Dodd's earliest works explore the background of Paul's writings. Dodd's first book, *The Meaning of Paul for To-day* (1920), was written after World War I. This book offers insights from ancient history and the new field of psychology in Dodd's reading of Paul's writing and its impact for his day. In *The Mind of Paul: A Psychological Approach* (1933), Dodd approaches Paul's writings again with the tool of psychology, exploring the background of Paul's writings. Dodd also wrote an influential commentary on Romans that delineates the foundational message of the prophets in contrast to the legalism of the Judaism of Paul's day.[5]

2. Theological Writings

Dodd's theological writings are among his greatest contributions. Many of these works are still a source of encouragement and controversy today. While Dodd's theology is quite diverse, most of his scholarship focuses on two major areas of his theology: his view of the authority of Scripture and his eschatology.

In Dodd's first major work of theology, *The Authority of the Bible* (1928), he establishes four areas of biblical authority: (1) authority of individual inspiration, giving the prophets as examples; (2) authority of corporate experience, describing the relationship between the

---

4. Elsewhere I have laid out a modified version of this history of Dodd's work in Beth M. Stovell, "C. H. Dodd as New Testament Interpreter and Theologian," in *Pillars in the History of Biblical Interpretation: Volume 1: Prevailing Methods before 1980*, eds. Stanley E. Porter and Sean A. Adams, McMaster Biblical Studies Series 2 (Eugene, OR: Wipf and Stock, 2016), 341–66.

5. Dodd argues that Paul "appeal[s] to the prophetic strain in biblical religion against the legal strain which prevailed in the Judaism of his own time." C. H. Dodd, *The Epistle of Paul to the Romans* (London: Hodder and Stoughton, 1932), 74. Dodd is also known for his minimization of the wrath of God in Romans. In Romans 1:18, for example, Dodd argues that God's wrath is impersonal, pointing to God's numinous quality (21–23). As Dodd explains, "in the long run we cannot think with full consistency of God in terms of the highest human ideals of personality and yet attribute to Him the irrational passion of anger" (Dodd, *Epistle to the Romans*, 24). Dodd argues further that we must translate ἱλαστήριον as expiation rather than propitiation. "The rendering of propitiation is therefore misleading, for it suggests the placating of an angry God" (Dodd, *Epistle to the Romans*, 55). Several scholars have examined and refuted Dodd's interpretation of ἱλαστήριον. For brief and succinct overviews on the issue, see J. A. Fitzmyer, *Romans*, AB 33 (New York: Doubleday, 1993), 349–50 and George Eldon Ladd, *Theology of the New Testament* (Grand Rapids: Eerdmans, 1989), 429–33. I am indebted to Jacqueline C. R. De Roo for this list of scholars. See Jacqueline C. R. De Roo, "Was the Goat for Azazel Destined for the Wrath of God?" *Biblica* 81 (2000): 242 n. 35.

Bible and the community (this concept of corporate experience links to Dodd's view of the Old Testament, which witnesses to "a process which taken as a whole reveals God")[6]; (3) authority of the incarnation, describing the role of Christ coming in a particular time and space and the Hellenistic context of the gospel; (4) authority of history, explaining the necessity of historical grounding for our faith in the biblical message. These same four themes are present in Dodd's *The Bible To-day* (1943), but with a greater emphasis on history. This focus on the relationship between history and the biblical message is also a theme in *History and the Gospel* (1938), *The Study of Theology* (1939), and *The Founder of Christianity* (1970).

Parables of the Kingdom (1935) introduces another continuing theological theme developed further in Dodd's later work: realized eschatology. In *Parables of the Kingdom* Dodd uses form-critical analysis with a central focus on the place of the parables in the context of the whole gospel story and Jesus's original intent within history in telling the parable.[7] Dodd surmises that the kingdom of God referenced throughout the Synoptic Gospels is realized in the ministry of Jesus:

> The absolute, the "wholly other," has entered into time and space. And so the Kingdom of God has come and the Son of Man has come, so also judgment and blessedness have come into human experience. The ancient images of the heavenly feast, of Doomsday, of the Son of Man at the right hand of power, are not only symbols of supra-sensible, supra-historical realities; they have also their corresponding actuality in history. Thus both the facts of the life of Jesus and the events which He foretells within the historical order, are 'eschatological' events, for they fall within the coming of the Kingdom of God.[8]

This work marked a crucial turning point in the study of eschatology and the parables during his time and still has effects on modern scholarship in these areas. After this work, Dodd's realized eschatology becomes a hallmark of his theological interpretation.[9] As William

---

6. C. H. Dodd, *Authority of the Bible* (London: Nisbet, 1955), 190.
7. On Dodd's use of form-critical analysis in his book *Parables of the Kingdom* (New York: Scribner, 1961), see Edgar V. McKnight, *What Is Form Criticism?* (Philadelphia: Fortress Press, 1969), 51–56.
8. Dodd, *Parables of the Kingdom*, 82.
9. A key part of Dodd's position on realized eschatology centers on his translation of the verb φθάνω. Dodd argues that this verb means "to arrive" in the same way as ἤγγικεν. Dodd argues this based on the Greek verbs translation of the Hebrew and LXX equivalents. See Dodd, *Parables of*

Baird states, "Without question, realized eschatology is a central, unifying feature of Dodd's total theological-historical project."[10] As we will see in our discussion of Dodd's work on Johannine literature below, this focus on realized eschatology was essential to Dodd's overall impact on Johannine studies.

3. Johannine Writings

In his inaugural lecture as Professor of Divinity at Cambridge, Dodd pointed to the importance of the fourth gospel for our understanding of early Christianity. Dodd stated that the study of the fourth gospel is the "keystone of an arch" that holds together the New Testament.[11] Thus the two largest and most in-depth works of Dodd centre on the interpretation of the fourth gospel (*Interpretation of the Fourth Gospel*, 1953) and its historical tradition (*Historical Tradition in the Fourth Gospel*, 1963). *Interpretation of the Fourth Gospel* is often considered Dodd's *magnum opus* and both books are still frequently cited today in scholarly debate.[12]

Dodd relies heavily on form criticism in these two works in order to interpret the gospel's message and to validate its historicity. One of the essential contributions Dodd's works provided to Johannine

---

the Kingdom, 43–46. J. Y. Campbell argues against Dodd's translation of φθάνω, ἤγγικεν, and Dodd's subsequent conclusions based on his translation. Campbell notes that Dodd's conclusions are not grammatically consistent across other accounts of usage and contain some logical errors when viewed in this light. See J. Y. Campbell, "Contributions and Comments," *ExpTim* 48 (1936): 91–94. Dodd replies to Campbell's critique the following month in the same journal, defending his position. It is interesting to note that Dodd bases a portion of his case on the Greek perfect as "durative-punctiliar" in its *Aktionsart* citing the grammar of A. T. Robertson (Robertson, *Grammar of the Greek New Testament in the Light of Historical Research* [New York: Hodder and Stoughton, 1914}, 895). Dodd uses this grammatical construct to argue that the meaning of ἤγγικεν could move developmentally from "approach" to "arrive." This theory is certainly unstable particularly in light of current arguments of verbal aspect theory. For Dodd's argument against Campbell, see C. H. Dodd, "Contributions and Comments," *ExpTim* 48 (1936): 138–42. For discussion of verbal aspect theory, see Stanley E. Porter, *Verbal Aspect in the Greek of the New Testament: With Reference to Tense and Mood*, SBG 1 (New York: Peter Lang, 1993).

10. William Baird, *History of New Testament Research: From C. H. Dodd to Hans Dieter Betz*, vol. 3 (Minneapolis: Fortress Press, 2013), 42.

11. C. H. Dodd, *The Present Task in New Testament Studies* (Cambridge: Cambridge University Press, 1936), 29.

12. Examples include Marianne Meye Thompson, "Eternal Life in the Gospel of John," *Ex Auditu* 5 (1989): 35–55; Christopher Skinner, "Another Look at 'the Lamb of God,'" *Bibliotheca Sacra* 161 (2004): 89–104; C. R. Koester, *Symbolism in the Fourth Gospel: Meaning, Mystery, Community* (Minneapolis: Fortress Press, 1995); Jan van der Watt, "Symbolism in John's Gospel: An Evaluation of Dodd's Contribution," in *Engaging with C. H. Dodd*, 66–85. All of these scholars deal with Dodd's discussion of symbolism specifically.

studies besides emphasizing the historical backgrounds to the fourth gospel was his emphasis on realized eschatology. Urban C. von Wahlde explores the impact of Dodd's contribution of realized eschatology to Johannine studies in his article "C. H. Dodd, the Historical Jesus, and Realized Eschatology." Von Walde argues that Dodd's view of a non-apocalyptic Jesus provides a unique approach to New Testament eschatology that fits nicely with some of the pre-existing forms of Jewish thought present at Jesus's time.[13] Besides Dodd's view of realized eschatology having a major impact of subsequent scholars, it has also impacted whole theological traditions. For example, realized eschatology has been widely accepted within Catholic tradition as a standard way of explaining their particular amillenial perspective on the kingdom of God.[14]

In addition, in each of these two works, Dodd bases substantial portions of his analysis on allusions and citations in the primary sources of Hellenistic Judaism and the Old Testament. For example, in *Historical Tradition in the Fourth Gospel*, Dodd spends an entire chapter specifically looking at the Old Testament allusions via testimonies and their impact on our understanding of John's gospel as a source in relation to the Synoptic Gospels.[15] In *Interpretation of the Fourth Gospel*, references to the literature of Hellenistic Judaism and to the Old Testament function as essential means of explaining the major themes that Dodd focuses on throughout the book. For example, Dodd devotes an entire chapter to Philo as representative of Hellenistic Judaism, which serves as a major background to the fourth gospel.[16]

4. Use of the Old Testament in the New Testament

Besides noting Dodd's contributions within Johannine studies, it is valuable to note Dodd's works that specifically contribute to the study of the use of the Old Testament in the New Testament. In *The Apostolic Preaching and its Developments* (1936), Dodd argues that underlying the New Testament are two oral sources: the *kerygma* and the *didache*.

---

13. Urban C. von Wahlde, "C. H. Dodd, the Historical Jesus, and Realized Eschatology." in *Engaging with C. H. Dodd*, 149–162.

14. For example, Pope Benedict XVI comments in his book *Jesus of Nazareth* praising Dodd's realized eschatology. See Pope Benedict XVI, *Jesus of Nazareth* (New York: Doubleday, 2007), 188.

15. C. H. Dodd, *Historical Tradition in the Fourth Gospel* (Cambridge: Cambridge University Press, 1963), 31–49.

16. C. H. Dodd, *Interpretation of the Fourth Gospel* (Cambridge: Cambridge University Press, 1953), 54–73.

The *kerygma* is the proclamation of the gospel, "not the action of the preacher, but that which he preaches, his message." The *kerygma* "is the public proclamation of Christianity to the non-Christian world."[17] The *didache*, on the other hand, is the teaching of ethical instruction.[18]

As Dodd explains the *kerygma* further, we see the influence of his realized eschatology on his description:

> *Kerygma* is a proclamation of the facts of the death and resurrection of Christ in an eschatological setting which gives significance to the facts. They mark the transition from "this evil Age" to the "Age to Come." The "Age to Come" is the age of fulfilment. Hence the importance of the statement that Christ died and rose "according to the Scriptures." Whatever events the Old Testament prophets may indicate as impending, these events are for them significant as elements in the coming of "the Day of the Lord." Thus the fulfilment of prophecy means that the Day of the Lord has dawned: the Age to Come has begun.[19]

Dodd arrives at an outline for this *kergyma*:

> The prophecies are fulfilled, and the new Age is inaugurated by the coming of Christ. He was born of the seed of David. He died according to the Scriptures, to deliver us out of the present evil age. He was buried. He rose on the third day according to the Scriptures. He is exalted at the right hand of God, as Son of God and Lord of quick and dead. He will come again as Judge and Saviour of men.[20]

Notably these descriptions of the *kergyma* point to the essential role of the Old Testament in the expectations of the New Testament authors. Locating Dodd's discussion of the *kerygma*, it is helpful to see in what ways Dodd's discussion of *kergyma* is similar to that of Martin Dibelius

---

17. C. H. Dodd, *The Apostolic Preaching and its Developments: with an Appendix on Eschatology and History* (repr., Grand Rapids: Baker, 1936), 7.

18. In his work, *Jesus the Divine Teacher*, Eugene Kevane has used the categories of *didache* and *kergyma* to discuss the role of catechetical teaching (*didache*) in relation to the message of Jesus (*kergyma*), which were a set of truths coming directly from God. This places Dodd's two categories in a Catholic context. See E. Kevane, *Jesus the Divine Teacher* (New York: Vantage Press, 2003). This is particularly interesting considering Pope Benedict XVI's recent comments in his book *Jesus of Nazareth* praising Dodd's realized eschatology. See Pope Benedict XVI, *Jesus of Nazareth*, 188.

19. Dodd, *Apostolic Preaching*, 8.

20. Ibid., 17.

and in what way Dodd differs.[21] Dodd follows Dibelius in his belief that a traditional outline can be found beneath the gospels. Dodd devotes much of his scholarship to excavating the foundational *kerygma* in such works as his *Apostolic Preaching, Interpretation of the Fourth Gospel,* and *According to the Scriptures.* Unlike Dibelius, Dodd did not judge the various forms within the Gospels to contain varying degrees of historical material nor did he see disunity in the text because of its various forms.[22]

The differentiation between *kerygma* and *didache* in Dodd's work influences Dodd's attribution of influential biblical texts to each category in his book. In *According to the Scriptures* (1952), Dodd seeks not only the form of the *kerygma*, but the form behind the form of the *kerygma*.[23] Dodd argues that behind the New Testament is the oral tradition of the *kerygma* and behind the *kerygma* are the Old Testament prophecies fulfilled by Jesus in his life, death, and resurrection, memorized as oral tradition. Further Dodd argues against the prevailing theory at the time that these quotations were part of *testimonia,* which were collections of proof texts in written form. Instead Dodd argues that these testimonies were oral in their nature and that the New Testament authors had entire passages in mind.[24] These Old Testament prophecies form the "substructure of New Testament theology."[25]

---

21. Dibelius and Dodd were friends and Dodd refers to his agreement with Dibelius's work in C. H. Dodd, "The Framework of the Gospel Narrative," *ExpTim* 43 (1931–1932): 396–400.

22. McKnight, *What is Form Criticism,* 33–37. This is a debatable point. D. A. Carson and J. S. King have argued over this specific point in Dodd's *Historical Tradition* (C. H. Dodd, *Historical Tradition in the Fourth Gospel* [Cambridge: Cambridge University Press, 1963]). Carson maintains that Dodd's use of form criticism moves him further away from establishing a historical background to the fourth gospel, because Dodd uses the language of form critics to discuss certain passages within the Johannine account as "coloured" and "shaped" by the needs of the early church. Carson argues that Dodd is undercutting his argument towards historicity here and that while Dodd argues for the essential need for history, his use of form criticism is inconsistent with this view. King believes Carson has "been unfair to Dodd" in this and many other respects. For the debate, see D. A. Carson, "Historical Tradition in the Fourth Gospel: After Dodd, What?," in *Gospel Perspectives II,* eds. R. T. France and David Wenham (Sheffield: JSOT, 1981), 83–145; J. S. King, "Has D. A. Carson Been Fair to C. H. Dodd?," *JSNT* 17 (1983): 97–102; D. A. Carson, "Historical Tradition in the Fourth Gospel: A Response to J. S. King," *JSNT* 23 (1985): 73–81.

23. Dillistone discusses in detail this care for the background of the New Testament in Dodd's work, describing it as the "form behind the forms." Frederick William Dillistone, *C. H. Dodd: Interpreter of the New Testament* (London: Hodder & Stoughton, 1977), 117.

24. C. H. Dodd, *According to the Scriptures* (London: Nisbet, 1952), 59–60. Baird provides a helpful description of the differences between Dodd's work and Rendal Harris's work on testimonies on these main points. See Baird, *History of New Testament Research,* 44; William Baird, *History of New Testament Research: From Jonathan Edwards to Rudolf Bultmann,* vol. 2 (Minneapolis: Fortress Press, 2003), 405–406.

25. This phrase is the subtitle of *According to the Scriptures.*

Dodd's work on *kerygma*, *didache*, and the notion of the Old Testament prophecies as a substructure of the New Testament in turn can be seen in Dodd's subsequent Johannine writings as he references his own work to explain the nature of Johannine sources and their dependence on the Old Testament.[26]

DODD, BULTMANN, AND INTERTEXTUALITY IN JOHANNINE STUDIES

To understand Dodd's contributions to Johannine studies, it is helpful to locate Dodd in relation to other Johannine scholars of his time. Much recent scholarship has been done articulating Dodd's relationship to Bultmann as Bultmann and Dodd stood as key figures in Johannine studies around the same time period. This section will review such research and highlight their impact on Johannine studies.

One way of evaluating the relationship between Bultmann and Dodd is in terms of their mutual relationship to the ability of form criticism to get us back to a historical Jesus.[27] Bultmann and Dodd stand at either end of the spectrum of form critics. While Dodd is more conservative than the conservative Dibelius, Bultmann is the most radical of the three originators in this approach. Whereas Bultmann has little or no confidence in getting back to Jesus's career and person, Dodd believes that we can get back to the historical Jesus.[28]

Koester highlights how the differing worldviews of Dodd and Bultmann impact the differences between Dodd and Bultmann's view of history, tradition, and their impact on Johannine studies. "Where Dodd emphasized continuity in the way Jesus's message

---

26. For example, in *Historical Tradition in the Fourth Gospel*, Dodd cites his *According to the Scriptures* as foundational to his approach concerning the Old Testament in the fourth gospel. Dodd, *Historical Tradition*, 31–49.

27. Much of the following discussion of Bultmann and Dodd is elsewhere developed in my chapter on Dodd and form criticism. See Stovell, "C. H. Dodd as New Testament Interpreter and Theologian."

28. Both Dillistone and McKnight note this key difference between Dodd and Bultmann. McKnight, *What Is Form Criticism*, 57; Dillistone, *C. H. Dodd*, 223. Dodd takes aim at Bultmann's form-critical analysis of the gospel of John, pointing to the critical issue of proving historical relationship. Dodd, *Interpretation*, 122–24. Dodd's belief in retrieving the original story of Jesus seems to intensify over the course of his life, eventually leading him to write a book reconstructing the life and personality of Jesus, which has taken a good deal of critique for its conservative beliefs (C. H. Dodd, *The Founder of Christianity* [New York: Macmillan, 1970]). For the critiques of *The Founder of Christianity*, Dillistone provides a helpful list. Dillistone, *C. H. Dodd*, 178–79.

was elaborated for a Hellenized world, Bultmann emphasized the discontinuity."[29] Koester points out that for Dodd faith is revealed through theological tradition and the history beneath the gospel accounts. In contrast, Bultmann eschews all availability to reach the historical Jesus because he believes true faith involves acknowledging the radical mystery of the gospel. For Dodd, history and continuity are not simply helpful but essential. We can see this in such statements from Dodd as this: "Christianity recognizes no spiritual revelation which is not directly related to the historical reality of Jesus."[30]

Due to Dodd's emphasis on continuity compared to Bultmann's view of paradox, it is also not surprising to find that those working toward seeing continuity between Old Testament and New Testament in John's gospel (and elsewhere) would see Dodd's approach as more in line with their purposes.

John Painter examines six agreements among disagreements between Dodd and Bultmann.[31] Several of these places of agreement (and disagreement) provide valuable insight into discussions of intertextuality and Dodd as they pertain to the fourth gospel.

1. Both Dodd and Bultmann see the need to grasp the worldview that John's gospel presupposes in order to understand the meaning of John's gospel. However, what composes these backgrounds is substantially different in Dodd than in Bultmann.[32] This area of agreement leads to one of the valuable insights of Dodd's work. In seeking this worldview of the fourth gospel, Dodd's research explores intertextual references that create a foundation for modern scholars of intertextuality.[33]

---

29. Craig R. Koester, "Progress and Paradox: C. H. Dodd and Rudolf Bultmann on History, Jesus Tradition, and the Fourth Gospel," in *Engaging with C. H. Dodd,* 57.

30. C. H. Dodd, *History and the Gospel* (New York: Scribners, 1938), 58. Koester quotes this statement to point to Dodd's belief in the plausibility of the historical message behind the gospels, contrasting this with Bultmann's view of such attempts as an offense. Koester, "Progress and Paradox," 59.

31. John Painter, "The Fourth Gospel and the Founder of Christianity: The Place of Historical Tradition in the Work of C. H. Dodd," in *Engaging with C. H. Dodd,* 262–67.

32. Painter, "The Fourth Gospel," 262–63.

33. One such example of Dodd's influence is the work on the intertextual references in the term "logos" in the prologue of the fourth gospel. See Lars Kierspel, *The Jews and the World in the Fourth Gospel: Parallelism, Function, and Context,* WUNT 2/220 (Tübingen: Mohr Siebeck, 2006), 88–89, 114 n. 114, 120.

2. Both Dodd and Bultmann see the interpreter's task as a hermeneutical circle, which is aware of how the parts make the whole
   and how the whole connects the parts. Thus it is Dodd's implicit
   assumption that the reader knows the whole story while reading
   a part.[34] The role of the *kerygma* is key to Dodd's understanding
   here. Dodd argues that behind the *kerygma* are the Old Testament prophecies. Thus, a whole and parts approach necessitates
   continuity with past tradition in intertextual ways. For example,
   Dodd points to the Old Testament "plot" around heroic figures
   like the Servant in Isaiah 53 and the Son of Man in Daniel 7 as
   impacting the quotation of these sources.[35]

3. Dodd and Bultmann agree about the fragmentary nature of
   evidence, but Dodd still believes in the plausibility of historical
   evidence behind the gospels.

4. Dodd and Bultmann both use the two document hypothesis and as
   noted above, use a form-critical approach to oral traditions.

5. Dodd and Bultmann both accept to some degree the conclusions of
   form criticism that oral tradition transmitted individual units and
   that the result of this is that designating a chronology of Jesus's life is
   problematic.[36] While chronology is problematized due to form critical assumptions, Dodd's focus on oral tradition encouraged him to
   explore how the Old Testament and other sources were transmitted
   by oral tradition leading to modern explorations of intertextuality.

6. Dodd and Bultmann agree that the fourth gospel is largely independent of the Synoptics. In the exploration of these unique Johannine
   elements within the Johannine tradition, Dodd highlighted the use
   of language, images, and symbols unique to the fourth gospel and
   explored the potential backgrounds of these symbols.[37]

Dodd's critiques of form criticism show his continuities and
his discontinuities with the presuppositions of this approach along

---

34. Painter, "The Fourth Gospel," 263.
35. C. H. Dodd, *The Old Testament in the New* (Philadelphia: Fortress Press, 1963), 12–13.
36. Painter, "The Fourth Gospel," 265–66.
37. For more on symbolism in Dodd, see Van der Watt, "Symbolism in John's Gospel," 66–85.

with one of the ways that Dodd would differ from Bultmann. Dodd maintains the form-critical method of seeking the oral tradition behind the texts and of designating various types of forms in this endeavour. Yet there are key differences in Dodd's approach. Dodd believes in recovering history behind the text, Dodd focuses on forms with the goal of reading the biblical text as unified rather than disparate, and he believes that this history is essential to a life-giving faith in Jesus Christ.[38] Dillistone summarizes the difference of Dodd's approach nicely:

> Behind all traditions and testimonies Dodd looked for the lineaments of a *Person,* a Person who was himself the image of the invisible God, a Person who brought to fulfilment all that could otherwise be known of the activity of God in the whole process of history. The concern for *forms* he shared to the full. But whereas Bultmann wished to operate dialectically, separating the authentic form from the inauthentic by a continuous exclusion of alternatives, Dodd wished to proceed organically, detecting the life-substance in each tradition and pointing to the way in which each element contributed to the process of integration into a living whole.[39]

This difference is likely connected to the general difference between British scholarship and German scholarship. Dodd represents the British emphasis on historicity over and against the German traditions of Bultmann. Both N. T. Wright and Dillistone point to this difference as key to understanding Dodd's approach.[40] Koester has observed that one can trace many of the differences between Dodd and Bultmann to the differences in their worldview: Dodd as a Congregationalist and Bultmann as a Lutheran.[41] Pointing to these differences alongside agreements allows us to highlight some of the key elements of Dodd's viewpoints.

---

38. Dodd makes clear the importance of history to faith in several of his books including *History and the Gospel* (1938), *The Study of Theology* (1939) and *The Founder of Christianity* (1970).
39. Dillistone, *C. H. Dodd,* 224.
40. This is well demonstrated by Dodd's debate with Tillich described in Appendix 1, Dillistone, *C. H. Dodd,* 241–43. Wright emphasizes this distinction in his writings as well, using Dodd as characteristic of a line of scholarship. See N. T. Wright, *The New Testament and the People of God* (Minneapolis: Fortress Press, 1996), 12, 22ff., 39.
41. Koester, "Progress and Paradox," 51–55.

DODD, THE OLD TESTAMENT, JOHN'S GOSPEL, AND INTERTEXTUALITY

This section will examine the positive impact that Dodd's work has had on the use of the Old Testament and sources from within Hellenistic Judaism in the study of John's gospel as well as highlight some of the faults with Dodd's approach that have been developed in more constructive ways in recent years.

Positive Impact of Dodd on Intertextuality and Old Testament Sources in Johannine Studies

We will now focus on three core ways that Dodd's work has influenced Johannine studies in terms of intertextuality and Old Testament and Hellenistic Judaism sources:

1. Dodd's use of Old Testament and Hellenistic Judaism as sources for the gospel of John in the sense of background has provided initial grounding in sources for intertextual study in the gospel of John.

2. Dodd's methodology laid out in *According to the Scriptures* has impacted the methods of intertextual studies. Essential to Dodd's approach is highlighting particular passages that are meaningful to the gospel of John and arguing for entire passages of the Old Testament to be referenced and essential to the message of the gospel of John.

3. Besides providing a starting point for intertextual method, Dodd's work also provides a theological reason why these Old Testament passages are being used the way that they are in the New Testament. This theological explanation is intertwined with Dodd's views on the value of history to theology and his view of realized eschatology.

Sources and Method

In his study of the use of Psalm 118 in the gospel of John, Andrew Brunson points to Dodd as the initiator of the contemporary debate around the role of context in New Testament citation of the Old Testament. Brunson cites Dodd's explication of the use of entire passages of the Old Testament in his *According to the Scriptures* as standing in contradiction to the proof-texting arguments made by other New Testament scholars. As Brunson points out, while Dodd's method has received its share of critics, scholars like I. Howard Marshall have demonstrated that even the critics like A. J. Sandberg's own statistics bolster Dodd's claims rather than undermining them.[42] Brunson builds on Dodd's method to argue that within the gospel of John, we see the Fourth Evangelist referencing what comes before and after his particular quotation of Psalm 118, demonstrating that he is aware of the context surrounding his referenced verses.

Two Johannine scholars point to Dodd as they explore the intertextual links around the term *logos*. In each case they note the complexity of the sources Dodd provides. In Lars Kierspel's *The Jews and The World in the Fourth Gospel*, Kierspel points to Dodd's view of the prologue and its depiction of *logos* as a Hellenistic opening to the gospel that builds on intertextual links. Kierspel demonstrates how Dodd accomplishes this by pointing to Philo and other Hellenistic sources as transitioning into the historical person of Jesus Christ, thus linking Hellenistic to Jewish sources. Kierspel notes how the work of Peter Phillips has built on Dodd's theories in his *The Prologue of the Fourth Gospel: A Sequential Reading*.[43] As Painter points out, Phillips's work extends Dodd's suggestion of Hellenistic readers to a larger group of "outsiders."[44] Both Phillips and Kierspel demonstrate the lasting impact of Dodd's use of these complex sources and how developments have come out of Dodd's original theories related to these sources. In each case, Dodd's use of sources and his methology have become the initial groundwork for further intertextual analysis.

From Method to Meaning

One of the keys to understanding Dodd's approach is that Dodd is interested in not only *how* the Old Testament is used in the New Testament, but also *why* the Old Testament is used in the New Testament. As Dodd notes in his book *The Old Testament in the New*, "it is clear that in

---

42. Andrew C. Brunson, *Psalm 118 in the Gospel of John: An Intertextual Study on the New Exodus Pattern in the Theology of John* (Tübingen: Mohr Siebeck, 2003), 18 n. 95.

43. Kierspel, *Jews and the World in the Fourth Gospel*, 114. Kierspel points specifically to Peter Phillips. *The Prologue of the Fourth Gospel: A Sequential Reading* (New York: T & T Clark, 2006), 73.

44. See Painter, "The Fourth Gospel," 263 n. 11 where Painter discusses Phillips's work in Phillips, *The Prologue of the Fourth Gospel*.

many places the New Testament writers have a more serious purpose in view [when citing the Old Testament in the New Testament]. In adducing passages from the Old Testament they are consciously appealing to an *authority* (here authority is in italics in Dodd). A quotation may be introduced to provide an unassailable premise upon which an inference may be founded, or to test a conclusion drawn by logical argument or put forth as a corollary of experience."[45] Thus Dodd's argument is not simply that a substructure of the Old Testament exists underneath the New Testament, but that this substructure functions as a supporting foundation to the validity of the New Testament itself.

Yet these Old Testament forms were not left unchanged in the process, but a new lens was applied for a Greek world. Dodd describes Philo of Alexandria as a chief example of this kind of application.[46] However, Dodd is also careful to not suggest the Philo's allegorical approach is the same as the New Testament authors. Instead, Dodd explains the ways that New Testament authors historically contextualized their uses of the Old Testament.[47] Dodd demonstrates this development in his discussion of the use of Old Testament passages and figures like the Son of Man in Daniel 7 and the figure described in Zechariah 9–14 and their impact on the fourth gospel.[48] Dodd describes how in each case "the reader is invited to study the context as a whole, and to reflect upon the 'plot' there unfolded. In some way, an understanding of the plot will help him to see the significance of the strange events of the life and death of Jesus, and what followed."[49]

Later when discussing the use of Day of the Lord passages, Dodd argues that by referencing the Old Testament Scriptures, the "New Testament writers imply that they and their contemporaries are in some sense living through the drama of disaster and glory, of death and resurrection, which in a variety of ways, and with greater or less elaboration, is the 'plot' of them all."[50] Thus the purpose of quoting the Old Testament is theological in its scope, both by locating itself within the authority of the Old Testament, and also by showing that the early Christian community is in fact *living* the great story of Scripture in

---

45. Dodd, *Old Testament in the New*, 4.
46. See Dodd's description of Philo on this account in ibid., 5.
47. Ibid., 6–7.
48. Ibid., 17–18.
49. Ibid., 20.
50. Ibid., 24.

their midst. In this way Dodd's approach to intertextuality is never a neutral enterprise, but one informed by faith, history, and tradition.

Critiques of Dodd's Use of the Old Testament and Other Sources in Johannine Studies

While Dodd's writings have been a rich source for subsequent Johannine scholars, providing insight into the use of sources in John's gospel, yet Dodd's approach to the use of the Old Testament and other sources is not without its faults. While van der Watt demonstrates the contribution that Dodd has made to understanding symbolism in John's gospel, he also notes weaknesses in Dodd's methodology where recent studies of intertextuality would provide greater clarity. Van der Watt notes that in Dodd's explanation of the vine imagery in John 15,

> Dodd also recalls that the vine/vineyard is a "standing symbol of the people of God" in the Old Testament (Isa. 5:1–7; Ps. 80:9–15; Jer. 2:21; see 1953: 136). Dodd does not explain how that should be applied to the viticulture language of John 15, though he does reflect a little on this elsewhere (1953: 411–12), by remarking that John applied the vine symbolism to Jesus, now making him and his disciples the people of God. He does not go any further than this.[51]

Van der Watt further critiques Dodd's method stating that Dodd "does not explain the dynamics of the intertextuality between the Old Testament usages and that of John in chapter 15, neither does he consider any references to the vine/vineyard imagery outside of the Old Testament." Yet with one of the single elements of John 15, Dodd uses many sources outside of the Old Testament, but not with the entire passage. Van der Watt notes that Dodd sometimes references other sources outside of the Old Testament and other times does not without any consistency.[52] Yet these critiques have not kept scholars from using Dodd throughout the years since the publication of his first works.

---

51. Van der Watt, "Symbolism in John's Gospel," 69–70.
52. Ibid.

DODD'S LASTING LEGACY

As Thatcher and Williams's volume demonstrates, the legacy of Dodd has continued to impact Johannine scholarship for more than sixty years. Dodd has impacted the study of Johannine narrative, the study of John's gospel in relation to oral traditions, the understanding of John's gospel as it relates to history, the advancement of form-critical method in Johannine studies, examinations of the *kerygma* and the *didache* as related to John's gospel, and understanding the diverse backgrounds to John's gospel including purely Greek sources, sources in Hellenistic Judaism, and sources within the Old Testament itself. Besides these advances, Dodd's work has encouraged scholars in studying intertextuality to think more broadly about the impact of the Old Testament and other sources, but also to think carefully about *why* these particular sources are being referenced and how they relate to the larger canonical story of the Scriptures. Finally, Dodd's work has impacted the field of New Testament eschatology. Dodd's exploration of realized eschatology has impacted not only the field of Johannine studies, but theology more broadly spanning out into other theological disciplines. While Dodd's methods are not without their flaws and his work has been built upon alongside much critique, nevertheless Dodd's work continues to hold a valuable place in Johannine studies.

RUDOLF BULTMANN AND THE JOHANNINE LITERATURE

Bryan R. Dyer

INTRODUCTION

I n his 1991 book *Understanding the Fourth Gospel*, John Ashton divides the history of interpretation on the gospel of John into three periods: "Before Bultmann," "Bultmann," and "After Bultmann." There have been many scholars who have offered significant contributions to interpretation of the Johaninne literature—several of these names are being presented in this volume, but to which we might add Walter Bauer, F. C. Baur, C. K. Barrett, or more recently Francis Moloney, I. Howard Marshall, Richard Bauckham, and several other names. Yet none of these scholars, as significant as they are, have impacted the study of John's gospel, the Johannine literature, or the New Testament as a whole, in the same way that Rudolf Bultmann has. In the words of Ashton, Bultmann is "unmatched in learning, breadth, and understanding" and "towers like a colossus" among scholars of the fourth gospel.[1]

---

1. John Ashton, *Understanding the Fourth Gospel* (Oxford: Oxford University Press, 1991), 45. I should note that Ashton's comments here do not appear in the second edition published in 2007.

Yet this declaration is ironic. It is ironic because, as Ashton states, "in spite of his pre-eminence, every answer Bultmann gives to the really important questions he raises—is wrong."[2] How can it be that this towering figure to whom all scholars before and after are compared—whom everyone working in Johannine studies (let alone New Testament studies) must engage with—is wrong in nearly every major conclusion that he came to? It may be that Ashton is exaggerating, but it is certainly true that in many aspects of Bultmann's work on the gospel of John—his hypotheses regarding its sources, its relationship to Gnosticism, and his restructuring of the entire gospel—have been taken up by relatively few scholars since. So where is Bultmann's influence? How are we to understand how Bultmann approached Scripture and influenced Johannine scholarship? These questions are the impetus for the writing of this essay.

As is often the case, a key to understanding a person is to know something of the context from which they emerged. One of the impressive things about Bultmann is the extent of his learning and the many hats that he wore as a scholar. He was a biblical exegete but also a theologian, philosopher, and historian. He drew upon many different sources for his work, including Karl Barth, Søren Kierkegaard, and Martin Luther. As a result, Bultmann left a lasting imprint on numerous methods for approaching Scripture such as form criticism, existential interpretation, and the history-of-religion approach. Just as he once called early Christianity a "syncretistic phenomenon,"[3] so too could we describe Bultmann's own theology and method.

To provide some background to Bultmann and his impact on Johannine scholarship, I will explore a few sources which Bultmann incorporated into his approach to the New Testament. I wish to focus on his interaction with the history-of-religion school, but also existentialism and dialectical theology. Next this paper will look closely at Bultmann's quest to "demythologize" the New Testament, which will lead us to examine his interpretation of the gospel of John.

---

2. Ashton, *Understanding the Fourth Gospel*, 45.

3. Rudolf Bultmann, *Primitive Christianity in Its Contemporary Setting*, trans. R. H. Fuller (London: Collins, 1956), 209–13.

THE *RELIGIONSGESCHICHTLICHE SCHULE*

Coming to prominence in the late nineteenth and early twentieth century, the *religionsgeschichtliche Schule* ("history-of-religion school") concerned itself with the study of the Old and New Testaments in light of other religions.[4] Its members sought to approach their study of religions without theological or philosophical assumptions. Therefore, they focused most of their attention on historical and comparative analyses.[5] The *religionsgeschichtliche Schule* was interested in how a religion, like early Christianity, developed over time within the context of other religions. They also gave special attention to religious practice, custom, and expression.

Rudolf Bultmann entered into the academy as a student amidst a hotbed of activity within the history-of-religion school.[6] While at the University of Berlin, he studied under Hermann Gunkel who provided impactful work toward both form criticism and history-of-religion. Bultmann received his doctorate from Marburg University where he studied under other history-of-religion scholars such as Wilhelm Heitmüller and Johannes Weiss. It was during this time that he was introduced to the works of Richard Reitzenstein and Wilhelm Bousset. This was the setting of Bultmann's academic career in which he built upon the work and thoughts of these scholars. Upon Heitmüller's retirement in 1921, Bultmann succeeded him at Marburg University and remained there until his retirement in 1951.[7]

All of these scholars had a hand in developing the *religionsgeschichtliche Schule* as well as the theology of Bultmann. Of all those within this school of thought, four were particularly impactful on Bultmann's thinking—Gunkel, Bousset, Reitzenstein, and Heitmüller. Hermann Gunkel's work has been accredited with the "inauguration of *religionsgeschichtliche Schule* research."[8] In *Creation and*

---

4. For more on the *religionsgeschichtliche Schule*, see Richard S. Ascough, "Historical Approaches," in *Dictionary of Biblical Criticism and Interpretation*, ed. Stanley E. Porter (London: Routledge, 2007), 157–59; William Baird, *History of New Testament Research*, 3 vols. (Minneapolis: Augsburg Fortress, 1992–2013), 2:238–52; Karen L. King, *What Is Gnosticism?* (Cambridge, MA: Belknap, 2003), 71–109; John Riches, *A Century of New Testament Study* (Valley Forge, PA: Trinity, 1993), 14–49.
5. Ascough, "Historical Approaches," 157.
6. For a wonderful essay that situates Bultmann within the larger history-of-religion project, see Helmut Koester, "Early Christianity from the Perspective of the History of Religions: Rudolf Bultmann's Contribution," in *Bultmann, Retrospect and Prospect: The Centenary Symposium at Wellesly*, ed. E. C. Hobbs (Philadelphia: Fortress, 1985), 59–74.
7. Roger A. Johnson, *Rudolf Bultmann: Interpreting Faith for the Modern Era* (London: Collins, 1987), 10.
8. Ascough, "Historical Approaches," 157.

Chaos in the Primeval Era and Eschaton, Gunkel identified mythological elements in Genesis 1 and Revelation 12 and attributed them to an
influence from Babylonian religions.[9] Gunkel argued not for a literary
dependence between the texts, but, as William Yarchin describes, "rather
a reception of the Babylonian elements in ancient Israelite worship via
oral tradition."[10] This stress on the mythological character of the biblical
accounts was later picked up by Bultmann in the bulk of his scholarship.

Wilhelm Bousset's work also did much to advance history-of-
religion thought and Bultmann's theology. In fact, Bultmann refers
to Bousset's book *Kyrios Christos* as "brilliant," showing that early
Christianity was "essentially a cult-piety which sent forth as its flower:
mysticism."[11] An important contribution that Bultmann incorporated
into his own work was Bousset's distinction between Palestinian and
Hellenistic Christianity. In an article concerning the Synoptic Problem, Bultmann shows how Bousset impacted his work:

> The importance of this distinction was made clear by W. Bousset in his
> *Kyrios Christos* (second edition, 1921). He showed that primitive Pales-
> tinian Christianity was very different from Hellenistic Christianity. The
> former remained within the limits of Judaism and regarded itself as the
> true Israel; its piety was eschatological and it awaited Jesus as the coming
> Son of Man. Primitive Hellenistic Christianity, on the other hand, was
> a religion of cult, in the center of which stood Jesus Christ as the "Lord"
> who communicated his heavenly powers in the worship and the sacra-
> ments of the community. It goes without saying that the recognition of
> this difference is of great importance in the analysis of the synoptic tradi-
> tion. It means that the elements of cult-religion contained in the Synop-
> tic Gospels are secondary, coming from Hellenistic sources.[12]

9. Hermann Gunkel, *Creation and Chaos in the Primeval Era and the Eschaton: A Religio-Historical Study of Genesis 1 and Revelation 12*, trans. K. W. Whitney, Jr. (Grand Rapids: Eerdmans, 2006), 250. Gunkel concludes: "We have recognized, with the assistance of the Creation myth, how the Babylonian tradition has fructified the Israelite tradition at many different points. For the kinds of acquired materials and the appropriation thereof Genesis 1 and Revelation 12 are characteristic. It is basically the same materials which appear here two times, although in a different form. In the early periods it is a myth of primal times, a myth which made its way from Babylon to Israel. In the later period it is a prophecy about the end time. The mood and the needs of humanity had changed between the two periods, in Babylon no less than in Israel."

10. William Yarchin, *History of Biblical Interpretation: A Reader* (Peabody, MA: Hendrickson, 2004), 238.

11. Rudolf Bultmann, *Theology of the New Testament*, 2 vols., trans. Kendrick Grobel (New York: Scribners, 1951–1955), 2:247.

12. Bultmann, "A New Approach to the Synoptic Problem," *Journal of Religion* 6 (1926): 337–62 (360–61). In his introduction to the fifth edition of *Kyrios Christos*, Bultmann writes: "Among the

The distinction between early Palestinian and later Hellenistic Christianity plays a significant role in how Bultmann understands the early Church and tradition.

Richard Reitzenstein's work paid special attention to the influence of Oriental mythology upon early Christianity. He argued that much of early Christian thought originated as Oriental myth and passed through Jewish thought to Christian thinkers—especially Paul. Of his task he writes:

> A large and attractive task is opened up for the researcher, to demonstrate on the one hand the Oriental origin, and on the other hand the stages of the occidentalizing of this thought-world by the Jewish, the Greek, and finally the general Western feeling. It is not Christian by birth, but it has become Christian through powerful religious personalities.[13]

For example, in a chapter entitled "On the Developmental History of Paul," Reitzenstein argues that Paul's Christology was built upon an earlier myth of the divine *Anthropos*. He writes, "I am convinced that for the elaboration of his interpretation of Christ, Paul used a conception, already present in both Hellenistic and Palestinian Judaism, but ultimately stemming from the Iranian sphere, of the divine Anthropos as the bearer of the true religion." However, Paul's Christ differs from the divine mythological Anthropos in that it dies for our sins. This, according to Reitzenstein, is uniquely Pauline: "In spite of the borrowing, his religion remains new and his very own."[14]

---

works of New Testament scholarship the study of which I used to recommend in my lectures to students as indispensable, above all belonged Wilhelm Bousset's *Kyrios Christos.* . . . In this work the demands raised by Bousset's predecessors and contemporaries of the so-called history-of-religions school (I mention only W. Wrede, H. Gunkel, J. Weiss, and W. Heitmüller) for the first time have been brought to fulfillment in a coherent and comprehensive presentation" (Rudolf Bultmann, "Introductory Word to the Fifth Edition," in Willhelm Bousset, *Kyrios Christos*, trans. J. E. Steely [Nashville: Abingdon, 1970], 7).

13. Richard Reitzenstein, *Hellenistic Mystery-Religions: Their Basic Ideas and Significance*, trans. J. E. Steely (Pittsburgh: Pickwick, 1978), 421.

14. Reitzenstein, *Hellenistic Mystery-Religions*, 540. He writes: "That Anthropos did not die, and for Paul the fact that Christ, himself innocent, suffered the death of a criminal stands at the center of the religious feeling; that other Anthropos has no connection with our sins, and for Paul the conviction that his own sins made this death necessary and that he himself has been set free from his sins by that death forms the very foundation; finally, the other Anthropos indeed worked on earth, ascended, and will come again, but Christ has arisen from the dead and has shown himself to Paul himself. This is for him the actual content of his message; the ardor of religious feeling that binds him to his Lord can only be explained from this perspective, not from the doctrine of the Anthropos."

Reitzenstein also made the argument that Gnosticism did not originate after Christianity but an early form of it was present before Christ. "By reversing the chronological precedence of Gnosticism and Christianity, he increased the importance of non-Jewish materials for understanding early Christianity."[15] Bultmann adopted Reitzenstein's findings into his own research:

> The researches of the philologist Reitzenstein, have led to the probable conclusion that already in certain circles of Judaism there were stronger influences than had hitherto been supposed of oriental, Iranian-Babylonian redemptionist religion and speculation, such as we find later in Gnosticism.[16]

This gnostic influence on early Christianity is a theme which Bultmann will further develop in his own writing.

Another significant history-of-religion scholar was Wilhelm Heitmüller. Along with Bousset and Reitzenstein, Heitmüller taught Bultmann to view the New Testament literature in light of a comparison between the early church and its contemporary religions movements— particularly Jewish apocalyptic and Hellenistic Gnosticism.[17] Heitmüller's work *Baptism and the Lord's Supper* argued that baptism was a mystical rite that had its origin in the Oriental religions of the Hellenistic world.[18] Bultmann praised Heitmüller's work in that it "pointed out the meaning and importance of the sacraments to earliest Christianity."[19]

Bultmann's Assessment and Critique of the History-of-Religion School

As we have seen, many of Bultmann's colleagues and mentors played a pivotal role in the *religionsgeschichtliche Schule*. While he was active within the scholarly work of the history-of-religion school, it is better understood as the groundwork upon which Bultmann developed his approach to Scripture. Many of the findings from this school of thought influenced Bultmann, but he also found some aspects to criticize. So here, briefly, we will look at how Bultmann viewed the *religionsgeschichtliche Schule*.

---

15. King, *Gnosticism*, 89.
16. Bultmann, "New Approach," 361.
17. Johnson, *Rudolf Bultmann*, 9–10.
18. Baird, *History of New Testament Research*, 2:242.
19. Bultmann, *Theology of the New Testament*, 2:247.

Helmut Koester has written on how Bultmann engaged with and furthered the investigation of the history-of-religion school. He writes that Bultmann "was never actively involved in pursuing the more universalistic ambitions" of the school, that is, "searching for the underlying common denominator of all specific religions and theologies."[20] However, as Koester points out, Bultmann was "fascinated by the history-of-religions discovery of the predominance of myth and mythological language in the New Testament and of the syncretistic character of early Christianity."[21]

At several places in Bultmann's own writing he pauses to reflect upon the history-of-religion school.[22] A concise articulation of its strengths according to Bultmann is tucked away in his introduction to the fifth edition of Wilhelm Bousset's *Kyrios Christos*. Written in 1964, Bultmann presents "a few points to illustrate the significance which *the history-of-religions school* has had for the study and understanding of the New Testament."[23] Speaking of the *religionsgeschichtliche Schule* in general and Bousset's work in particular, Bultmann highlights six significant contributions to New Testament studies: (1) the significance of eschatology; (2) Hellenistic Christianity is to be distinguished from the primitive Palestinian community; (3) flowing out of the Hellenistic/Palestinian distinction are "Jesus and Paul" and "the historical Jesus and the kerygmatic Christ"; (4) emphasis on the sacrament and the church; (5) the peculiarity of Hellenistic Christianity; and (6) the removal of "the wall of separation between New Testament theology and the history of doctrine in the early church."[24] Bultmann goes on to say that the *religionsgeschichtliche Schule* signified a "decisive step toward a better understanding of the New Testament."[25]

The *religionsgeschichtliche Schule* was a "decisive step" for Bultmann as he built upon the work of these scholars and corrected what he viewed as their shortcomings. The biggest complaint voiced by Bultmann concerning the work of the *religionsgeschichtliche Schule* consists of the "tearing apart of the act of thinking from the act of living and

---

20. Koester, "Early Christianity," 66.
21. Ibid.
22. See Rudolf Bultmann, "New Testament and Mythology: The Problem of Demythologizing the New Testament Proclamation," in *New Testament and Mythology and Other Basic Writings*, trans. S. M. Ogden (Philadelphia: Fortress, 1984), 1–44 (13–14); *Theology*, 2:245–51; "New Approach," 359–62.
23. Bultmann, "Introductory Word," 7.
24. Ibid., 7–8.
25. Ibid., 9.

hence a failure to recognize the intent of theological utterances."[26] More specifically, he pointed out that the history-of-religion school did not regard God as "wholly other," but as a human phenomenon. While Bultmann was indebted to the *religionsgeschichtliche Schule* in their identification of myth in early Christian expressions of their faith, he argued that their attempts at removing those myths were at the cost of losing what was essential about the faith, or to use the term that Bultmann so often did, the *kerygma*.

To put it simply, the *kerygma* was to Bultmann the essential element that the New Testament expressed. It is the proclamation of the early church concerning God's act of salvation through the person Jesus Christ. While communicated in mythological language, Bultmann considered this to be the core message of early Christianity. He writes: "It [the *kerygma*] proclaims precisely Jesus's person as the decisive event of salvation. It talks about his person mythologically. But can this be a reason for setting the proclamation of his person aside as sheer mythology? That is the question."[27]

For Bultmann, the *religionsgeschichtliche Schule* lost what is indispensable to Christianity in their attempts to demythologize. Expressing Bultmann's thought, André Malet states: "the 'history of religion school' does not demythologize christology but abolishes it."[28] Bultmann sums up his concern:

> Through such interpretation [of the history-of-religion school], also, the New Testament proclamation loses its character as kerygma. Here, too, there is no talk of a decisive act of God in Christ which is proclaimed as the salvation event. The decisive question, therefore, is whether precisely this salvation event, which is presented in the New Testament as a mythical occurrence, or whether the person of Jesus, which is viewed in the New Testament as a mythical person, is nothing but mythology. Can there be a demythologizing interpretation that discloses the truth of the kerygma as kerygma for those who do not think mythologically?[29]

---

26.   Bultmann, *Theology of the New Testament*, 2:250–51.
27.   Bultmann, "New Testament and Mythology," 13.
28.   André Malet, *The Thought of Rudolf Bultmann*, trans. R. Strachan (Garden City, NY: Doubleday, 1971), 150.
29.   Bultmann, "New Testament and Mythology," 14.

It is this question that drives his quest to demythologize the New Testament while not losing its essential kerygma. Bultmann continued to be indebted to the *religionsgeschichtliche Schule* scholars who went before him as he approached the early Christian documents.

PRIMITIVE CHRISTIANITY IN ITS CONTEMPORARY SETTING

Building upon the work of his predecessors while granting attention to his own concerns, Bultmann made a significant contribution to the work of the *religionsgeschichtliche Schule* in a work entitled *Primitive Christianity in its Contemporary Setting*. The goal of this composition is made clear in the Introduction: "[Christianity] was no more an inevitable product of historical causes than was any other great movement of the past, yet its uniqueness is thrown into sharper relief by setting it against the background of its environment."[30] He continues, "Only by paying attention to what Christianity has in common with these other movements shall we be able to discern its difference from them."[31]

In this book Bultmann takes on the role of historian—describing distinctive qualities of the various religious worldviews contemporary to Christianity. He begins by looking at Judaism and its Old Testament background. Christianity's proclamation of Jesus, according to Bultmann, "must be considered within the framework of Judaism."[32] Further, its proclamation was a protest against the legalism and piety of Judaism in the tradition of the prophets. Bultmann continues to describe the Greek background of thought and the various religious worldviews within Hellenism—including Stoicism, star worship, mystery religions, and Gnosticism. He draws further parallels between Gnosticism and Christianity in reference to their understanding of how humans situate themselves in the world. Bultmann writes: "The situation of natural man to the world appears to Christian eyes very much as it does to Gnosticism. In fact, Christianity may employ gnostic ideas and terminology to describe it."[33]

Roger A. Johnson points out a critical aspect of Bultmann's description of these various worldviews. "[A]ll of the religions of the

---

30. Bultmann, *Primitive Christianity*, 11.
31. Ibid.
32. Ibid., 84.
33. Ibid., 224.

Hellenistic era . . . shared in common a particular form of thought which was as prominent in that culture as scientific thinking is in our own: namely, a mythological form of thought."[34] All of these religious movements spoke and thought in terms of angels, demons, and other supernatural expressions. According to Bultmann, Christianity too used mythological language and imagery to proclaim its *kerygma*. He does not develop a method of extracting such mythology here, but this historical study certainly laid the foundation for that quest.

So, for example, Bultmann establishes how early Christianity adopted the features of the gnostic "redeemer myth."[35] Like Gnosticism, Christianity saw redemption as only possible through a divine action. For the early church, this action happened in the death and resurrection of Jesus. According to Bultmann, the Hellenistic church began to interpret the man Jesus in terms of the gnostic redeemer. Already in existence at the time of Paul, these gnostic concepts were combined with the "already traditional interpretation of the death of Jesus as an atoning sacrifice, which came partly from the Jewish cultus, partly from the juridical notions prevalent in Judaism."[36] In Paul, then, is a combination of Jewish and gnostic ideas.

Despite all the overlap in imagery and terminology, Bultmann holds that early Christianity was radically different from its surrounding religious movements. As Johnson writes, "For Bultmann, the self-understanding of Christian faith is as unique and different from the religions of its age as it is similar in its form of expression."[37] That is, while early Christianity borrowed mythological language in how it communicated its proclamation, that *kerygma* was unique to Christianity. Again, this unique message was of God's salvific action in the death and resurrection of Christ. As Bultmann puts it, "Although [Primitive Christianity] presents the Cross and Resurrection of Jesus in mythological terms, the preaching of the Cross is nevertheless a

---

34. Johnson, *Rudolf Bultmann*, 29.
35. Bultmann, *Primitive Christianity*, 232–37. Earlier, Bultmann articulates the redeemer myth in his description of Gnosticism: "The supreme deity takes pity on the imprisoned sparks of light, and sends down the heavenly figure of light, his Son, to redeem them. This Son arrays himself in the garment of the earthly body, lest the demons should recognize him. He invites his own to join him, awakens them from their sleep, reminds them of their heavenly home, and teaches them about the way to return. . . . The Gnostic redeemer delivers discourse in which he reveals himself as God's emissary: 'I am the shepherd,' 'I am the truth,' and so forth. After accomplishing his work, he ascends and returns to heaven again to prepare a way for his own to follow him" (195).
36. Bultmann, *Primitive Christianity*, 233.
37. Johnson, *Rudolf Bultmann*, 31.

decisive summons to repentance." The redemptive significance of the cross, according to Bultmann, is only apparent to those who "accept him as Lord in their daily lives."[38]

This last point establishes the framework from which Bultmann begins his quest to *demythologize* the New Testament. Through his analysis of early Christianity in light of its contemporary religious movements, it is concluded that primitive Christianity expressed a unique *kerygma* in borrowed mythological language. It follows, then, that in order to obtain the original message (or the core theological truth) of Christianity one must identify and remove the mythological expressions and imagery. It is to this quest that we now turn.

DEMYTHOLOGIZING THE NEW TESTAMENT

As we have seen, the work of the *religionsgeschichtliche Schule*—which greatly influenced Bultmann's early academic career—laid the foundation upon which the effort to extract the mythological elements from the New Testament grew. It was also shown that Bultmann saw in the *religionsgeschichtliche Schule* a serious mistake in that it lost the essential proclamation of early Christianity in its efforts to "demythologize." This served as a warning to Bultmann as he began his own quest to remove the core Christian *kerygma* from the heavily mythologized New Testament texts. However, Bultmann's motivation for his quest extends beyond the *religionsgeschichtliche Schule* and its influence/shortcomings. To understand why and how he approached the New Testament, a few more elements impacting Bultmann should be introduced. These include the contemporary liberal theology of Bultmann's time, dialectical theology, and existential biblical interpretation. With these issues addressed, we may more fully understand what drove Bultmann's quest to demythologize the New Testament and his approach to the Johannine literature in particular.

Liberal Theology, Dialectic Theology, and Existential Biblical Interpretation

Bultmann's method of interpretation was not only a response to the shortfalls of the *religionsgeschichtliche Schule*, but also of liberal theology. By "liberal theology," Bultmann is addressing the dominant view

---

38. Bultmann, *Primitive Christianity*, 238.

of Scripture and Christianity of his day. This involved many elements including: a historical-critical approach to the Bible, a focus on the historical Jesus as God's decisive revelation to humanity, a connection of God to moral goodness, and confidence in humanity as the partner for building the kingdom of God.[39]

Bultmann's criticism of liberal theology contained several parts.[40] First, he believed that liberalism reduced Christianity to simply religious values or morals. "Bultmann has often shown how, by applying outside criteria to the New Testament, the leading liberals came to regard Jesus as nothing more than a great historical and religious figure who most nobly manifests the divine."[41] According to Bultmann, the *kerygma* in liberal theology is reduced to "basic religious and moral ideas" and "is eliminated as kerygma."[42] Second, Bultmann took issue with the "historical Jesus" which liberal scholars often appealed to. Bultmann thought that one could know very little of the historical Jesus: "The Christ who is preached is not the historic Jesus, but the Christ of faith and the cult."[43] Lastly, Bultmann writes that the "chief charge to be brought against liberal theology is that it has dealt not with God but with man."[44] Or, to put it in a term that defined Bultmann's later scholarly work, liberal theology does not approach God as "wholly other."[45]

This concept of the "wholly other," along with reservations about liberal theology, provided common ground between Bultmann and another prominent thinker of the time: Karl Barth. In a review of Barth's second edition of *Epistle to the Romans*, Bultmann found much to appreciate and the two began a friendship and (brief) theological alliance.[46] Bultmann and Barth (along with Emil Brunner

---

39. Johnson, *Rudolf Bultmann*, 332, note 4.
40. For a summary of Bultmann's criticism of liberal theology, see Johnson, *Rudolf Bultmann,* 10–17; Malet, *Thought of Rudolf Bultmann*, 30, 145–47. Within Bultmann's body of work, see especially Rudolf Bultmann, "Liberal Theology and the Latest Theological Movement," in *Existence and Faith: Shorter Writings of Rudolf Bultmann*, trans. S. M. Ogden (Cleveland: World, 1960), 28–52; idem, "Ethical and Mystical Religion in Primitive Christianity," in *The Beginnings of Dialectic Theology*, eds. J. M. Robinson and J. Moltmann (Richmond: John Knox, 1968), 230–33; and idem, "New Testament and Mythology," 12–13.
41. Malet, *Thought of Rudolf Bultmann*, 146.
42. Bultmann, "New Testament and Mythology," 12.
43. Rudolf Bultmann, *The History of the Synoptic Tradition*, rev. ed., trans. John Marsh (Oxford: Blackwell, 1968), 370.
44. Bultmann, "Liberal Theology," 29.
45. See Rudolf Bultmann, "What Does It Mean to Speak of God?" in *Existence and Faith*, 53–65.
46. Johnson, *Rudolf Bultmann*, 15.

and Friedrich Gogarten) are credited with the development of *dialectical theology*, or neo-orthodoxy.[47]

The basic premise of dialectical theology is that "God is the 'wholly other' and that man therefore really encounters God only where he and all *his* possibilities are completely brought to nothing."[48] Thus, God is regarded as a subject not an object and can only be known in personal encounter and not through abstract propositions. Further, within dialectical theology there is an acknowledgement that truth is paradoxical in nature and so seemingly conflicting statements in Scripture should be understood as paradoxes and not explained rationally. The work of Bultmann overlaps with certain aspects of Barth and dialectical theology, but these similarities between the two scholars might be outweighed by their differences.[49] While the two were united in their criticism of liberal theology's weakness, Bultmann and Barth's theologies soon went in different directions.

The final aspect of Bultmann's scholarship that we address in this section is existential biblical interpretation. Many of the major themes of existentialism have already appeared in our examination of Bultmann. These include a turn away from "objectivity," a focus on the individual's existence and an acknowledgement of paradoxes. While existentialism is often associated with Kierkegaard, Bultmann's use of the philosophy was more in line with the tradition of Neo-Kantianism.[50]

To understand Bultmann's use of existentialism, we must differentiate between "existential" and "existentialist."[51] By "existential," Bultmann refers to an individual's self-understanding while "existentialist" refers to a systematic method of understanding human existence. So, for example, Bultmann discusses "faith" as an existential decision—

---

47. See Rudolf Bultmann, "The Significance of 'Dialectical Theology' for the Scientific Study of the New Testament," in *Faith and Understanding*, trans. L. P. Smith (New York: Harper & Row, 1969), 145–64.

48. Walter Schmithals, *An Introduction to the Theology of Rudolf Bultmann*, trans. John Bowden (London: SCM, 1967), 7. On dialectical theology, especially in relation to Karl Barth, see Dietrich Korsch, "Dialectical Theology," *The Westminster Handbook to Karl Barth*, ed. R. Burnett (Louisville: WJK, 2013), 51–55.

49. For a comparison between Bultmann and Barth, see Johnson, *Rudolf Bultmann*, 16; and Malet, *Thought of Rudolf Bultmann*, 376–426; on their relationship and disagreements, see Christophe Chalamet, "Bultmann," in *Westminster Handbook on Karl Barth*, 22–25.

50. For more on Neo-Kantianism and its use in Bultmann's theology, see Roger A. Johnson, *The Origins of Demythologizing: Philosophy and Historiography in the Theology of Rudolf Bultmann* (Leiden: Brill, 1974), 38–86.

51. This section is indebted to Johnson's treatment of Bultmann's existentialist approach to Scripture (Johnson, *Rudolf Bultmann*, 21–28).

an altering of one's self-understanding based upon the innovation of God, the "wholly other." Bultmann then refers to "theology" as the task of explaining the meaning of faith. Therefore, to approach the New Testament in existential terms is to do so with existential concepts (including those mentioned above). Further, we must ask the question "is there in such [mythological] talk a view of human existence that offers even to us today, who no longer think mythologically, a possibility for understanding ourselves?"[52]

New Testament and Mythology

"The world picture of the New Testament is a mythical world picture."[53] So begins one of Bultmann's most famous and controversial essays and thus he inaugurates his quest to demythologize the New Testament. As is clear, Bultmann begins with the foundational element to which the *religionsgeschichtliche Schule* spoke: the biblical accounts are expressed in mythological terms. At this point, Bultmann uses "myth" to refer to a way of thinking about the world in a pre-scientific era. Furthermore, the New Testament uses this way of communicating truth in a way that is completely unacceptable in a post-scientific era. "Insofar as it is mythological talk it is incredible to men and women today because for them the mythical world picture is a thing of the past."[54] It is important at this point to make clear that Bultmann believes that by removing the mythological elements from the New Testament, there remains the *kerygma*.[55] This, he argues, is not itself mythology but the attempt to understand it calls for demythologizing.

This task is not an attempt to recreate the mythological world of the New Testament—as if such an endeavor were possible. Rather, Bultmann argues that we must remove the layers of mythology to arrive at the core of the New Testament proclamation. He poses the challenge in this way: "We simply have to ask whether it [the proclamation, or *kerygma*] really is nothing but mythology or whether the very attempt to understand it in terms of its real intention does not lead to the elimination of myth."[56] This task, Bultmann argues, is posed by both the nature of myth and the New Testament. First,

---

52.   Bultmann, "New Testament and Mythology," 15.
53.   Ibid., 1.
54.   Ibid., 2–3.
55.   Ibid., 9.
56.   Ibid.

he writes that the point of myth is not to provide an objective world picture, but to express how we understand ourselves in the world.[57] In a later essay, Bultmann clarifies how the nature of myth warrants this task: "Demythologizing seeks to bring out the real intention of myth, namely, its intention to talk about human existence as grounded in and limited by a transcendent, unworldly power, which is not visible, to objectifying thinking."[58] Here we see a second understanding of myth in Bultmann's thought: myth as a way of thinking about God using objectifying concepts and images.[59] To demythologize is, in a sense, to "de-objectify" the New Testament's portrayal of God and the divine.

Second, Bultmann argues that the New Testament itself warrants the task of demythologizing. This is due to the contradictory elements within it. According to Bultmann, that Jesus can be presented as born of a virgin contradicts the concept of his preexistence. Or, as another example, how can humans be understood as "cosmically determined" yet, at other places, "summoned to decision"?[60] The reality of these contradictory themes in the New Testament serves as further motivation for Bultmann's demythologizing quest. As we will see, this is especially true of the Johannine literature as Bultmann sees there the first attempts at demythologizing within the New Testament canon.

So the question facing Bultmann at this point is how to move forward in the task of demythologizing. Built upon his *religionsgeschichtliche Schule* background, he has established that the *kerygma* of the New Testament is communicated in mythological imagery and terminology which must be removed in order for it to speak to a contemporary audience. The mythological worldview present in the New Testament is so far removed from our modern mind that it acts as a stumbling block in understanding the essential proclamation of the salvific act of God through Jesus Christ. Furthermore, the use of myth has taken the transcendent, *wholly other* God and objectified him. The goal, therefore, is to free Scripture from a mythological worldview and objectifying thinking.[61] With this goal in mind, Bultmann

---

57. Ibid.
58. Bultmann, "Problem of Demythologizing," 99.
59. Johnson, *Rudolf Bultmann*, 41.
60. Bultmann, "New Testament and Mythology," 10–11.
61. Bultmann, "Problem of Demythologizing," 102. Bultmann also argues that the point is not to make the New Testament "scientifically respectable." Both science and myth objectify God, according to Bultmann.

understands that the only context in which to discuss theology and to understand the *kerygma* is in existential terms.

By this, Bultmann attempts to read the New Testament with the question of how it presents an existential understanding for the modern reader. "Therefore, the issue is whether the New Testament offers us an understanding of ourselves that constitutes for us a genuine question of decision."[62] Bultmann later elaborates on this point:

> That the Bible, like other historical documents, not only *shows* me a possibility for understanding my existence, which I can decide either to accept or to reject, but beyond this becomes a word addressed to me personally, which *gives* me existence—that is a possibility that I cannot presuppose and reckon with as a methodical principle of interpretation. That it is ever actualized is—in traditional terminology—the work of the Holy Spirit.[63]

The intention of the New Testament—the proclamation of God's salvific act in Jesus Christ—is comprehensible through the act of demythologizing and is understood existentially. It communicates an understanding of human existence—particularly to the one approaching the text—and calls for a decision. Will one respond in faith or not?

BULTMANN AND THE JOHANNINE LITERATURE

Nowhere is this more true for Bultmann than in the gospel and epistles of John.[64] Bultmann's magisterial commentary on John's gospel, published in 1941 and translated into English thirty years later, demonstrates his most significant work as a biblical exegete and theologian. For Bultmann, John's gospel and epistles are the high point of the theological development of the New Testament.[65] It is the fourth gospel, in particular, where Bultmann makes his most important contribution to New Testament studies and where he

---

62. Bultmann, "New Testament and Mythology," 15.
63. Bultmann, "Problem of Demythologizing," 106.
64. On Bultmann and Johannine literature, see D. Moody Smith, "Johannine Studies since Bultmann," *Word & World* 21 (2001): 343–51; Jörg Frey, "Johannine Christology and Eschatology," in *Beyond Bultmann: Reckoning a New Testament Theology*, eds. B. W. Longenecker and M. C. Parsons (Waco, TX: Baylor University Press, 2014), 101–32; Richard Bauckham, "Dualism and Soteriology in Johannine Theology," in *Beyond Bultmann*, 133–54.
65. Bultmann, *Theology of the New Testament*, 2:9–10.

finds the motivation and justification for his theological approach and his quest for demythologizing.[66]

There are several aspects of Bultmann's approach to the fourth gospel that are worthy of extended examination: his view of the gospel's redaction history, his hypothesis of its literary structure, and emphasis on Jesus as Revealer. However, with the space that I have remaining, I would like to touch briefly on the relationship between the fourth gospel and Gnosticism and then conclude with a short comment on the significance of Bultmann's scholarship.

With his interest in the history-of-religion school, it is no surprise that a major question for Bultmann was of the background for the gospel of John. From where did the evangelist draw his imagery and language? It was not the Palestinian Christianity found in the Synoptic Gospels. While Bultmann saw some parallels in their accounts, he argued that the fourth gospel was independent of the Synoptics.[67] The fourth gospel likewise did not emerge from the Hellenistic Christianity of the first century CE, which the Pauline corpus represents. Nor did the gospel come out of the Jewish-Hellenistic Christianity of Hebrews or *1 Clement*.[68] This is, of course, a simplistic portrait of early Christianity, but Bultmann's point is that the fourth gospel seems to be derived from a unique stream of Christianity distinct from the rest of the New Testament writings.

The answer to the question, for Bultmann, was that the gospel of John emerged from an early oriental Gnosticism that had already been under the influence of Judaism.[69] The dualism found in the fourth gospel, for Bultmann, makes a connection to Gnosticism clear—as does the adapted use of the gnostic redeemer/revealer myth of the gospel's prologue. It is important, however, to be clear on this point

---

66. When I presented this paper it was suggested that Bultmann's work on the Synoptic Gospels rivals his work on the gospel of John as his "most important contribution to New Testament studies." It may be that his work on the Synoptics, especially his *History of the Synoptic Tradition*, has fared better under scholarly scrutiny than the conclusions he articulates in his commentary on John. However, in my opinion, Bultmann's *The Gospel of John* is his most interesting and influential work. It is here that he integrates his vast knowledge and research and presents a creative and influential interpretation of the fourth gospel, the development of early Christianity, and his quest to demythologize. Any scholar working in Johannine studies ignores Bultmann to their own discredit.

67. Bultmann, *Theology of the New Testament*, 2:3–5.

68. Rudolf Bultmann, "Die Bedeutung der neuerschlossenen mandäischen und manichäischen Quellen für das Verständnis des Johannesevangeliums," *ZNW* 24 (1925): 100–46 (100).

69. Rudolf Bultmann, *The Gospel of John: A Commentary*, trans. G. R. Beasley-Murray, R. W. N. Hoare, and J. K. Riches (Philadelphia: Westminster, 1971), 29–30.

as Bultmann is often misunderstood here: Bultmann argues that the author of the fourth gospel uses gnostic imagery and language but adapts these sources for his own purposes. In fact, for Bultmann, the gospel writer's source is drenched in mythology and he ultimately demythologizes these gnostic images and concepts. To use Bultmann's words: "John . . . frees himself from this mythology, but at the same time he retains its terminology."[70]

Let us consider briefly the opening words of the fourth gospel: "In the beginning was the Word, and the Word was with God, and the Word was God." Bultmann found this concept of Jesus as the preexistent λόγος—which (as the gospel writer continues) returns to the world he created, only to be rejected by its inhabitants—hard to believe as an invention of an early Christian writer. Rather, he argues, since there are parallels between it and pre-Christian sources, it is best to conclude that John is adopting an earlier idea. The most obvious connection, according to Bultmann, is to the Jewish Wisdom myth in which preexistent Wisdom, who assisted God at the creation, seeks a dwelling-place on Earth but is rejected. However, Bultmann argues that this Wisdom myth actually finds its source in the gnostic redeemer/revealer myth. The similarities between the prologue and Jewish literature exist because both go back to this same tradition for their source.[71]

Bultmann then develops the mythological and philosophical thinking behind the gnostic concept of Logos. This motif, he argues, was taken over from Gnosticism at a very early stage by Christianity and made fruitful for Christology. He summarizes:

> The *Johannine Prologue*, or its source, speaks in the language of Gnostic mythology, and its Λόγος is the intermediary, the figure that is of both cosmological and soteriological significance; it is the divine being that, while existing from the very beginning with the Father, became man for the salvation of men.[72]

Bultmann notes a tension with the application of this gnostic myth in the prologue revolving around how the Logos is understood in relation

---

70. Ibid., 251.
71. Ibid., 23.
72. Ibid., 28.

to God. How is one to understand the relationship between God and the λόγος? The answer, he says, is given in mythological language: and the Word was with God. This seems to point to two divine beings that were present at creation but this is quickly followed by the phrase: and the Word was God. Bultmann argues that this phrase "shows that no simple identification is intended. A *paradoxical* state of affairs is to be expressed which is inherent in the *concept of revelation*."[73] He continues: "The truth to be expressed lies between the alternating and apparently contradictory ways in which the Logos is defined: for it cannot be adequately expounded in the language of the myth; it has rather to be grasped from the succession of contradictory propositions."[74]

Bultmann argues that this tension exists throughout the gospel: The Father and Son are one (10:30), yet the Father is greater (14:28); the Son carries out the will of the Father (5:30), yet whoever sees the Son sees the Father (14:9). Bultmann writes, "God is there only in his revelation, and whoever encounters the revelation, really encounters God: θεὸς ἦν ὁ Λόγος. . . . God is only encountered in the revelation, when it is understood that it is his *revelation*: ὁ Λόγος ἦν πρὸς τὸν θεόν."[75] Thus Jesus is understood as the Revealer—the λόγος—insofar as he makes God known. Thus, John uses gnostic language and sources but radically changes, or demythologizes, them for his own theology.

As another example, take the dualism found in the gospel. It is not connected, as it was in Gnosticism, to cosmological determinism but rather to the "possibility of human choice and destiny based upon present, existential decision."[76] To quote from Bultmann:

> The membership of a person to a world of darkness or to the world of light is determined not by his fate or by his 'nature' but by his decision. The Gnostic dualism of fate has become a dualism of decision. And faith is neither more nor less than the *decision*, achieved in the overcoming of the offence, *against the world* for God.[77]

This notion of a dualism of decision points to a significant influence of Bultmann upon Johannine studies: the urgent and personal dimension

73. Ibid., 34.
74. Ibid.
75. Ibid., 35.
76. Smith, "Johannine Studies," 344.
77. Bultmann, *Theology of the New Testament*, 2:76.

of the text. We can squabble, and countless scholars since Bultmann have, about the merits of understanding the fourth gospel's background in early Gnosticism. Gnosticism was, of course, a later development than early Christianity and all of the literature from which Bultmann drew was probably later than the fourth gospel and likely was influenced by it. Yet, there is urgency to Bultmann's commentary on John as he fleshes out the concept of Jesus as Revealer and emphasizes the author's dualism of decision. This is no mere exercise in historical research. For Bultmann, the gospel of John calls its readers to a decision. They are confronted with Jesus as the revealed Word and must respond. This urgency and call to decision that Bultmann found in the gospel of John is, I believe, one of his greatest contributions to Johannine scholarship.

We can begin to see why Bultmann, despite being challenged on his major conclusions regarding the gospel of John, continues to be a towering figure in Johannine scholarship. It may be that his answers to the important questions he raises of the text have not been followed in the years since his commentary was published. However, it is the questions that he raises that are so important. Further, as I hinted at above, it is Bultmann's urgency and emphasis on how the fourth gospel speaks to a contemporary audience, calling them to respond to Jesus as the Revealer, that is unparalleled in commentaries since.[78]

CONCLUSION

The goal of this essay has been to situate Rudolf Bultmann within his historical and theological context and to present, in broad strokes, his approach to Scripture—especially the Johannine literature. I have emphasized the influence of the *religionsgeschichtliche Schule* upon Bultmann because I believe that this is foundational for his understanding of the New Testament and his task as an interpreter. We have touched on dialectical theology and existential interpretation because these, too, influenced Bultmann's quest to demythologize the New Testament.

While demythologization is commonly seen, especially in conservative circles, as a disruption or even corruption of the text, I hope that Bultmann's desire for the Christian proclamation of God's salvific

---

78. Bauckham, "Dualism and Soteriology," 139.

work through Christ to be heard shines through. Bultmann was not interested in discrediting or diluting the gospel message. Rather, he saw the task of demythologizing as "parallel to the Pauline-Lutheran doctrine of justification through faith alone without the works of the law."[79] Or, as Bultmann clarifies, "it is the consistent application of this doctrine to the field of knowledge."[80] Through the process of demythologizing, Bultmann argues that every security on which man relies is pulled away.[81] Whether or not one finds his quest to be misguided, Bultmann endures as an influential and profound scholar whose desire that the Christian message speak to the modern world should motivate new generations of New Testament scholars.

---

79. Bultmann, "Problem of Demythologizing," 122.
80. Ibid.
81. Johnson elaborates: "Just as Luther sought to eliminate any tangible, visible merits or works which one could claim as an aid for faith, so demythologizing is clearing away all false props for faith, whether historical evidence for Jesus, rational foundations for faith, or miracles" (*Rudolf Bultmann*, 42).

JOHN A. T. ROBINSON: PROVOCATEUR AND PROFOUND JOHANNINE SCHOLAR

Stanley E. Porter

INTRODUCTION TO ROBINSON'S LIFE AND WORK

J ohn A. T. Robinson was born John Arthur Thomas Robinson on June 15, 1919 in the precincts of Canterbury Cathedral; and died in Arncliffe, a village in the English Dales, on December 5, 1983 at the age of sixty-four.[1] Robinson was no stranger to either the church, in particular the Church of England—as the son and grandson of a canon of Canterbury—or the academy—his father being a well-known scholar of the time and candidate for the Lady Margaret's Professor of Divinity in Cambridge, and his being the nephew of J. Armitage Robinson, who was Dean of Christ's College, Cambridge, and then became Dean of Westminster and then of Wells, and is now best known for a commentary on Ephesians.[2] Even though his father

---

1. For biographical information, I rely throughout upon Eric James, *A Life of Bishop John A. T. Robinson: Scholar, Pastor, Prophet* (Grand Rapids: Eerdmans, 1987).

2. J. Armitage Robinson, *St Paul's Epistle to the Ephesians* (London: Macmillan, 1903). Among other things, he also wrote *The Study of the Gospels* (London: Longmans, Green, 1919) and *The Historical*

died when he was nine, John went to Marlborough school as a scholarship student, and then to Jesus College, Cambridge, where he first
studied classics and then theology. He went to Westcott House, the
Anglican theological college known for producing bishops, to train for
the ministry, and then got a scholarship to stay on for the PhD at Trinity College, awarded in 1946. During this time, he was heavily influenced by a variety of contemporary theologians and read widely in
theology and other subjects (he kept notebooks in which he recorded
the titles of all of the books he read).

After ordination, John first served as a curate in Bristol in an inner-
city church from 1945 to 1948, during which time he also married. In
1948, he was appointed Chaplain of Wells Theological College, where
he found the environment somewhat isolated, until he was appointed
the Dean of Clare College, Cambridge, in 1951, succeeding C. F. D.
Moule, who had been appointed Lady Margaret's Professor of Divinity
at Cambridge. This college position was much more to John's liking, as
he was also appointed as a lecturer in the faculty of theology. His positions enabled him to develop both his ecclesial and academic interests,
including discovering the first inklings of some of his ideas regarding
John's writings that I will discuss further below. When his former vicar
in Bristol, Mervyn Stockwood, was appointed the Bishop of Southwark,
he wanted John to join him as suffragan (or assistant) bishop, but the
current Archbishop of Canterbury (Fischer) at first strongly objected.
This controversy was a harbinger of more controversy to come. After
much debate and the exchange of numerous letters by Stockwood,
Fischer, and Robinson, in 1959 John was appointed Bishop of Woolwich. In some ways, he was singularly unsuited to such a ministry in
a very unchurched part of London on the south bank of the Thames.
However, John, again showing his colors early, innovated a number
of programs that made Christianity popular in the area. John's time
as bishop was highly productive for him again on both ecclesial and
academic fronts. He testified in a court case that brought questions
about the role and beliefs of Anglican bishops, and he published a book
that made him world famous, or infamous in some circles. I will return
to some of his publishing accomplishments, if that is the best term, in
a moment. I wish first to note the court case. In 1960, Penguin was
intending to publish an unedited version of D. H. Lawrence's book,

---

Character of St. John's Gospel (London: Longmans, Green, 1929).

Lady Chatterley's Lover, but which had been deemed pornographic and therefore illegal to publish in the UK. On the basis of his social activism and his already published works in the area (it probably did not help that Robinson had published a book called *The Body*), the publishers called upon Robinson to offer an opinion as a bishop on the nature of the book, which led to his testifying in a well-publicized trial at the Old Bailey essentially that sex is sacred and that Lawrence's depiction of it is spiritual and that Christians ought to read it. The headlines write themselves and the reaction was predictable—with the Church of England ending up involved in a great amount of damage control, especially when the verdict agreed that the work was not pornographic.

The workload of a suffragan bishop, however, whether he is causing public outcry or not, is apparently quite immense, especially in a difficult diocese, and so John was exhausted by the job over the years—to say nothing of his increasing notoriety, so that he came to be known as the "notorious Bishop of Woolwich."[3] He thus welcomed the opportunity when he was appointed Dean of Chapel of Trinity College, Cambridge, in 1969. Despite his success as a dean, with a staff of chaplains, John did not find life at Trinity as welcoming as he had hoped. Nevertheless, he continued to work on many fronts, both ecclesially and academically. He also had several professional disappointments, including his not being appointed as either a regular bishop or as a professor in one of the British universities, although he applied and was rejected several times (which did not help his college relations). John also had a number of sabbaticals and numerous speaking engagements that often took him away from his College, which no doubt heightened the frustration or envy of some of his colleagues. Robinson was in Hamilton, Ontario, Canada, for a three month sabbatical from September to December 1982 at McMaster University, and while there also delivered a lecture at McMaster Divinity College, as well as at other educational institutions in the area.[4] However, during his time at Trinity, John initiated ways of making the chapel services and liturgy more appealing and wrote the two most important single books for which he is probably still known as a

---

3. James, *Life*, 95.
4. See ibid., 263–65. The lecture delivered at McMaster Divinity College is John A. T. Robinson, "What Future for a Unique Christ?" in Robinson, *Where Three Ways Meet: Last Essays and Sermons* (London: SCM, 1987), 9–17, and in *The Christological Foundation for Contemporary Theological Education,* ed. Joseph D. Ban (Macon, GA: Mercer University Press, 1988), 217–24.

scholar, where he is known at all. John was contemplating his future, whether at Trinity or elsewhere, when in 1983 he was diagnosed with inoperable cancer and given six months to live. He continued his work up until the day he died, including preparing the Bampton Lectures on John's gospel, which were delivered instead by his longtime friend Moule and published later as his final authored book.

As a result of this very brief recounting of John Robinson's life, how would we evaluate his scholarly life and career? I think that the jury is out on that. For one, he appears to have been a complex individual with mixed and diverse interests. He was born and reared in a very elite social and educational stratum, yet he had an abiding interest in and concern for the poor and less privileged, including concern for their spiritual well-being. He was full of personal contradictions as well. He apparently rubbed many people the wrong way, including many of his colleagues at Trinity College, who were frequently suspicious of him and his most recent belief or action. He also, however, had a small group of very dedicated students who responded warmly to him, and he seems to have made many friends on the wider academic scene.

John Robinson's scholarly interests and production are surprisingly wide and diverse. At the end of his life, he categorized his own writings into three major groupings: theological exploration, biblical interrogation, and social responsibility.[5] It will probably come as a surprise to note that he wrote a total of twenty-nine books in these three areas (two of them appearing after his death, as I will comment upon momentarily), with eight of them being in New Testament studies, along with writing numerous articles, chapters, and book reviews in all three areas. He clearly had diverse interests and published accordingly, so as to be characterizable as a theologian, a New Testament scholar, and a Christian ethicist.

Robinson is perhaps most enduringly remembered for his controversial book *Honest to God*, published in 1963, which, according to Amazon, has sold over 750,000 copies (the initial print run was six thousand copies in the UK and two thousand in the US).[6] This book today seems rather tame and even dated. It read then and reads today as a second-order popularization of neo-orthodoxy and existential theology, with much dependence upon Paul Tillich (ground of being),

---

5. See James, *Life*, 297–98.
6. John A. T. Robinson, *Honest to God* (London: SCM, 1963; Philadelphia: Westminster, 1963). The original print figures are from James, *Life*, 115.

Dietrich Bonhoeffer (Christianity without religion), and Martin Buber (I and thou), along with a good dose of Joseph Fletcher's situational ethics.[7] If you didn't know already, you could have guessed that the book was published in the 1960s and captured and popularized ideas already well known in scholarly circles (the book appeared as a paperback for general readers). This is consonant, however, with what we find in Robinson's *Thou Who Art*, the published version of his PhD dissertation (not published until 2006).[8] This work shows Robinson's theological and philosophical roots to be clearly of his time. He begins with the fundamental (mis-)conception of the disjunction between Hebraic and Greek thought, the one being static and the other dynamic, found also in other writers of the time especially influenced by the biblical theology movement and soundly criticized by James Barr.[9] On the basis of this foundation, Robinson pretty much dismisses all of Christian theology to the end of the Middle Ages as having been influenced by Greek thought. He tackles the question of the personality of God on the basis of contemporary neo-orthodox and existential thought, including the works of Martin Buber, Soren Kierkegaard, Emil Brunner, and Karl Barth,[10] among a wide range of others, including continental thinkers. The work is not technical philosophy, but a theological treatment of human and divine personality, which ends up addressing and challenging traditional doctrines such as Christology and the Trinity, finding what is retainable in them in the notion of their intersubjective relations. I summarize this book as extensively as I do, because one can see pretty much the basis of all of Robinson's subsequent theological and ethical, and even for the most part biblical, thought in this initial work.

---

7. See, for example, Paul Tillich, *Systematic Theology*, vol. 1 (Digswell Place: Nisbet, 1951), esp. 181–321; Dietrich Bonhoeffer, *Letters and Papers from Prison*, 2nd ed., ed. Eberhard Bethge, trans. Reginald H. Fuller (London: SCM, 1956); Martin Buber, *I and Thou*, trans. Ronald Gregor Smith (Edinburgh: T&T Clark, 1937); and Joseph Fletcher, "The New Look in Christian Ethics," *Harvard Divinity Bulletin* (October 1959): 7–18. An excellent study of this period is William Hordern, *A Layman's Guide to Protestant Theology*, rev. ed. (New York: Macmillan, 1968). See also John A. T. Robinson, Review of *Martin Buber: An Intimate Portrait*, by Aubrey Hodes, *JTS* 23.1 (1971): 330; Robinson, Review of *Dietrich Bonhoeffer: Theologian of Reality*, by André Dumas, trans. R. M. Brown, *JTS* 23.2 (1972): 539–41.

8. John A. T. Robinson, *Thou Who Art: The Concept of the Personality of God* (London: Continuum, 2006), with a very helpful introduction by Rowan Williams (ix–xi) used in my summary.

9. One of the best known arguing similarly is Thorlief Boman, *Hebrew Thought Compared with Greek*, trans. Jules L. Moreau (London: SCM, 1960). See in response James Barr, *The Semantics of Biblical Language* (Oxford: Oxford University Press, 1961).

10. See Hordern, *Layman's Guide*.

Some of the other books that might still be mentioned occasionally are his *The Honest to God Debate*, which includes Robinson's further
thoughts on the issues,[11] his *Exploration into God*, which began as lectures
delivered at Stanford University,[12] and *But That I Cannot Believe!*, where
he reassesses a wide range of traditional Christian beliefs, such as Adam
and Eve, the virgin birth, miracles, the resurrection, the second coming
(to which he devoted two further books),[13] life after death, and instead
redefines God, the Holy Spirit, the Trinity, and prayer, among other
things—a book thoroughly and explicitly neo-orthodox to the core.[14]

I think that the most appropriate summary of Robinson's scholarship is found in his biography in the following quotation by former
student Paul Hammond, then lecturer (now professor) in English at
Leeds University:

> When his books were re-issued, [Robinson] often said that he found
> little that he wanted to change. His theology wasn't on the move in these
> years [at Cambridge]—indeed, was he ever, strictly speaking, a theologi-
> cal thinker? His theology was characteristically a bundle of quotations. I
> don't mean that disparagingly at all, but he did not seem to have enough
> of an original philosophical streak to make him a creative theologian. He
> was much more of an apologist, an interpreter of the church to the world
> and vice versa, insisting that you started your theology from where you
> really were, not from where others thought you should be.[15]

I think that this is an apt summary of Robinson's work in all three
areas, even in Johannine studies to an extent, although in the area of Johannine studies I think that he did have a bit more of a creative streak—or
at least a rebellious streak that was not simply or merely popularizing the
opinions of others. There was no doubt that for Robinson his theological,
biblical, and social views were entangled with the thought of the times, to

11.   David L. Edwards, ed., *The Honest to God Debate* (London: SCM, 1963), which is not technically
       an authored book by Robinson, though he lists it. It contains essays and responses to his *Honest to
       God*, with a new chapter by Robinson at the end (pp. 232–75) as well as some of his other writings.
12.   John A. T. Robinson, *Exploration into God* (London: SCM, 1967).
13.   The first is John A. T. Robinson, *In the End, God... A Study of the Christian Doctrine of the Last
       Things* (London: James Clarke, 1950), which appeared in the "Theology for Modern Men" series. I
       treat the second book on the topic below.
14.   John A. T. Robinson, *But That I Can't Believe!* (London: Fontana, 1967), with the words Bishop
       of Woolwich in bigger letters than those of his name on the cover of the edition I have—no doubt
       playing on the fact that a bishop of the church does not believe a number of things.
15.   James, *Life*, 226.

the point that it is sometimes hard to separate them. This is perhaps best captured by a statement by one of Robinson's students pointing him out to another: "That is the Bishop of Woolwich, who wrote *Honest to God*. He also wrote a book about *Lady Chatterley's Lover* called *The Body!*"[16]

This brings me to Robinson's biblical and primarily New Testament scholarship. I will concentrate here on his books, before turning to John's gospel, where I will deal with his articles and chapters as well as his major book.

Robinson's first book of biblical scholarship was entitled *The Body: A Study in Pauline Theology*.[17] Though labeled a work of Pauline theology, it is more properly a work of biblical theology that argues against individualism (he even claims the "age of individualism is over," which shows Robinson was not a prophet) and for communal and interdependent understandings of humans, as found in Paul's notion of the body. He draws upon Old Testament thinking as the basis of his distinctions, and then deals expressly with the "concept of σάρξ" and the "concept of the body (σῶμα)," all under three rubrics of the body as flesh, cross, and resurrection.[18]

The second book shifts from Paul to *Jesus and His Coming*, where he in fact argues that the church has entirely misunderstood the notion of Jesus's second coming, in that there was only the one coming of Christ that has already occurred but is ongoing, and which leads to all of humanity becoming one with God.[19] Robinson argues both that Jesus was misunderstood by his earliest interpreters and that a belief in a second coming was later formulated.

Robinson's first of two collections of previously written essays was published in 1962, entitled *Twelve New Testament Studies*.[20] The earliest essay dates to 1947, and two to the 1960s, with the others all

---

16. James, *Life*, 158.
17. John A. T. Robinson, *The Body: A Study in Pauline Theology*, SBT 5 (London: SCM, 1952).
18. Robinson was soundly criticized for his approach in Robert H. Gundry, *Soma in Biblical Theology with Emphasis on Pauline Anthropology*, SNTSMS 29 (Cambridge: Cambridge University Press, 1976), which takes a more limited view of the evidence. Robinson critically reviewed Gundry's book in *JTS* 28 (1977): 163–66.
19. John A. T. Robinson, *Jesus and His Coming: The Emergence of a Doctrine* (London: SCM, 1957). I cannot help but citing the last sentence of the book, which all too well illustrates Robinson's attempt to theologize everything, including Greek itself: He refers to the already inaugurated coming of Christ as showing "that tremendous aorist in which the Apostle to the gentiles declares (Eph. 1.10) that it was the design of God, once and for all, in the fullness of time, 'to sum up all things' in Christ." See also Robinson, Review of *The Fulness of Time*, by John Marsh, *Theology* 56 (1953): 107–109; cf. James Barr, *Biblical Words for Time*, SBT 33 (London: SCM, 1962).
20. John A. T. Robinson, *Twelve New Testament Studies*, SBT 34 (London: SCM, 1962).

published in the 1950s, with five on John's gospel, including three that continue to be cited, on John the Baptist and Qumran, his new look on the fourth gospel, and the destination and purpose of John's gospel (to which I will refer again below). Robinson's standing was such that when in 1971 the renowned C. H. Dodd (his former undergraduate teacher) published his final book, a treatment of the historical Jesus, in the British edition Robinson provided a foreword.[21]

Robinson wrote what is probably his most enduring book on the question of *Redating the New Testament*.[22] This book, in some ways an introduction to the books of the New Testament, but primarily concerned with the dates of all of the books of the New Testament, argues that AD 70, with the fall of Jerusalem and destruction of the temple, marks a decisive barrier to any of the books being written after that date. He contends that the impact of that event, as illustrated in reference to it in virtually all important subsequent Jewish literature, compels but also supports finding an earlier date for all of the other books. He ends up reconstructing the entire early history of early Christianity. Some of the more noteworthy conclusions—besides the obvious one already mentioned regarding dating all books early—are that virtually all of the books of the New Testament can be attributed to their purported authors, the Pastoral Epistles are genuine and placed within the chronology of Paul's missionary journeys with a single Roman imprisonment, and a concomitant early date is necessary for other early Christian literature, such as the *Didache* (AD 40–60), *1 Clement* (early AD 70), the *Epistle of Barnabas* around AD 75 and the *Shepherd of Hermas* up to around AD 85. Robinson closes this book by quoting in full a letter he had received from Dodd, expressing sympathy for his position but thinking that few would follow him (perhaps Dodd had a better chance of being a prophet).[23]

---

21. John A. T. Robinson, "Foreword," in C. H. Dodd, *The Founder of Christianity* (London: Collins, 1971), vii-viii (though unnumbered), with the US version having been published by Macmillan in 1970.

22. John A. T. Robinson, *Redating the New Testament* (London: SCM, 1976; Philadelphia: Westminster, 1976). I note that my edition, by Westminster, on the dust jacket, promotes Robinson as author of *Honest to God*, which shows that even in the 1970s academic publishers used popular reputation to sell important scholarly works.

23. Robinson wrote several commendations of Dodd: John A. T. Robinson, "A Tribute to C. H. Dodd—England's Greatest Biblical Scholar," *The Church of England Newspaper*, 25 May 1956; Robinson, "Theologians of our Time. XII. C. H. Dodd," *ExpTim* 75 (1964): 100–102; Robinson, "Charles Herold [sic] Dodd," in *Tendenzen der Theologie im 20. Jahrhundert*, ed. H. J. Schultz (Stuttgart: Kreuz, 1966), 237–42; cf. Robinson, *C. H. Dodd*, by F. W. Dillistone, *Theology* 81 (1978): 148–49.

Soon after, Robinson published a book that might come as a surprise in the light of his *Redating*, when he asks the question, *Can We Trust the New Testament?*[24] In this book, Robinson describes four different profiles of popular readers of the Bible, and argues that none of them is correct. This book is less about the substance of the New Testament and more about how we can trust the theology of the New Testament, even if many of its traditional doctrines, such as who Jesus was, cannot now be accepted.

Robinson at this point returns to Paul in a commentary entitled, aptly for him, *Wrestling with Romans*.[25] This was his last New Testament book published while he was alive. Robinson says that "I have vowed never to write a biblical commentary. For in a commentary you have to say something on everything, whether you have anything to say or not. This is why most commentaries in my experience are duller than books written by the same persons, even on the same subject."[26] If not exactly a prophet, Robinson certainly is an astute observer on this point. Despite this being a commentary based on lectures for students and addressed to a lay audience (at least then), it is full of the kind of witty writing for which Robinson had become known—as well as his neo-orthodox theology in which Paul's grounded language becomes interpreted highly metaphorically.

The final two books by Robinson were published after his death, but were being worked on by him when he died. The first is the second collection of his essays, *Twelve More New Testament Studies*.[27] This collection includes three previously unpublished essays, and draws upon essays that Robinson published as early as 1948, two in the 1960s, three in the 1970s, and three in the 1980s. The essays in this collection are not as well known as his previous ones, but do include five on John's gospel, including his essay on John's prologue and "His Witness Is True: A Test of the Johannine Claim." There is also an essay on the Shroud of Turin, something that fascinated Robinson and to which he refers elsewhere, along with his use of the secret gospel of Mark—again indicating that he was definitely a person of his times,

24. John A. T. Robinson, *Can We Trust the New Testament?* (London: Mowbray, 1977; Grand Rapids: Eerdmans, 1977). I note that my Eerdmans front cover describes Robinson as "Author of 'Honest to God.'"
25. John A. T. Robinson, *Wrestling with Romans* (London: SCM, 1979; Philadelphia: Westminster, 1979).
26. Robinson, *Wrestling with Romans*, vii.
27. John A. T. Robinson, *Twelve More New Testament Studies* (London: SCM, 1984).

and perhaps even a little too willing to accept the newest discovery and attempt to integrate it into his framework of understanding.

The final book is his major work on John's gospel, *The Priority of John*.[28] As I will point out below, this book argues that John's gospel has as much priority as the Synoptic Gospels. He does not claim that it is earlier than the Synoptics, but that (following his teacher, Dodd) it is independent and as reliable and needs to be taken into consideration in reconstructing the life of Jesus, as he does.

At this point, I turn to Robinson's significant contribution to Johannine studies.

JOHN ROBINSON ON JOHN

John Robinson's interest in John's gospel was no doubt formed early, perhaps in the New Testament seminar led by C. H. Dodd that Robinson was invited to attend while he was an undergraduate. We do know that he had continued respect for Dodd throughout his life, and Dodd has more entries in the index of *Priority of John* than any other author. When Robinson is telling the story of the trends in discussion of John's gospel in his *Redating the New Testament* and *Priority of John*, he cites Dodd's and Percival Gardner-Smith's work as indicating the shift from belief in John's dependence upon the Synoptics to its independence.[29]

Robinson's own indications of his views of John's gospel, however, begin early in his scholarly career. In 1955, Robinson treated the parable of the shepherd in John 10:1–5, and attempts to show, following his teacher Dodd and against Joachim Jeremias, that this parable does not evidence any of the signs that Jeremias identifies as indicating later treatment, so that this parable, according to Robinson, provides "a record which compares favourably with that of any of the Synoptic material" and its "significance for the historical value of the fourth gospel as a whole lies in the fact that this should be true of a section which is typically Johannine and which cannot possibly be attributed to any kind of

---

28.   John A. T. Robinson, *The Priority of John*, ed. J. F. Coakley (London: SCM, 1985; Oak Park, IL: Meyer Stone, 1987). By now, on the cover of my US edition, Robinson is listed as author of both *Honest to God* and *Redating the New Testament*, two very different books.

29.   Robinson, *Redating the New Testament*, 262; *Priority of John*, 10–15; Percival Gardner-Smith, *St. John and the Synoptic Gospels* (Cambridge: Cambridge University Press, 1938); C. H. Dodd, *Historical Tradition in the Fourth Gospel* (Cambridge: Cambridge University Press, 1963).

dependence on the Synoptics."[30] Already in 1955 the basic framework of Robinson's viewpoint of John's gospel is clearly articulated.

In 1959, Robinson published the article for which he is perhaps still best known on "The New Look on the Fourth Gospel."[31] Reflecting directly the influence of Dodd and reappraising the current situation regarding John's gospel, Robinson argues against five presuppositions. First, he rejects the dependence of John's gospel on the Synoptic Gospels, but instead argues for the author using oral tradition. Second, he rejects the notion that the author of the gospel reflects a different background than that of the events conveyed. In other words, he rejects the idea that John is writing long after the situation in Palestine has changed, under the influence of the fall of Jerusalem—based to a large extent on the evidence found in the Dead Sea Scrolls, which show a Judaism depicted in very similar terms to that in John's gospel. Third, Robinson rejects the distinction that John's gospel is only concerned with the Christ of faith and not the Jesus of history. On the basis of the Dead Sea Scrolls, John's use of parables, and the gospel's environmental features, Robinson argues for an accurate depiction of the people and events surrounding Jesus. Fourth, he rejects the idea of John's gospel being the culmination of first-century theological development. Robinson thinks that John's gospel does not reflect a realized eschatology (as usually defined) or an increasing and refined apocalypticism, but instead reflects the primitive, unified eschatology of Jesus himself: "the vindication and the visitation of the Son of man."[32] Fifth and finally, Robinson rejects the idea that the author is not necessarily John the apostle or a non-eyewitness. Robinson shows his regard for the neglected work of J. B. Lightfoot on John's gospel,[33] by recognizing the strength of the argument for the author as an eyewitness, a plausible conclusion on the basis of the previous four points. Robinson does not go as far here as he later does regarding authorship, but many of the planks of his objection to traditional views of John's gospel are taking shape.

---

30.   John A. T. Robinson, "The Parable of the Shepherd (John 10.1–5)," *ZNW* 46 (1955): 233–40, repr. in *Twelve New Testament Studies*, 67–75, here 75.

31.   John A. T. Robinson, "The New Look on the Fourth Gospel," in *Studia Evangelica*, TU 73, ed. Kurt Aland (Berlin: Akademie, 1959), 338–50 (originally a paper given in Oxford in 1957), repr. in *Twelve New Testament Studies*, 94–106.

32.   Robinson, "New Look," in *Twelve New Testament Studies*, 103.

33.   J. B. Lightfoot, *Biblical Essays* (London: Macmillan, 1893), 1–198.

In 1960, Robinson published an important article on the destination and purpose of John's gospel.[34] Robinson argues several major
points. The first is that John's gospel is the most Jewish gospel (again
following Lightfoot), and along with that arguably the most anti-Jewish
but not pro-Gentile, with the gospel focused entirely upon Israel. He
also claims that there is a cosmic perspective to John's gospel, in which
the world might be saved (though not mentioning the Gentiles), but
this is in the context of how Judaism relates to those who are the true
Israel, Jesus Christ, who is the Messiah. Robinson places the gospel
in the Judaism of southern Palestine, which means the gospel is written in Greek for Greek-speaking Jews (not Gentiles) of the Diaspora,
which reveals some of the major tensions within Judaism. Further,
the purpose of Jesus's death was to create one Israel with Jesus as its
shepherd, one people of Israel. Finally, John's address of "the Jews" is
of his fellow Jews of Palestine, standing as a bridge between them and
his audience, as a means of evangelizing Diaspora Judaism into the
church. In this essay, we can see developed Robinson's view of John's
gospel as not indicating the traditional stance of it reflecting a Hellenistic environment or influence, a late date after separation from the
synagogue, or a primarily Gentile audience.

In 1962, Robinson published an article on "The Relation of the
Prologue to the Gospel of St John."[35] In this article, he affirms the
authorial integrity of the prologue and epilogue of the gospel, but
goes further and claims that the body of the gospel was written first,
then the Johannine epistles, and then the epilogue and the prologue.
This can account for both differences between the prologue and the
body of the gospel and the fact that the prologue seems to be a suitable introduction to the gospel, perhaps written to place it in a new
context (relying upon the work of a number of scholars who see the
heavy Semitic elements in the prologue, such as C. F. Burney and
others since). Robinson draws several conclusions from this finding.
One is that the prologue is part of the environment of the gospel, not
a reflection of its background. The second is that, if this reconstruction
is correct, then the proper way to read the gospel is not that the time-

---

34.   John A. T. Robinson, "The Destination and Purpose of the Johannine Epistles," *NTS* 7 (1960–
      1961): 56–65, repr. in *Twelve New Testament Studies*, 107–25; and repr. in *New Testament Issues*, ed.
      Richard Batey (London: SCM, 1970), 191–209.
35.   John A. T. Robinson, "The Relation of the Prologue to the Gospel of St John," *NTS* 9 (1962–1963):
      120–29, repr. in *Twelve More New Testament Studies*, 65–76.

less truths of the prologue are to be read into the body of the gospel but that the timeless truths emerge out of the realities that the gospel depicts. Robinson is further developing his view on John's gospel, in this article showing further how he treats its relationship to the epistles but also how he counters some of the objections to its integrity and early Jewish situation.

In 1963, Robinson published "The Place of the Fourth Gospel," in a collection of essays gathered by Gardner-Smith.[36] Robinson begins with the question of whether John's gospel is among the Synoptic Gospels. He of course recognizes a number of differences between the Synoptics and John's gospel, but believes that such distinctions are often overdrawn merely for the sake of convenience and marginalization of John's gospel. However, he thinks that the three-against-one formulation of the issue is misleading. He prefers to think of there being five independent sources, Mark, Q, L, M, and John, so that when sayings appear in any two of them they can be compared (use of Dodd's criterion of multiple forms is applied to John as well).[37] Robinson then treats four areas in which objections to such an approach might be made. The first is history. Robinson thinks that this criterion has been greatly overdone, and that John's gospel in its details regarding Palestine reveals its attention to historical detail. Some have been led in the wrong direction by John's prologue with its timeless truths, which, as already noted above, Robinson believes was added later to a fundamentally historical document. The second is literary form. While there are differences in form, there are also many similarities, including small units of independent tradition, as Robinson, using the work of Dodd, has already argued. Third is vocabulary. Without minimizing differences in style, Robinson again notes those who exaggerate them. There are many passages where Synoptic wording is found in John and vice versa. The merger of both types of vocabulary is found in the P. Egerton 2 papyrus, which attests to the early church not finding it difficult to merge traditions, as both Synoptic and Johannine traditions are utilized in P. Egerton 2. The fourth is theology. Here Robinson repeats the results of a number of his previous studies

---

36.   John A. T. Robinson, "The Place of the Fourth Gospel," in *The Roads Converge: A Contribution to the Question of Christian Reason*, ed. Percival Gardner-Smith (London: Edward Arnold, 1963), 49–71.

37.   C. H. Dodd, *History and the Gospel* (London: Nisbet, 1938). On this criterion, see Stanley E. Porter, *The Criteria for Authenticity in Historical-Jesus Research: Previous Discussion and New Proposals*, JSNTSup 91 (Sheffield: Sheffield Academic Press, 2000), 85–89.

regarding such topics as eschatology and Christology, where he finds John more in continuity with the teaching of Jesus than the Synoptics.

I could cite other articles, but these suffice to show the major contours of Robinson's thought to this point. In other words, many of his major ideas regarding John's gospel, as we shall see, had already been formed in the 1950s and early 1960s. However, it took until 1976 for him to publish his first full-length treatment of John's gospel within the context of his reconstructed history of early Christianity.

In *Redating the New Testament*, Robinson devotes two chapters to the Johannine writings, one chapter to Revelation and another to the gospel and epistles. In the chapter on Revelation,[38] Robinson notes that Revelation is one of the few books that had its date of composition indicated in ancient tradition, although the tradition is confusing. Irenaeus attributes Revelation to the time of Domitian (AD 81–96) (*Adv. Haer.* 5.30.3),[39] Eusebius links it to the persecution (banishment) by Domitian (*D.E.* 3.5; *Hist. Eccl.* 3.20–809), as does Victorinus (*In Apoc.* 10.11), and Clement of Alexandria, cited by Eusebius, refers to the tyrant's death as allowing John to return from Patmos (*Quis div. salv.?* 42.1–15, in Eusebius, *Hist. Eccl.* 3.23.5–19). Robinson notes that only Eusebius links authorship with persecution, and that the specification of the emperor is shaky. Robinson remarks also that there is tradition that links John with Rome (Tertullian, *Prescr.* 36.3), while Epiphanius attributes John's exile to Claudius Caesar (*Haer.* 51.12, 33). Robinson notes that F. J. A. Hort, Lightfoot, and B. F. Westcott all argued for a date for Revelation of AD 68–70, which apparently was the consensus for the nineteenth century, despite modern objections. Robinson then evaluates the internal arguments. He thinks that there is good reason for dating Revelation to before the separation of Christianity and Judaism (e.g., Rev. 2:9; 3:9). Further, he also notices the failure to make any clearly found reference to the imperial cult in the seven letters, even though such references are found throughout the rest of the book. Robinson also believes that the seven letters address an early state of affairs. As for the rest of the book, Robinson dismisses the statements of Eusebius regarding Domitian (e.g. *Hist. Eccl.* 3.17–20), because Eusebius does not note a single Christian dying during this time. Robinson believes instead that

---

38. Robinson, *Redating the New Testament*, 221–53.
39. Quoted in Eusebius, *Hist. Eccl.* 3.18.2–3; 5.8.6.

the persecution of Nero was far greater, even though not mentioned by the church fathers in this regard. As for the imperial cult, Robinson believes that worship by Christians was not required early on but only increased later, under Trajan (AD 98–117). Instead, the temple is depicted in Revelation 11:1–2, with images of its destruction based upon the Old Testament, not the actual events of AD 70. This is especially true of the image of partial destruction. The seven kings of Revelation 17:9–11 have resulted in a variety of calculations (depending upon when the counting begins, etc.), but Robinson believes the most plausible calculation of the sixth king is Galba, who reigned from AD 68–69. The final argument concerns the fire connected with the whore of Babylon of Revelation 17:16. Robinson thinks that this represents the burning of Rome that occurred in AD 69 with Vitellius and Vespasian contending for the throne. Thus, according to Robinson, Tertullian is to be believed that the author shared the sufferings (Rev. 1:9) of Revelation in Rome after Nero's persecution (*Apol.* 5, cited in Eusebius, *Hist. Eccl.* 4.20.7).

Robinson's discussion of John's gospel and the epistles follows on from his discussion of Revelation.[40] He begins by noting that a number of scholars, such as Hort, Lightfoot, and Westcott, could only argue for the same author for Revelation and John's gospel and epistles if they were not written at the same time (Revelation was written in the 60s, and the gospel and epistles later). Robinson rejects the argument that John's Greek improved but sees it as a colorful and intentional use of language. As with Revelation, Robinson begins his discussion with the traditional evidence. As with Revelation, this evidence only indicates that John lived to be quite old and into the reign of Trajan (AD 98–117) (Irenaeus, *Adv. Haer.* 2.22.5; 3.3.4, cited in Eusebius, *Hist. Eccl.* 3.23.3–4) and that he wrote last of the gospel writers (Irenaeus, *Adv. Haer.* 3.1.1; Clement of Alexandria in Eusebius, *Hist. Eccl.* 6.14.7; Eusebius, *Hist. Eccl.* 3.24.7). The Muratorian fragment assumes John and his fellow disciples are still alive. Others writing that the gospel was dictated to Papias and that John rejected Marcion (Anti-Marcionite Prologue) or that he wrote to oppose Valentinus (Victorinus) are simply impossible, and Epiphanius is simply

---

40. Robinson, *Redating the New Testament*, 254–311. See also Robinson, "Zur Datierung des Johannesevangeliums: Eine Antwort an Professor Josef Ernst," *IBW Journal* (Paderborn, Germany), June 1983, 94–96.

confused in his details (*Haer.* 51.12). There is also a tradition found in the Syriac *History of John* that dates John's exile to Patmos to Nero. Thus Robinson concludes that the evidence for the traditional date of late in the first century is highly problematic. Nevertheless, modern scholarship has followed two courses in dating John's gospel—either the traditional date of late first century since the early church fathers and the late date of sometime in the second century proposed by the radical critics, starting with F. C. Baur, David Friedrich Strauss, and their followers—though this latter date has now been discredited with the discovery of P52 and the P. Egerton 2. This leaves simply one date under consideration, the late first century, which constitutes a very firm consensus.

Robinson indicates, however, that the evidence for such a date during Domitian's reign is lacking. Robinson also notes a further change in Johannine scholarship, from John being thought to be dependent upon one or more of the gospels to Johannine independence, proposed first by Gardner-Smith and then more strongly by Dodd. This, Robinson admits, is the position from which he had undertaken his previous Johannine scholarship.[41] However, he now wishes to challenge this. He first examines Dodd's view of John's material and finds that, though Dodd recognizes early elements, he places the writing of the gospel late, but does not account for how John received his tradition. Robinson finds that, despite various viewpoints, all recognize that there is early material in John's gospel. The solution, Robinson believes, is in the account of being ejected from the synagogue (John 9:42; 12:42; 16:2), which supposedly reflects the eighteenth benediction. The similarity of exclusion in Qumran, the lack of references to Gentiles in John, the failure to find a specific post-AD 70 situation, and especially the failure to mention the fall of Jerusalem in John's gospel of all gospels (with its supposed exclusion of Christians from the synagogue) indicate that, in fact, the temple is still standing and John's gospel is to be dated before the fall of Jerusalem. This is confirmed by reference in John 2:20 to the length of the temple's building process and the reference in John 5:2 to there being a pool in Jerusalem. Robinson now tests his theory against the gospel, claiming that both the epilogue (John 21) and the

---

41. Robinson cites four articles in this regard: "New Look"; "Destination and Purpose"; "Relation of the Prologue"; and "Place of the Fourth Gospel."

prologue were later additions. The prologue of the gospel reflects the same type of "pre-existence Christology" as does Paul in Philippians and Colossians, as well as Hebrews and Revelation. The language of John is similar to that of Qumran.

As for the Johannine epistles, Robinson rejects his earlier late first-century dating as in his previous writings and endorses an earlier date as written to Jewish Christians in Asia Minor in danger of false gnostic teachers. There is a recent docetic tendency that must be addressed by the biblical author, but the epistles lack any mention of persecution. Robinson concludes for a date in the early 60s. With the body of the gospel written, and then the epistles, Robinson looks at how the prologue and epilogue were then added, which accounts for their similarities to the epistles (e.g., Christology). The original milieu of the gospel preaching appears to Robinson to be both Palestinian and Greek, that is, in contact with Greek-speaking Jews. The author had what Robinson calls an "internal" relation to the tradition, even in those passages where Jesus is recorded as speaking in Greek within a Palestinian context. All of these factors lead Robinson to consider authorship of John's gospel. The evidence points to John the son of Zebedee. Robinson thus thinks that there were various gospel traditions developing at the same time, of which John's was one of them, not drawing upon another account. John's gospel, with its two editions, took longer to form but it did occur at the same time as the other gospels, that is, AD 50–55 for the first edition, 60–65 for the Johannine epistles, and AD 65+ for the form with the prologue and epilogue. In this sense, as Robinson states, "I believe that John represents in date, as in theology, not only the *omega* but also the *alpha* of New Testament development."[42] Despite the stimulating nature of Robinson's argument, it is generally ignored in New Testament scholarship.

In *Priority of John*, Robinson provides both his fullest arguments and his clearest rationale for accepting an early date of John's composition. This book was the basis of Robinson's Bampton Lectures of 1984 delivered by Moule in abbreviated form. The book itself was edited from the fuller manuscript by one of Robinson's former students, J. F. Coakley (then at Lancaster, now at London). As is evidenced by his use and expansion of arguments found in previous publications, this book represents the culmination of Robinson's work on John's gospel.

---

42. Robinson, *Redating the New Testament*, 311.

In the first of his eight chapters, Robinson addresses the presumption of priority.[43] He picks up the argument that he had developed elsewhere, in particular his argument in "The Place of the Fourth Gospel," in which he raises the question of whether John's gospel should be considered one of the Synoptics. He further notes and develops the change in perspective on John's gospel brought about especially by Dodd, to the point where he presumes, subject to confirmation by further evidence, that John's gospel is not just an independent source but an early source. He rejects how other contemporary Johannine scholarship has created various historical redactional layers and thereby attempted to confirm John's late date, but instead sees the gospel as both early and late. Although he refers to the criterion of multiple attestation, following Dodd, Robinson minimizes its significance by relegating its use to smaller details, while taking the larger view that John's gospel is one of the independent sources, alongside the other major ones, Mark and Luke (especially for the passion narrative).

The second chapter, the largest in the book, addresses the supposed distance in space, time, and person of John's gospel from the events that it purports to describe.[44] In each of these sections, Robinson argues against the standard views that have been used to distance John's gospel from the pre-AD 70 period. Citing his article on "The New Look on the Fourth Gospel," Robinson claims that his few straws in the wind are now all blowing in his direction. He not only cites the Dead Sea Scrolls, to which he made reference in that article, as further confirming this, but also cites the five other possible backgrounds to John's gospel cited by Dodd: the hermetic literature, Hellenistic Judaism, rabbinic Judaism, Gnosticism, and Mandaism—all of which now show that John's gospel need not be Hellenistic or late, as traditionally thought. In more particular detail, Robinson then turns to the supposed distance in space, arguing both that the gospel originated in Ephesus and that there is no geographically based theological agenda to the gospel that indicates community involvement. Instead, he thinks that the geographical evidence points to intimate knowledge of Palestine (e.g., Pool of Bethesda, John 5:1–9), and that the Greeks mentioned in the gospel are Greek-speaking Jews from the Diaspora. He concludes with the evidence of connection of the

---

43. Robinson, *Priority of John*, 1–35.
44. Ibid., 36–122.

gospel with the high priest (John 18:15–16). Regarding the supposed distance in time, Robinson notes his previous work on absolute dating and turns to related issues. Revisiting what the tradition says about the date of composition, Robinson again rejects the implication that the date of composition was late. He instead turns first to factors such as the nature of the church's ministry and the emphasis upon "sound doctrine"—where he finds the issue of church structure only in the epilogue (which he argues was added later) and in 2 John 9. More important to note is that Jewish-Christian relations are not mentioned in John's gospel, and that there is even less mention of events that might look like the fall of Jerusalem than in the Synoptics. Robinson also considers the banishment from the synagogue, but argues that the twelfth of the eighteen benedictions or *birkat ha-minim* has no bearing at all on John's gospel, as it indicates that those who departed from strict observance were judged on their behavior. The supposed anti-Semitism in John's gospel is, according to Robinson, not racial anti-Semitism but anti-Jewish establishment, usually the Jewish authorities such as the Pharisees.

With the elimination of the *birkat ha-minim* as a credible explanation, Robinson thinks that there is no reason not to date the gospel early, especially as a date in AD 80–100 was a compromise, once the discovery of P52 and P. Egerton 2 made a later date impossible. Robinson deals last with the supposed distance in person. Robinson examines both the external and internal evidence regarding authorship. He disputes the external evidence that tries to distance the apostles from the elders, and shows that it is "the elder John" or John the son of Zebedee. When he turns to the internal evidence, Robinson finds it compelling to see the beloved disciple as the author, but then asks who the beloved disciple is. The author of the gospel is a Greek-writing Jew (whose first language was Aramaic, as reflected in subtle ways in his Greek usage), who had connections with Galilee, Samaria, and especially Jerusalem, and who was associated with Capernaum. In other words, Robinson says that the person seems an awful lot like John the son of Zebedee, as attested in the external tradition. This would fit his being able to write the kind of Greek of the gospel, his not being formally educated (not illiterate), and his contacts in Jerusalem. There is one final piece of evidence that Robinson introduces. According to John 19:25, Jesus's mother had an unnamed sister in the gospel, whom Robinson equates with the Salome of Mark 15:40–41 and the mother of James and John in Matthew 20:20. This, for Robinson, explains Jesus's instruction to the beloved disciple, his own relative, to take care of Mary in John 19:26–27 (they would also have been related to John the Baptist).

At this point, Robinson turns to the chronology of Jesus's ministry, and then includes analysis of the beginning, middle, and end of the gospel. In discussing the chronology, Robinson believes that apparent discrepancies between the Synoptic Gospels and John's gospel are overdrawn.[45] The major area that is usually cited is the length of Jesus's ministry. Robinson concedes that if one begins with the Synoptics there are problems in reconstructing the chronology, but not if one begins with John's gospel. Robinson believes that John's gospel, with its reference to three Passovers—one each at the beginning, middle, and end of Jesus's ministry (John 2:13, 23; 6:4; and 11:55; 12:1; 13:1)—indicates a ministry of two years. The ministry begins in Jerusalem, with the cleansing of the temple, which is better explained and located early in Jesus's ministry rather than at the end. The date of the commencement of Jesus's ministry can be calculated from the reference to the temple having been built for forty-six years (John 2:20). After his meeting with Nicodemus, Jesus spends time in the countryside, then goes to Samaria and Galilee, probably because Jesus was causing concern among the Pharisees by the crowds he was attracting (John 4:12). Jesus returns to Jerusalem (John 5:1, not Passover) and then goes back to Galilee. Jesus then spends another Passover, quite possibly in Galilee (John 6:4), followed by ministry outside of Israel proper (Tyre and Sidon and Caesarea Philippi). The turning point of Jesus's ministry is reached when he leaves Galilee and goes into Judea, and then eventually to Jerusalem. The Synoptics, especially Luke's gospel, do not make the extent or time of Jesus's Judean period clear. At that point, Jesus makes his way to Jerusalem for Passover, staying in Bethany at the home of Lazarus, Mary, and Martha (John 12:1–2). According to Robinson, his calculations indicate that Jesus entered Jerusalem on a Monday, not Sunday (so-called Palm Sunday). By Robinson's estimation, Jesus on Thursday, 14 Nisan, ate a meal the day preceding Passover that has features of a Passover meal (interpreted by the Synoptics as a Passover meal). This would have occurred in April of AD 30.

---

45. Robinson, *Priority of John*, 123–57.

Robinson then reconstructs the major temporal points in Jesus's ministry. In the first of three chapters on the content of John's gospel, Robinson reconstructs the early period of Jesus's ministry, especially its relationship to John the Baptist.[46] Referring to his article on "The Relation of the Prologue to the Gospel of St. John," Robinson notes that the prologue was added later, and its theological statements grew out of the historical statements of the body of the gospel. Robinson notes a number of clear temporal indicators in the opening chapters of John's gospel, some of which are usually dismissed as theologically oriented. He does not see them as having theological significance but historical significance. He recognizes some symbolism in John's gospel, but not here. Instead, he sees that Jesus already had disciples before his Galilean ministry, and attempts to reconstruct how this came about. In effect, Robinson sees a close relationship between Jesus and John the Baptist, such that Jesus in some way identified with John and John had aspirations for Jesus. When Jesus first flees Judea, he goes to where John the Baptist is located, Bethany beyond the Jordan. Robinson, referring to his own article on "The Baptism of John and the Qumran Community," thinks that John had some connection to the Qumran community, which explains John's message of redemption.[47] John, following Qumran, believed that an individual would come who would exemplify the ideal servant of the community. John tried to force this person to emerge by his eschatological message. When Jesus appears, John's gospel makes clear that Jesus's disciples had a connection to John the Baptist, and Jesus was seen by John as "the one in my following" (not the one following after me). Jesus at first preaches as a representative of John, accepting the role John had set for him (John 3:29–30), including the cleansing of the temple. However, soon after Jesus breaks his relationship with John and goes his own way (John 4:1–4), with Jesus preaching a message of "deliverance" rather than "judgment."

The next chapter, the shortest in the book, is concerned with the middle portion of John's gospel.[48] Robinson notes that there are many difficulties with reconstructing the chronology of the middle period of Jesus's ministry. Although there is an abundance of material to work

---

46. Ibid., 158–89.
47. John A. T. Robinson, "The Baptism of John and the Qumran Community: Testing a Hypothesis," *HTR* 50 (1957): 175–91, repr. in *Twelve New Testament Studies*, 11–27.
48. Robinson, *Priority of John*, 190–211.

with, there are only eight events that are found in John and two of the Synoptics in the same order. From this, Robinson believes that we can see that there are some episodes that are duplicated (e.g., feedings), while there are others that are conveyed especially by the Synoptics that make no sense without John's gospel (and, in that sense, rely upon John's gospel to be understood). One of these concerns the relationship of John 5 and 6, which some (such as Rudolf Bultmann) have reversed because of the apparent unexplained transition in John 6:1.[49] Robinson has an alternative explanation that maintains the canonical ordering. This passage occurs around the time of the second Passover, one that Jesus does not go to Jerusalem to celebrate. Jesus instead is involved in events around the Sea of Galilee, including the feeding of the five thousand, whose geography, Robinson believes, is best explained by the Johannine account. The reason for Jesus's not going to Jerusalem for Passover, Robinson thinks, is the political situation in Judea at the time. The crowd's reaction to the feeding indicates that Jesus was aware that the crowd might attempt to make him king, indicating the highly politicized messianic expectation of the day. Drawing upon some of his work in "His Witness Is True: A Test of the Johannine Claim,"[50] Robinson argues that Jesus may early have been labeled as Jesus the Christ, with popular connotations regarding kingship (similar to the way John named the Baptist became John the Baptist). This interpretation would also explain the issue of the messianic secret, and why Jesus wished for his followers not to address him in this way. That Jesus stayed away, Robinson thinks, may have been wise especially as a mob from Galilee went to Jerusalem and some were killed (Luke 13:1–3), which may have been the reason for Herod's being in Jerusalem during the subsequent Passover (Luke 23:7). Jesus instead withdrew with his followers, after the missionaries returned and he heard that John the Baptist had been killed.

The third chapter of content deals with the passion story, divided into nine parts.[51] The first concerns the approach to Jerusalem, where Robinson notes the variety of theories regarding this material.[52] John's

49.   See Rudolf Bultmann, *The Gospel of John: A Commentary*, trans. G. R. Beasley-Murray (Oxford: Blackwell, 1971), 203.

50.   John A. T. Robinson, "'His Witness Is True': A Test of the Johannine Claim," in *Jesus and the Politics of his Day*, eds. Ernst Bammel and C. F. D. Moule (Cambridge: Cambridge University Press, 1984), 453–76, repr. in *Twelve More New Testament Studies*, 112–37.

51.   Robinson, *Priority of John*, 212–95.

52.   Ibid., 212–22.

gospel, however, provides the most orderly details of the account, with indications of the time period and the order of events, including the events surrounding Lazarus. Robinson unfortunately draws upon the secret gospel of Mark as confirmation of his support for the Johannine account. The second is the proscription of Jesus, where John provides a number of important technical details.[53] These include: the timing of the legal actions against Jesus, their being done by the Jews alone, the role of Caiaphas, and Jesus's withdrawal from public ministry. The third section is Jesus's arrival in Jerusalem.[54] The independence of John's account is seen by Robinson in the fact that it has virtually no wording in common with the Synoptic account apart from the words of the quoted Psalm (117:25). The arrest of Jesus, the next section, is again independent of the form found in the Synoptic Gospels.[55] John's contribution is the introduction and identification of those involved, using appropriate terminology that suggests that he has firsthand information. The next section is the Jewish trial.[56] Robinson emphasizes that John's gospel is correct in emphasizing Annas as the power behind the high priest and giving the details of Jesus's interrogation (is this based upon the association of the gospel with the high priest?). The charges against Jesus, Robinson contends, are found throughout the gospel and related to the charge of being a political Messiah (John 1:51; 2:19; 6:62; 7:12; 8:28; 10:24–25; 10:36). The Roman trial makes clear that this trial was not simply an affirmation of the Jewish trial, as Pilate rejects the idea of Jesus as a political threat.[57] Jesus claimed a different political status, and Pilate did not see him as a threat, which resulted in the presentation of other charges. The charge of Jesus being "Son of God" also fails to convince Pilate. The result is an appeal to the crowd that realistically reflects how Pilate was viewed. As a result of this trial, Robinson calls into serious question the charge that John's gospel handles these matters in a highly theological way. The trial is not one that is anti-Semitic, but that reflects Pilate trying to evade his responsibility and Caiaphas representing the Jews pushing for Jesus's death—something agreed even in early Jewish literature (e.g., *b. Sanh.* 43a). If anything, the Romans are depicted as being manipulated by

---

53. Ibid., 222–29.
54. Ibid., 229–38.
55. Ibid., 238–44.
56. Ibid., 245–54.
57. Ibid., 254–75.

others in the trial. The seventh section treats the crucifixion.[58] The Johannine account has a number of highly plausible historical details, including the tri-lingual *titulus*. The burial, the eighth part, notes that the garden setting is from John, as well as the involvement of Nicodemus.[59] Robinson discusses Nicodemus at length, finding that there is no good historical evidence to doubt either Nicodemus's involvement at the burial or his earlier encounter with Jesus (John 3). The ninth and final section addresses the resurrection.[60] Robinson finds the details related to the empty tomb, such as the death clothes, highly plausible, to the point of indicating support for those who find that John's account is earlier than that of the Synoptics.

Robinson concludes his volume with two chapters on the teaching of Jesus and the person of Christ. In the first, on Jesus's teaching, Robinson argues against those who distance John's view of Jesus's teaching from that of the Synoptics. He admits that John's style or presentation of Jesus is different from that of the Synoptics, but he draws the analogy with the teaching of Socrates as found in Plato and Xenophon. Xenophon may represent the words more as they would have been heard in the flesh, but Plato captures their meaning better (Robinson appeals here to what he calls a "criterion of verisimilitude").[61] Discussing common ground between John's gospel and the Synoptics, Robinson believes that Jesus's teaching is grounded by means of reference to places and times and more integrated into the gospel than theories regarding "signs" and "discourses" suggest. He also finds common ground in seeing Jesus's teaching reflecting Semitic influence, a common view of the Son of Man, the use of *abba* and *amen*, Jesus's apocalypticism, common sayings, and a number of common incidents (such as some parables). Robinson argues instead that John's gospel looks inwardly, while the Synoptics relate to outward phenomena. This does not mean that the author of John's gospel can be credited with a kind of individualism in which he, for example, gnosticizes Jesus's teaching or creates an introverted or exclusivist community. One of the major points of distinction has usually been Johan-

---

58. Ibid., 275–81.
59. Ibid., 281–87.
60. Ibid., 288–95. See also Robinson, "Resurrection in the NT," in *Interpreter's Dictionary of the Bible*, vol. 4, ed. George A. Buttrick (New York: Abingdon, 1962), 43–53; Robinson, "What Is the Resurrection?" in *More Sermons from Great St. Mary's*, ed. Hugh Montefiore (London: Hodder and Stoughton, 1971), 18–28.
61. Ibid., 298.

nine eschatology. Here Robinson sees John, contrary to Dodd, not as presenting the culminating eschatological teaching, but, as Robinson himself had intimated in his much earlier *Jesus and His Coming*, an early inaugurated eschatology, one that still awaits the work of the Holy Spirit (John 7:30; 14:25–26; 16:7–15) and the last day.

In his final chapter on the person of Christ, Robinson captures what John's gospel says about Jesus. He states that "what John gives us is basically the same Jesus of history who is the Christ of the church's faith, the Christ of the church's faith who is also the Jesus of history."[62] He sees this happening in a dialectical relationship that involves outward and inward levels, not an antithetical one that plays history off against theology. For example, Robinson notes that "Son of God" only appears once as a title in John's gospel on Jesus's lips (John 11:4), but he is depicted in relationship to God throughout the gospel. In this, John's gospel is similar to the Synoptics. Concerning the self-consciousness of Jesus, Robinson rejects the notion of discovering the inner psychological consciousness of Jesus, but instead believes that we can reconstruct Jesus's self-consciousness by inference in a number of key passages. Robinson finds it interesting that scholars are willing to see some glimmer of Jesus's self-consciousness in the Synoptic passages regarding Jesus's "eschatological consciousness"—the very point where the Synoptics and John's gospel converge. Against the work of James Dunn,[63] Robinson does not see the Johannine Christology as reflecting later creedal developments. This is to read John's gospel through later understandings of notions of incarnation and preexistence. Robinson sees the Christology of John's gospel instead in relational terms, speaking about how Jesus saw himself as one who had envisioned God and brought his message. This means that Jesus as the true son has what he calls a functional and ethical understanding of sonship, not an ontological one. John's understanding of the preexistence and incarnation of Jesus is, again against Dunn, similar to that found in Paul, especially in Colossians 1:19. This is not what Robinson calls a "*personal* pre-existence" but that of a human who completely

---

62. Ibid., 343.
63. James D. G. Dunn, *Christology in the Making: A New Testament Inquiry into the Origins of the Doctrine of the Incarnation* (London: SCM, 1980; Philadelphia: Westminster, 1980), with reference to numerous pages within Dunn's work. See also John A. T. Robinson, "Dunn on John," *Theology* 85 (1982): 332–38.

reflected God, what Robinson sees in Philippians 2:6–11. Jesus, therefore, when he uses "I," is neither an individual nor referring to God, but a type of "archetypal image of the self"[64] in a Jungian sense (also in a Buberian sense). This Jesus then becomes divine through the resurrection (Rom. 1:3–4), which the church has thus pushed back progressively earlier to Jesus's baptism, birth, and even further, culminating in John's account, to the point where the incarnation is the incarnation of God in Christ as the community, not the single individual Jesus.

CRITICAL EVALUATION OF ROBINSON'S JOHANNINE SCHOLARSHIP

So how might we evaluate the scholarship of John Robinson, and in particular his Johannine scholarship? I must admit that it is disappointing that he ends his life's work, and arguably his major monograph on John (and one of his two most important monographs), with rather dubious theologizing. After a strongly argued historical account, in his last chapter he takes a different tack and walks away from what would appear to be the force of his own arguments and engages in the very kind of unconvincing theologizing that he accuses others of doing.

I do not think that these final statements should negatively color our view of Robinson's scholarship. Nevertheless, he seems to have been greatly overlooked by those writing the history of New Testament interpretation. He is not mentioned in William Baird's three-volume history of New Testament research, does not figure into John Riches's history of the last one hundred years of scholarship, and was not treated in the first edition of Donald McKim's handbook of biblical interpreters, though he was included in the revised version.[65] Robert Morgan's book on biblical interpretation gives him a paragraph in his brief treatments of various scholars, and says that his testimony on *Lady Chatterley's Lover* and his *Honest to God* "made him a symbol of the 1960s," but attributes his views in *Redating the New Testament* and *Priority of John* to an "independent mind and innate Anglican

---

64. Robinson, *Priority of John*, 387.
65. R. A. Culpepper, "Robinson, John A.T. (1919–1983)," in *Dictionary of Major Biblical Interpreters*, ed. Donald K. McKim (Downers Grove, IL: InterVarsity Press, 2007), 874–77.

conservatism."[66] Gerald Bray (one of Robinson's students, listed at the beginning of *Redating the New Testament*)[67] mentions Robinson briefly in two places in his book on biblical interpretation—the first noting Robinson's "wildly radical theological views" but his "conservative exegetical" positions. He claims that the thesis of Robinson's *Redating the New Testament* "has not been convincingly refuted."[68] The most thorough treatment of Robinson is found in Tom Wright's portion of the history of New Testament interpretation first written by Stephen Neill. Wright mentions *Redating the New Testament* in conjunction with reexamining the fourth of Neill's twelve achievements of New Testament scholarship since 1861, on dating. Wright states that the reaction to the book was "polite but largely unsympathetic," although he adds that "relatively few arguments have been put up to contest it in the ten years since it appeared."[69] He mentions *Priority of John* in relation to the twelfth achievement, on how John's gospel cannot be treated like the Synoptic Gospels, when he states that Robinson "in his magnum opus" has tried to correct this.[70] Wright then later very ably and generally positively summarizes the entire book in a discussion of John's gospel.[71]

Robinson has a number of unmissable faults as a scholar. One is his tendency to jump on every bandwagon that comes his way: neo-orthodoxy and existential theology (even in his *Priority of John*), popular approaches to a variety of issues (the peace movement, vegetarianism, among others),[72] the secret gospel of Mark,[73] the Shroud

---

66. Robert Morgan with John Barton, *Biblical Interpretation* (Oxford: Oxford University Press, 1988), 327. See also p. 124 for brief mention.
67. Robinson, *Redating the New Testament*, ix, along with Chip Oakley and Paul Hammond, among others.
68. Gerald Bray, *Biblical Interpretation: Past and Present* (Downers Grove, IL: InterVarsity Press, 1996), 434. See also p. 444.
69. Stephen Neill and Tom Wright, *The Interpretation of the New Testament 1861–1986*, 2nd ed. (Oxford: Oxford University Press, 1988), 361. Note that Wright quotes a letter from Neill regarding Robinson's book: "he does have the knack of asking the right kind of question; he shows how fatally inclined [some scholars] are to accept dubious hypotheses as established facts just because one or two prominent theologians have loudly asserted them." Neill also claims that "A great deal of it is just wrong."
70. Ibid., 364.
71. Ibid., 433–39.
72. See James, *Life*, for a variety of stories. As examples, see John A. T. Robinson, "A Christian Response to the Arms Race," in *Debate on Disarmament*, eds. M. Clarke and M. Mowlam (London: Routledge & Kegan Paul, 1982), 81–96; Robinson, "A Christian Response to the Energy Crisis," in *Three Ways Meet*, 108–13.
73. See Robinson, *Redating the New Testament*, 109, where he notes that its "genuineness has yet to be established," though he thinks the trend is in that direction; Robinson, *Priority of John*, 34 n. 116, 46 n. 56, and 221 n. 19, where he refers to the text as "probably authentic," a highly questionable verdict.

of Turin,[74] and even Johannine scholarship in the form of his teacher, Dodd's, work on Johannine independence. There is an undeniable implicit grandstanding and popular apologetics to Robinson's writing that one cannot get away from. He was in many ways a publicity hound that reminds me of the kind of rock-star biblical scholars that we, unfortunately, have today (even a few is too many).

This verdict mostly applies, however, to his scholarship other than in Johannine studies. There is something different about his study of John's gospel in particular, as well as the issue of dating of the New Testament, that demonstrates an independence of mind that takes him beyond the fads of the day and even beyond his respected teacher Dodd. Robinson began his study of John's gospel relatively early in his scholarly career and continued to study that gospel throughout his life, ending it with his major volume on John's gospel. There is clear progression in his thought. He begins where his teacher Dodd left off, with the independence of John's gospel. He implicitly appeals to many of the traditional criteria for authenticity in historical Jesus research, such as Semitic language and Palestinian environment, but mostly multiple attestation.[75] Through the course of several essays, he tentatively and then more assertively lays out what would become the framework of his later thought by seeing not only the independence of John's gospel but its earliness and its historical reliability in comparison with the Synoptic Gospels. In his major books, however, there is a significant shift that occurs. In *Redating the New Testament*, Robinson shifts his emphasis to the fall of Jerusalem. Whereas this was a relatively minor issue in his earlier writings, and not the capstone to his argument, in *Redating the New Testament* it becomes central. This becomes the dividing point for his dating scenario. He also examines external tradition, internal evidence, and the relationship among the books, but the issue of the fall of Jerusalem becomes the single most important argument. In *Priority of John*, Robinson moves further along in his argument. He almost assumes the dating scheme that he has developed, and then concentrates upon argu-

---

74. See John A. T. Robinson, "Re-Investigating the Shroud of Turin," *Theology* 80 (1977): 193–97; Robinson, "The Shroud and the New Testament," in *Face to Face with the Turin Shroud*, ed. P. Peter Jennings (Great Wakering, UK: Mayhew-McCrimmon, 1978; Oxford: Mowbray, 1978), 69–80, repr. in *Twelve More New Testament Studies*, 81–94; Robinson, "The Holy Shroud in Scripture," *The Tablet*, 26 August 1978; Robinson, "If the Shroud Were Genuine What Difference Would It Make?" *The Examiner*, Bombay, October-November, 1978.

75. See Porter, *Criteria for Authenticity*, 63–102.

ing that John's gospel does not have the distinctives that have often been drawn upon to remove it from comparison with the Synoptic Gospels. In that sense, he draws at several points upon his previously published essays. However, he is always developing these arguments more thoroughly and more completely. For example, in his article on the priority of John, he draws directly upon the criterion of multiple attestation, which he rightly attributes to Dodd. In *Priority of John*, Robinson acknowledges the criterion (as well as one he calls "verisimilitude," which appears to be historical likeness), but states that, whereas it may add to some of the details, he does not rely upon it. He is viewing a bigger picture, in which there are three major independent sources to examine, and John's gospel is one of them (alongside Mark and Luke).

In the course of his arguments of his New Testament and especially Johannine scholarship—although not so much in his popular writings and even much more minimally in his theological writings—Robinson shows himself to be a master New Testament scholar. He is thorough in his analysis, knowledgeable of alternative views, well documented in his study, well argued in his development, and especially well written in his presentation. In his drawing upon a wide range of scholars, some of them relatively obscure, he knows English scholarship to be sure but also German literature, he respects traditional scholarship, and he knows and offers a critique of the ancient sources. One of the strengths of his *Redating the New Testament* is that he intertwines the relationships of all of the New Testament books, along with some of the early church fathers, into a coordinated whole.

To Robinson's credit, he takes the more difficult position in his New Testament and especially his *Redating the New Testament* and his Johannine studies. With his radical theological beliefs, in many ways it would have been much easier for him simply to accept late dates for the books of the New Testament as heavily theologized treatments that reflect later church developments. His task of asserting the essential and reduced theological core of a given belief (such as Christology) would have been much easier. He instead has accepted very early dates, and along with them traditional authorship, such as John the son of Zebedee (or at least one who seems an awful lot like him), for John's gospel and epistles, as well as Revelation, while retaining his theological views that are skeptical of traditional theological beliefs.

This tension is what results in the disappointing ending of *Priority of John*, when he does not continue down the same path as he has established in his own trajectory.

Further critical examination of Robinson's arguments is warranted. I do not believe that his arguments regarding John's gospel—or for the dating of the New Testament—have been taken seriously or seriously enough. The burden he has to overcome is significant, when we recognize that John's gospel does "sound" a lot different from the Synoptics and that there is an abundance of traditional interpretation to oppose. Robinson himself argues that everything in John's gospel sounds the same, as do the things within the Synoptics, and that the traditional view, while enduring, is not as well conceived as many might imagine. His argument regarding dating presents a strong challenge to the consensus view, especially as the traditional view of Johannine dating is as much a compromise based upon the lack of viability of the second-century date and overreliance upon the external evidence. I have recently teased out the implications of the various dates for the books of the New Testament, including the Johannine writings, and believe that we must reconsider how the various dates are interconnected.[76] The strength of Robinson's treatment of John's gospel is his use of it to reconstruct Jesus's ministry. This approach, somewhat like the interlocking tradition of Leon Morris and others since,[77] but extended beyond simply instances where one of the gospels informs the other, presents both a highly plausible historical reconstruction and motivation for a number of events and actions in the gospel and Jesus's life, such as his ministry in relation to John, his avoidance of Jerusalem and the messianic secret, and some of the events surrounding his death.

In the light of this, I think that it is surprising, though perhaps not without expectation, that Robinson has not been more widely heralded, especially but not only by evangelical scholars. I believe that, whether he is right or not, he stands out in relation to a number of other scholars for the boldness and innovativeness of his thought.

---

76. Stanley E. Porter, "Dating the Composition of New Testament Books and Their Influence upon Reconstructing the Origins of Christianity," in *In Mari Via Tua: Philological Studies in Honour of Antonio Piñero*, eds. Israel M. Gallarte and Jesús Peláez (Córdoba: Ediciones El Almendro, 2016), 553–74.

77. Leon Morris, *Studies in the Fourth Gospel* (Exeter: Paternoster, 1969), 40–62.

Far too many New Testament scholars are content simply to repeat and develop the ideas of others. John Robinson appears to have had some unique ideas of his own that he was able to plausibly support and defend.

CONCLUSION

John Robinson's life and especially his lifelong interest in John's gospel provide a fascinating portrait in contradiction and achievement. The contradictions revolve around both personal and public matters. Robinson seems to have been curious to the point sometimes of recklessness in his adoption of the latest thoughts and ideas that were circulating. As a result, he eagerly embraced and continued to embrace tenets of neo-orthodoxy, existential theology, and the biblical theology movement, while also arguing for very conservative historical positions. He was a popular and even attention-seeking apologist for his radical theological ideas, while devoting his major scholarship to the rather unspectacular issues of redating the New Testament and arguing for the priority of John's gospel. In these two areas, however, rest his lasting, even if still widely overlooked, contribution. Whereas many scholars have had their day, when their ideas have been weighed and either incorporated or rejected, even if their reputations remain, John Robinson is still probably better known in many circles for being the author of *Honest to God* than he is for his much more significant work *Redating the New Testament* or his even more substantial *The Priority of John*.

RAYMOND E. BROWN AND THE FOURTH GOSPEL: COMPOSITION AND COMMUNITY

Joshua W. Jipp

INTRODUCTION

I n his 1979 publication of *The Community of the Beloved Disciple*, Raymond Brown (1928–1998) reflects upon his scholarly research that began in 1955 with a seminar paper at Johns Hopkins University: "Little did I realize then that I was beginning a quarter-century love affair with the most adventuresome body of literature in the New Testament."[1] And while Brown has made a variety of significant and lasting contributions to the study of the New Testament, it is undoubtedly his pioneering research on Johannine studies for which he will most justly be remembered. Francis Moloney is not speaking hyperbolically when he says that Brown is commonly "regarded as the premier Johannine scholar in the English-speaking world."[2] In addition to his two-volume Anchor Bible commentaries on the gospel of John, his Anchor Bible commentary on

---

1. Raymond E. Brown, *The Community of the Beloved Disciple: The Life, Loves, and Hates of an Individual Church in New Testament Times* (New York: Paulist, 1979), 50.
2. Francis J. Moloney, "The Gospel of John: The Legacy of Raymond E. Brown," in *The Gospel of John: Text and Context*, Biblical Interpretation Series 72 (Leiden: Brill, 2005), 112–36, here 112.

the epistles of John, the previously noted volume on the history of the
Johannine community, his more popular book *The Churches the Apostles
Left Behind*,[3] and his substantial but uncompleted revision of his Anchor
Bible commentaries (the introduction to the gospel finished and edited
by Francis J. Moloney),[4] Brown estimates he wrote about an article per
year on the gospel between 1955 and 1979.[5] One might study with profit
Brown's argumentation for the independence of John's tradition from
the Synoptic traditions, his situating the thought of the gospel within
first-century Judaism due to its similarities to the Qumran literature,[6] his
rejection of Gnosticism as a source for the gospel's religious thought, the
gospel's significant use of Jewish Wisdom language as a source for John's
Christology, and his belief that the primary purpose of the gospel was to
edify the faith of believers rather than to convert unbelievers.

But it is almost certainly his research on the hypothetical Johannine community, along with the interrelated matter of the composition and various stages of the fourth gospel, that contributed to
an *almost* hegemonic way of reading the fourth gospel in the latter
half of the twentieth century. Although he later changed his mind,
Robert Kysar stated this strongly when he said that the fourth gospel
"cannot be read meaningfully apart from some understanding of the
community out of which and to which it was written."[7] Stated most
simply, Brown's project trades upon the belief that the fourth gospel is
a primary source for determining the history and beliefs of a particular community *and* that this history is partially determined or reconstructed by the various stages of the composition of the gospel. Given
the significant influence Brown's approach has had upon the interpretation of the fourth gospel, it may be of some value to: (a) examine
Brown's argumentation for community and composition, (b) make a
few remarks upon the methodological assumptions of Brown's proj-

---

3. Raymond E. Brown, *The Churches the Apostles Left Behind* (New York: Paulist, 1984).
4. Raymond E. Brown, *An Introduction to the Gospel of John*, ed. Francis J. Moloney, ABRL (New York: Doubleday, 2003).
5. Brown, *The Community of the Beloved Disciple*, 5.
6. Raymond E. Brown, "The Qumran Scrolls and the Johannine Gospel and Epistles," *CBQ* 17 (1955): 403–19.
7. Robert Kysar, *The Fourth Evangelist and his Gospel: An Examination of Contemporary Scholarship* (Minneapolis: Augsburg, 1975), 270. See also, John Painter, *The Quest for the Messiah: The History, Literature and Theology of the Johannine Community*, 2nd ed. (Nashville: Abingdon, 1993), 61: "the most significant single factor in shaping the Johannine tradition was the relation to the synagogue, a relationship which began with dialogue, became a conflict and ended in mutual execration."

ect, and (c) present a few of the most important criticisms of Brown's approach to community and composition.

COMPOSITION

"It is notorious that many biblical scholars are also passionate readers of detective stories."[8] Perhaps Brown's professed love affair for the Johannine writings stems from the way in which his questions and methods allow him to analyze the writings looking for clues that would give up the history of the community that produced them.[9] In his 1966 Anchor Bible commentary, Brown posits five stages of the literary composition of the fourth gospel, though he simplifies these stages to three in his revised *Introduction*.[10] The gospel is not, for Brown, the product of a single author such as John the son of Zebedee or John the Elder.[11] Differences in the style of Greek, dislocations, unnecessary repetitions, theological inconsistencies, and awkwardness in the literary sequencing (i.e., the Johannine aporias) are appealed to as evidence that the gospel underwent multiple stages of reworking, additions, and editing.[12]

Stage One: A particular disciple—perhaps the Beloved Disciple—functioned as the vehicle for the oral traditions of Jesus's words and deeds.[13]

---

8. Raymond E. Brown, *The Gospel According to John I–XII*, AB 29 (Garden City, NY: Doubleday, 1966), lxxxvii.

9. The amount of references to "detective-like" work gives an important insight into how Brown viewed his work. See also his references to Sherlock Holmes in order to illustrate his work in *The Community of the Beloved Disciple*, 61.

10. Despite the change in the numbering of stages (three instead of five), Brown's approach to these stages has not changed greatly. He appears to be a bit annoyed at the reviewers who complained of the complexity of the five stages: "In the original edition of this commentary (1966) I posited five stages in the composition of the gospel. I believed them to be minimal, for I am convinced that the full details of the gospel's prehistory are far too complicated to reconstruct. Nevertheless, a number of reviewers found counting up to five very difficult and complained about the complexity of my approach." And he indicates that he has decided to set forth three stages instead of five for the sake of "the arithmetically challenged" (Brown, *An Introduction to the Gospel of John*, 64).

11. In *The Gospel according to John I–XII*, xcviii, Brown noted the difficulties with assigning the fourth gospel to the son of Zebedee and yet could write: "When all is said and done, the combination of external and internal evidence associating the fourth gospel with John son of Zebedee makes this the strongest hypothesis, if one is prepared to give credence to the gospels' claim of an eyewitness source." Later, however, Brown moved from this position and argued, instead, that the Beloved Disciple was not one of the Twelve but was rather likely a disciple of John the Baptist (see John 1:35–51). See *The Community of the Beloved Disciple*, 33–34.

12. Brown, *An Introduction to the Gospel of John*, 40–42. For other explanations for the aporias, see John Ashton, *Understanding the Fourth Gospel*, 2nd ed. (Oxford: Oxford University Press, 2007), 100–107.

13. Brown, *An Introduction to the Gospel of John*, 64–66.

Stage Two: Jesus is proclaimed in the Johannine community. It is important to note that Brown sees the Jesus-tradition as being shaped here, *in part*, by the history of this "particularly close-knit community with a particular history."[14] Jesus's Samaritan following (John 4:42; cf. 8:48) "suggests that the community reflected in the fourth gospel brought into membership a number of Samaritans—thus a composite membership of Jews and Samaritans not present in the communities evangelized by the Twelve."[15] The Samaritan influence may also explain why the Johannine traditions emphasize Jesus as a Moses-like figure (1:17; 3:13–14; 5:45–46).[16]

Stage Three: In this stage the gospel is written, but Brown "detects" the hand of "the evangelist" who is responsible for writing the gospel and the "redactor" who later made some additions to the evangelist's work.[17] Both figures are probably disciples of the Beloved Disciple (who is already dead at the stage in which the gospel was written). The evangelist is a remarkable theologian-storyteller who is responsible for developing Jesus's miracles into christological dramas, weaving Jesus's sayings into coherent and poetic sermons, the literary techniques of irony and misunderstanding, and the signs.[18] The redactor, working *within* the Johannine school,[19] reworked the gospel and is probably responsible for the prologue (1:1–18), the epilogue (21:1–25), the inserted doublet discourses (6:51–58 with 6:35–50), and added settings to some discourses (3:31–36 and 12:44–50).[20] There are, then, for Brown three members of the Johannine community directly involved in the composition of the gospel: the Beloved Disciple, the Evangelist, and the Redactor.[21]

---

14. Ibid., 66.
15. Ibid., 67.
16. Ibid., 68.
17. Ibid., 78; cf. page 79 where Brown affirms "the history of the Johannine community can be read out of the gospel by a type of detective work."
18. Ibid., 79–82.
19. Unlike Rudolf Bultmann, Brown sees the redactor as one "who preserved Johannine material and who tried to make the Gospel as complete a collection of this material as possible..." Brown, *The Gospel According to John I-XII*, cxxi.
20. Brown, *An Introduction to the Gospel of John*, 82–85.
21. On distinguishing between the work of the evangelist and the redactor, see also Rudolf Schnackenburg, *The Gospel According to St John*, vol. 3: *Commentary on Chapters 13–21* (Crossroad: New York, 1982), 375–88; R. Alan Culpepper, *The Johannine School: An Evaluation of the Johannine-School Hypothesis Based on an Investigation of the Nature of Ancient Schools*, SBLDS 26 (Missoula, MT: SBL Press, 1975).

COMMUNITY

The stages of literary composition and redaction are invoked to explain the literary aporias, apparent contradictions, and theological tensions detected by Brown within the fourth gospel, but they also provide windows, as we have noted, for the interpreter to see the history of the community that is inscribed within the gospel. John Painter states this clearly: "The evidence suggests that Jn, as we now know it, came into being progressively through the re-interpretation of the tradition in various situations."[22] This commitment can be seen already in Brown's 1966 commentary: "We suggest that the adaptation of the Gospel to different goals meant the introduction of new material designed to meet new problems."[23] The seeds for Brown's later investigations of the Johannine community are already here, and he notes that the story of the expulsion of the healed blind man in John 9 has been adapted to "the new situation in the late 80s or early 90s which involved the excommunication from the Synagogue of Jews who believed in Jesus as the Messiah."[24]

But the Johannine community seeds have not yet germinated, for there is no reconstruction of the community such as we find in his 1979 *The Community of the Beloved Disciple*. Here Brown reads the gospel of John, at least in part, as "an autobiography of the Johannine community."[25] Brown discerns four stages of the Johannine community.

Stage One: The first stage of the community corresponds to the literary stage preceding the writing of the fourth gospel, and it begins with the event depicted in John 1:35–51 where a group of Jewish followers of John the Baptist confess Jesus to be Israel's Messiah.[26] The major event in the Johannine community in this stage is the entrance of a group of Samaritan converts (4:4–52; 8:48)[27] who provide the impetus for John's Moses-Christology (e.g., 1:16–18; 3:13–14) and this catalyzes a higher Wisdom Christology that emphasizes Jesus's

---

22. Painter, *The Quest for the Messiah*, 74. Moloney states this well in Brown, *An Introduction to the Gospel of John*, 3–4: "For Brown, many of the tensions, both literary and theological, can still best be understood by coming to grips with the various stages in the development of a gospel, which eventually became the Gospel."
23. Brown, *The Gospel According to John I–XII*, xxxvi.
24. Ibid., xxxvi.
25. Brown, *The Community of the Beloved Disciple*, 69.
26. Hence the titles "Messiah," "Rabbi," "Son of God" (1:34).
27. Brown, *The Community of the Beloved Disciple*, 37, comments on the slur leveled against Jesus that he is a Samaritan in 8:48: "This suggests that the Johannine community was regarded by Jesus as having Samaritan elements."

preexistence and a uniquely high Christology exemplified in the "I Am" statements (e.g., 1:9–10, 14; 8:12; 9:5; 10:30; 14:9).[28] This high Christology is at variance with the earlier Christology "articulated by the first followers of Jesus in 1:35–51."[29] And these Samaritans brought with them "categories for interpreting Jesus that launched the Johannine community toward a theology of descent from above and pre-existence" (e.g., 5:20; 6:46; 7:16).[30] Thus, John's Christology is indebted to and intertwined with community experience.

> Inevitably the combination of a different Christology, opposition to the Temple cult, and Samaritan elements, which were characteristic of the second group that entered the mainstream of Johannine Christianity, would have made the Johannine believers in Jesus particularly obnoxious to more traditional Jews.[31]

Thus, the development of the Johannine community's high Christology results in a situation where the Jews begin to expel Johannine Christians from the synagogues (9:22; 12:42; 16:2).[32] The mutual antagonism between the Johannine Christians and "the Jews" is responsible for the former's stressing "a realization of the eschatological promises in Jesus to compensate for what they had lost in Judaism (whence the strong theme of replacement in the Gospel)."[33] Thus, what Brown had recognized as a literary theme in John 5–10 in his Anchor Bible commentary, namely, how the presence of Jesus relativizes the significance of the Jewish feasts, is seen here to be the result of the Johannine Christians' expulsion from the synagogue.[34]

---

28. Brown here accepts and is using the results of Wayne A. Meeks, *The Prophet King: Moses Traditions and the Johannine Christology*, NovTSup 14 (Leiden: Brill, 1967).
29. Brown, *The Community of the Beloved Disciple*, 43.
30. Ibid., 45.
31. Brown, *The Community of the Beloved Disciple*, 39.
32. Note the difference from Martyn who thinks the high Christology is the result (not the cause) of the expulsions from the synagogue. Ashton, *Understanding the Fourth Gospel*, 23 (and chs. 2–3), agrees with Martyn that the "expulsion was the consequence, not the cause, of the Johannine group's adoption of beliefs incompatible with the strict monotheism of those whom the Gospel calls 'the Jews'."
33. Raymond E. Brown, *An Introduction to the New Testament*, ABRL (New York: Doubleday, 1997), 374–75.
34. Brown, *The Community of the Beloved Disciple*, 48–51. Brown, *An Introduction to the Gospel of John*, 76: "Expulsion had cut the Johannine Christians off from the rich liturgical life, and to compensate for that the Johannine tradition emphasized a strong motif of replacement: Jesus takes the place of many of the institutions of Judaism."

Stage Two: Brown locates the second stage of the Johannine community to the period when the basic gospel was written (ca. AD 90). In this stage, the rejection of Jesus by the majority of the Jewish leaders (John 12:37–40) *and* the inclusion of non-Jews within the Jewish community (12:20–23) give rise to the well-known Johannine dualistic tendencies. Johannine dualism nicely brings out the "universalist possibilities in Johannine thought, in an attempt to speak to a wider audience" (3:16–17) *and* establishes those who reject and persecute the community as belonging to Satan, the ruler of this world (17:15–16; 14:30; 16:33).[35] Brown finds this stage of the community to be primarily preoccupied with "the relation of the Johannine believers to various shades of non-believers and other believers."[36] This is mirror reading at its best (or at least most exaggerated) as Brown consistently detects real *contemporary* figures and groups behind the Johannine characters. The nonbelievers comprise three groups. The first group, "the world," includes both the Jews and broader non-Jewish society and has produced for the Johannine community "an increasing sense of alienation, so that now the community itself is a stranger in the world."[37] The second group, "the Jews" who have rejected Jesus and already expelled the Johannine Christians from the synagogue, are those who have catalyzed the controversy over Jesus's divinity (5:39–40, 45–47; 6:31–33; 7:23; 8:34–57; 10:34–36) and continue to persecute the Johannine community.[38] The third group of unbelievers are those who are disciples of John the Baptist and for whom the "Johannine Christians still held hope for their conversion."[39] Other non-Johannine Christians who appear include those Christians who refuse to publicly confess their belief in Jesus as Messiah out of fear that they will be expelled from the synagogue ("Crypto-Christians," 12:42–43; cf. 3:1–36; 7:50ff.), Christians with a low Christology who break away from the Johannine community (6:60–69; 8:31ff.), and apostolic Christians who are symbolized by Simon Peter and other members of the Twelve and are seen as less perceptive in their faith than the Beloved Disciple and the Johannine Christians (20:6–9).

---

35. Brown, *An Introduction to the New Testament*, 375.
36. Brown, *The Community of the Beloved Disciple*, 62.
37. Ibid., 64.
38. Ibid., 66–69.
39. Ibid., 69–71; cf. Painter, *The Quest for the Messiah*, 68–69.

Stage Three: This stage corresponds to the composition of the first and second Johannine epistles (ca. AD 100). The author of the Johannine epistles, along with the evangelist and redactor of the fourth gospel, belongs to a Johannine school that "shared a theological position and style." [40] Both groups, according to Brown, "*knew the proclamation of Christianity available to us through the Fourth Gospel, but they interpreted it differently*" (italics his).[41] Here the Johannine community splits. The "orthodox" community, represented by the author of 1 and 2 John, stresses now both the divinity and humanity of Jesus as a corrective to those who have seceded (1 John 2:18–19) and, according to the orthodox group, are deficient with respect to Christology *and* ethics.[42] The author of 1 John belongs to the Johannine school and his "genre, polemic, argumentation, and even structure" depend upon John's gospel.[43] The secessionists do not acknowledge that Jesus Christ has truly come in the flesh (1 John 4:1–3; 2 John 7), and they fail to love their brethren (1 John 2:9–11; 3:10–24; 4:7–21). Brown claims that every idea of the secessionists (so far as one can reconstruct it from 1 and 2 John) "*can be plausibly explained as derivative from the Johannine tradition as preserved for us in GJohn*" (italics his).[44] The group represented by 1 John has a more conservative approach to Christology, ethics, eschatology, and pneumatology.[45]

Stage Four: Brown sees this stage as corresponding to both the writing of 3 John and the time when the redactor added chapter 21 to the fourth gospel.[46] In this stage, the divided groups of the Johannine community are both "swallowed up respectively by the 'Great Church' and by the gnostic movement."[47] The secessionists' rejection

---

40. Brown, *The Community of the Beloved Disciple*, 96.

41. Ibid., 106; Raymond E. Brown, *The Epistles of John*, AB 30 (Garden City, NY: Doubleday, 1982), 69.

42. Brown, *The Epistles of John*, 71: "The amalgamation of the secessionists into the known gnostic movements of the second century would have required a heightening of the dualistic christology and perfectionistic anthropology criticized in I and II John."

43. Brown, *The Epistles of John*, 86. Here Brown points to the use of similar vocabulary and theological motifs, the use of the first person plural "we" of the Johannine school, and the likelihood that 1 John appeals to homilies from earlier Johannine tradition.

44. Ibid., 72.

45. Brown, *An Introduction to the Gospel of John*, 75.

46. Brown, *The Epistles of John*, 110, states that "in having Jesus assign a shepherding role to Simon Peter, John 21 has moved notably closer to the ideal of church order that would dominate the Great Church." The rest of the gospel betrays a privileging of the testimony of the beloved disciple over that of Peter who represents the Great Church. See Brown, *The Churches the Apostles Left Behind*, 91–95.

47. Brown, *The Community of the Beloved Disciple*, 145. Brown, *The Epistles of John*, 103, admits that this is speculative and that it is possible that both groups "did survive but left no traces in history."

of the "salvific importance" of Jesus's humanity was "exaggerated in a docetist direction" and this resulted in them making "common cause with docetists against church authorities who proclaimed the theology of a salvific humanity."[48] Alternatively, the high Christology of preexistence as well as its rejection of Docetism enables the author of 1 John's branch of the movement to merge with the apostolic Christians.[49] Given the checkered interpretation of the fourth gospel and its docetic/gnostic interpretations by the other branch of the Johannine community, however, the "Great Church . . . was at first wary of the Fourth Gospel because it had given rise to error and was being used to support error."[50] Here Brown points to the reception of John's gospel by heterodox authors and texts such as Heracleon's commentary, *Odes of Solomon*, Ptolemaus, *Tripartite Tractate*, the secret gospel of Mark,[51] and others.[52] Brown claims that the lack of evidence and appreciation for the gospel of John among so-called orthodox second-century authors is probably due to the fact that "the secessionist adversaries of 1 John were the bridge by which GJohn gained acceptance among the Gnostics."[53] The church's decision to welcome the fourth gospel into the canon along with the Synoptic Gospels holds great significance: "This means that the Great Church . . . has chosen to live with the tension. It has chosen not a Jesus who is either God or man but both; it has chosen not a Jesus who is either virginally conceived as God's Son or pre-existent as God's Son but both . . . not a Peter or a Beloved Disciple but both."[54]

---

48. Brown, *The Epistles of John*, 105.

49. Ibid., 113: the Great Church was "not unfavorable to the Johannine christology," but "they were not at ease with GJohn precisely because the secessionists, who constituted the larger part of the Johannine Community, had taken GJohn with them as they went down various paths to Cerinthianism, Montanism, Docetism, and Gnosticism. GJohn had proved too amenable to gnostic commentary and interpretation to suit many conservatives in the Great Church."

50. Brown, *The Community of the Beloved Disciple*, 146–47; Brown, *The Epistles of John*, 71: "we can understand why GJohn was better known among 'heretics' than among orthodox church writers of the second century . . . and why Irenaeus remembered a figure like Cerinthus when he discussed GJohn. The ultimate acceptance of GJohn into the church's canon, attested in the late second century, was in no small part due to the fact that 1 John offered an example of how GJohn could be read in a non-gnostic and even an anti-Gnostic way."

51. On which see Raymond E. Brown, "The Relation of 'The Secret Gospel of Mark' to the Fourth Gospel," *CBQ* 31 (1969): 357–69.

52. Brown, *The Community of the Beloved Disciple*, 147–50; Brown, *The Epistles of John*, 105–106. Brown's argument is bolstered by Ernst Käsemann's bold thesis that the gospel of John presents a naïve Docetism. See Käsemann, *The Testament of Jesus* (Philadelphia: Fortress Press, 1968).

53. Brown, *The Epistles of John*, 106.

54. Brown, *The Community of the Beloved Disciple*, 163–64.

FOUR BRIEF REFLECTIONS ON BROWN'S COMPOSITION AND COMMUNITY HYPOTHESIS

1. Brown's stages of literary composition give critical roles, as we have seen, to three figures: the Beloved Disciple, the Evangelist, and the Redactor (the latter two assumed to be faithful disciples of the former). As Richard Bauckham has noted, little interest is "given to the traditions of the early church about the origins and authorship of the gospel, since they are held to be incompatible with the internal evidence of the Gospel itself."[55] Reconstructions of the Johannine community depend, in part, on the belief that John the apostle (or an eyewitness) may not be *directly* responsible for its traditions. We have seen that Brown does not ignore, at least in his Anchor Bible commentaries, discussions of the traditional authorship of the gospel as John the son of Zebedee (though he later changes his mind), but there is minimal consideration that the traditions of the fourth gospel should be considered eyewitness testimony even if their origin is in the memory of a creative figure who experienced Jesus of Nazareth.[56] In Brown's evaluation of the work of Oscar Cullmann, he takes issue with his accounting for the differences between John and the Synoptics "on the basis of different styles of speech stemming from Jesus." For Brown, "precisely those differences make it implausible (nay impossible) that the Fourth Gospel was written by an eyewitness of the ministry of Jesus; the role of the Beloved Disciple was therefore not that of the evangelist."[57] The explicitly theological nature of John means that John's gospel was almost certainly not written by an eyewitness.[58] This further means that, for Brown, the story of the Johannine community can, in part, be reconstructed through detailed attention to the prehistory of the text. In fact, Ashton bluntly and rightly states that these aporias "are the foundation of all theories of layers of redaction

---

55. Richard Bauckham, *The Testimony of the Beloved Disciple: Narrative, History, and Theology in the Gospel of John* (Grand Rapids: Baker, 2007), 10.

56. This, of course, has important ramifications for using the gospel of John as a historical source: "And so, although we think that the Fourth Gospel reflects historical memories of Jesus, the greater extent of the theological reshaping of those memories makes Johannine material much harder to use in the quest of the historical Jesus than most Synoptic material." See Brown, *The Gospel according to John I–XII*, xlix.

57. Brown, *The Community of the Beloved Disciple*, 177–78.

58. See the evaluation of Brown's position here by Painter, *The Quest for the Messiah*, 90–91.

and successive editions of the Gospel."[59] The so-called Johannine aporias, then, cannot be explained by assuming the literary unity and coherence of the text.[60]

2. Brown's approach is a clear and fairly moderate example of the (or "a") historical-critical methodology that supposes meaning is found in the situations and settings that gave rise to the text.[61] In other words, as Robert Kysar has also noted, the method supposes that "the meaning of any text is dependent on the historical occasion for and in which it was written."[62] There is an obvious belief that despite the difficulty of reconstructing the historical occasion(s) and community/(ies) behind the text, the cracks, riddles, and aporias of the Johannine writings provide glimpses into this history and, therefore, into the meaning of the text. Brown uses enough illustra- tions from detective novels to hazard the nonscientific claim that he conceptualized his own research as a detective investigating clues left behind in the text. Thus, Brown largely *assumes* (so far as I can tell) that the fourth gospel is *the kind of literature* that is justifiably read as an autobiography of the Johannine community.[63] Involved in this method, as we have seen, is positing that behind literary

---

59. Ashton, *Understanding the Fourth Gospel*, 22.

60. See here the defense of those like Brown who examine the prehistory of the gospel in light of the aporias by Ashton, *Understanding the Fourth Gospel*, 14–19. See Painter, *The Quest for the Messiah*, 61: "This process [i.e., investigating the Johannine community] is reflected in the tradition and the observation of clues can lead to the detection that at first seems hidden."

61. He does not reject but reframes the form criticism of Wellhausen and Bultmann who insisted "the Gospels tell us primarily about the church situation in which they were written, and only secondarily about the situation of Jesus which *prima facie* they describe." Brown claims that "*Primarily*, the Gospels tell us how an evangelist conceived of and presented Jesus to a Christian community . . . a presentation that indirectly gives us an insight into that community's life at the time when the Gospel was written," and that "the Gospels offer a limited means for reconstructing the ministry and message of the historical Jesus." Brown, *The Community of the Beloved Disciple*, 17.

62. Robert Kysar, "The Whence and Whither of the Johannine Community," in *Life in Abundance: Studies in John's Gospel in Tribute to Raymond E. Brown*, ed. John R. Donahue (Collegeville, MN: Liturgical Press, 2005), 65–81, here 67. Luke Timothy Johnson, "What's Catholic about Catholic Biblical Scholarship?" in *The Future of Catholic Biblical Scholarship: A Constructive Conversation*, by Luke Timothy Johnson and William S. Kurz (Grand Rapids: Eerdmans, 2002), 3–34, here 12, includes Brown as an example of second generation Catholic scholarship: "The main distinguishing feature of this generation is its uncritical acceptance of the dominant historical-critical paradigm, and a style of scholarship that was increasingly directed to . . . other scholars."

63. Though not a critic in terms of method, Painter, *The Quest for the Messiah*, 67, rightly notes that Brown's method can give the "impression that the history of the community can simply be read out of the Gospel, suggesting that the evangelist set out to write a history of his community in the guise of a Gospel."

figures stand contemporary historical persons, groups, and theo-logical beliefs. These contemporary figures and persons that stand *behind the text* are central for determining the particular forma-tion of Johannine tradition, including its theological themes ("the Jews") and Johannine Christology (Mosaic and not Davidic).[64]

3. Brown's methodological approach to reconstructing the Johannine community is more asserted than it is argued for. Brown says he wants to study "the history of the Johannine community . . . by using a fruitful approach that has been opened up in Johannine scholarship of the last ten years. This is based on the suggestion that the Gospel must be read on several levels, so that it tells us the story both of Jesus and of the community that believed in him."[65] It is no surprise that Brown cites J. Louis Martyn's *History and Theology in the Fourth Gospel* (1968) as an example of this "fruitful approach."[66] The shift from his moderate suggestions regarding the Johannine community in 1966 to the much more complex, speculative, and at best probable ideas in his 1979 *The Community of the Beloved Disciple* is, if I myself may speculate, probably partially indebted to the successful reception of Martyn's *HTFG*.[67] Martyn, as is well known, proposes that portions of the gospel are to be read as a two-level drama whereby Jesus's words and deeds (the *einmalig*) are ciphers for the experiences and beliefs of the Johannine community. Martyn's major example comes from John 9 where Jesus stands in for the community of Christian prophets, the blind man for those Jews who convert, and the Jews for the synagogue leaders who expel those who confess Jesus (John 9:22; 12:42; 16:2). Martyn thereby understands this event, the expulsion of the Johannine community from the synagogue, to explain much of the particular character of the fourth gospel. The wide popular-ity of Martyn's argument, even when Johannine scholars did not agree with its details, almost certainly encouraged Brown, among

---

64. Kysar, "The Whence and Whither of the Johannine Community," 70; Painter, *The Quest for the Messiah*, 68.

65. Brown, *The Community of the Beloved Disciple*, 17.

66. J. Louis Martyn, *History and Theology in the Fourth Gospel*, 3rd ed. (Louisville: Westminster John Knox, 2003).

67. But the speculation is not too risky or far-fetched. See Kysar, "The Whence and Whither of the Johannine Community," 67–71. Ashton, *Understanding the Fourth Gospel*, 107, states of Martyn's book that it "is probably the most important single work on the Gospel since Bultmann's commentary."

others, to engage in more detailed, complex, and speculative investigations of the Johannine community.[68] Thomas Brodie is blunt and clear: "In comparison with the narrow drama depicted by Martyn, Brown's reconstruction depicts a community of immense complexity, complex in its composition and complex in its relationships."[69]

Another enormous contributor to Brown's investigations must be the work of Wayne Meeks whose 1967 *The Prophet King* is probably partially responsible for Brown's detecting that the inclusion of Samaritans within the Johannine community has led to the gospel's non-Davidic and Moses-oriented Christology. Likewise, Meeks's "The Man from Heaven in Johannine Sectarianism" argues that the social function of Jesus's discourses in the fourth gospel, particularly the ascent/descent schema of the Son of Man, makes best sense as stemming from the community's minority social location vis-à-vis the larger world of Judaism—a claim that further lends itself to support Brown's belief that the Johannine community (whether one uses or rejects the language of sectarian) can be distinguished from something like "apostolic Christianity."[70]

4. John Ashton notes that Rudolf Bultmann pointed to two significant riddles in the fourth gospel: (a) the gospel's relationship to the broader development of earlier Christianity, and (b) the central idea of the gospel as it stands.[71] The work of Brown, Martyn, and Meeks (among others) has demonstrated that the language, thought-world, and situation of the fourth gospel arose out of a Jewish matrix.[72] The beginnings of the Johannine community stem from Jewish followers of Jesus who held to a traditional Jewish-Christian Christology (John 1:35–51); the similarities between the fourth gospel and the Qumran scrolls suggest John's religious thought-world is not to be

---

68. For praise of Martyn's book, see Kysar, "The Whence and Whither of the Johannine Community," 68, who states: "Without a doubt this remarkable research is one of the grand achievements of Johannine research in the twentieth century." Also, see D. Moody Smith, "The Contribution of J. Louis Martyn to the Understanding of the Gospel of John," in *History and Theology in the Fourth Gospel*, 1–23.

69. Thomas L. Brodie, *The Quest for the Origin of John's Gospel: A Source-Oriented Approach* (Oxford: Oxford University Press, 1993), 18–19.

70. Wayne E. Meeks, "The Man from Heaven in Johannine Sectarianism," *JBL* 91 (1972): 44–72.

71. Ashton, *Understanding the Fourth Gospel*, 2.

72. See also Terence L. Donaldson, *Jews and Anti-Judaism in the New Testament: Decision Points and Divergent Interpretations* (Waco, TX: Baylor University Press, 2010), 100–102.

found outside of Judaism;[73] the polemic between the Johannine community and "the Jews" stems from the break with the Jewish synagogue and (partially) accounts for the particular language of the gospel. The primary point here is that Brown's work, among others, seems almost certainly partly responsible for the current consensus that situates John and the Johannine community within a Jewish framework (rather than a gnostic, Philonic, Hermetic, etc.).

CHALLENGES TO RAYMOND BROWN ON COMPOSITION AND COMMUNITY

Brown's professed love affair with the fourth gospel, and the enigmatic community that stands behind it, suggests that were he still alive he would continue to refine his argument (not to say reject or abandon) by evaluating recent research that challenges his way of reading the fourth gospel. I offer here, very briefly, three of the most pressing challenges to his thesis.[74]

1. The Limits of the Historical-Critical Enterprise

Growing dissatisfaction with the methods and fruitfulness of historical criticism is, in part, responsible for the proliferation of new methods. Robert Kysar, despite once affirming its broad components, claims

---

73. Brown, *An Introduction to the Gospel of John*, 115–50. See here also Painter, *The Quest for the Messiah*, 35–52. Though this is challenged strongly by Bauckham, "The Qumran Community and the Gospel of John," in *The Testimony of the Beloved Disciple*, 125–36.

74. Obviously, more challenges could be offered and some of them quite major. I think, for example, of challenges to Brown's argument (representative of many New Testament scholars) that the orthodox had a case of "Johannophobia" due to its popularity among gnostic interpreters and that it was later appropriated or rescued by Irenaeus for the cause of the orthodox. See here Charles E. Hill, *The Johannine Corpus in the Early Church* (Oxford: Oxford University Press, 2004), 3, who seeks to overturn the dominant thesis that "so deep was the affinity for this Gospel among Valentinians and gnostics, and so close was its identification with these groups in the popular Christian mind, that many Church leaders suspected it or opposed it." See also Martin Hengel, *The Johannine Question*, trans. John Bowden (London: SCM, 1989), 1–23; Titus Nagel, *Die Rezeption des Johannesevangeliums im 2. Jahrhundert: Studien zur vorirenäischen Aneignung und Auslegung des vierten Evangeliums in christlicher und christlich-gnostischer Literatur*, ABG 2 (Leipzig: Evangelische Verlagsanstalt, 2000). But see Francis Watson, *Gospel Writing: A Canonical Perspective* (Grand Rapids: Eerdmans, 2013), 411–509, who thinks that Hill has strongly overstated his case. Others have argued that the gospel of John is a literary unity and have made strong arguments that John's prologue (1:1–18) and epilogue (ch. 21) fit well with the author's theology and style. See Bauckham, "The 153 Fish and the Unity of the Fourth Gospel," in *The Testimony of the Beloved Disciple*, 271–84; D. A. Carson, *The Gospel according to John* (Grand Rapids: Eerdmans, 1991), 665–68.

that the "reconstruction of the Johannine community is based on both historical and interpretative methods now under siege and being dismantled piece by piece."[75] One need not turn to the most radical forms of so-called postmodern literary criticism to agree with Kysar that the meaning of a text is not found in the circumstances that gave rise to the text but within the text itself.[76] Kysar is also concerned about the hypothetical nature of the Johannine community hypothesis.[77] Its central thesis, in fact, the expulsion of the Jewish Christians from the synagogue, might not even refer to an event that had already taken place.[78] And others have argued that the expulsion passages (John 9:22; 12:42; and 16:2) are historically plausible within Jesus's own lifetime.[79] More and more voices have raised concerns about the speculative nature of the Johannine community hypothesis that results from the fact that the community is "unlocatable either temporally or geographically."[80] Johnson challenges Brown's attempt to reconstruct the history of the community based on his stages of literary composition:

---

75. Kysar, "The Whence and Whither of the Johannine Community," 76. This is also admitted by John Painter, a well-known proponent and practitioner of the search for the Johannine community: "Even in Jn, however, where the reflections are clearest, there are no straightforward data upon which the history of the Johannine community can be based." Painter, *The Quest for the Messiah*, 68.

76. Kysar, "The Whence and Whither of the Johannine Community," 73–74: "If postmodernism prevails it will mean the death of the historical critical method of biblical interpretation and all the historical reconstructions that were the results of the method, including those involving the Johannine community." This is a complete turnabout from his earlier work, which claimed that contemporary scholarship had proved the gospel to be a community document. See Robert Kysar, *The Fourth Evangelist and His Gospel* (Minneapolis: Augsburg, 1975), 269–70. In large agreement with the later Kysar is Hans-Josef Klauck, "Community, History, and Text(s)—a Response to Robert Kysar," in *Life in Abundance*, 82–90.

77. See especially, Robert Kysar, "The Expulsion from the Synagogue: The Tale of a Theory," in *Voyages with John: Charting the Fourth Gospel* (Waco, TX: Baylor University Press, 2006), 237–46. Also important here is Ruth Langer, *Cursing the Christians? A History of the Birkat Haminim* (Oxford: Oxford University Press, 2012).

78. See here, for example, those who suggest that the Johannine expulsion texts should not be related to the *Birkat ha-Minim*. Raimo Hakola and Adele Reinhartz, "John's Pharisees," in *Quest of the Historical Pharisees*, eds. Jacob Neusner and Bruce D. Chilton (Waco, TX: Baylor University Press, 2007), 131–47; Warren Carter, *John and Empire: Initial Explorations* (Harrisburg, PA: Trinity Press, 2008).

79. Jonathan Bernier, *Aposynagogos and the Historical Jesus in John: Rethinking the Historicity of the Johannine Passages*, Biblical Interpretation Series 122 (Leiden: Brill, 2013).

80. See Luke Timothy Johnson, *The Real Jesus: The Misguided Quest for the Historical Jesus and the Truth of the Traditional Gospels* (San Francisco: HarperCollins, 1996), 100. See also Brodie, *The Quest for the Origin of John's Gospel*, 20: "Each of these reconstructions is built on a reading of the New Testament, particularly of the Johannine literature, and also of other external evidence. Consequently each has its own plausibility. Yet given the diversity of views, it is clear that the actual process of reconstructing is extremely hazardous. As indicated earlier, the gospel supplies no evidence, for instance, that unbelieving adherents of John the Baptist even existed in 90 CE. The reasons given for their existence involve a bypassing of the theological nature of the text and in its place a projection of polemic."

The problems inherent in such an attempt ought to be obvious. What guiding principles attend the discrimination between sources and stages? What reasons are there for arranging the pieces in the suggested sequence? What would happen if the order were changed? . . . I mention Raymond Brown as an example precisely because he is the embodiment of scholarly respectability and sobriety. His name is not associated with the fanciful or faddish. Yet his entire reconstruction of Johannine 'history' rests upon no more solid basis than a series of subjective judgments and suspect methodological presuppositions.[81]

Johnson is not rejecting the historical analysis of the gospel of John, but is rather, as I understand him, challenging the historical-critical method for front-grounding what is behind the text rather than the text itself as well as frequently failing to "operate within the intrinsic limitations imposed by the scarcity of evidence and controls."[82] Martin Hengel voices a similar concern over reconstructions of the Johannine community, stating: "They are doomed to failure, because we know nothing of a real history which even goes back to Palestine, and conjectures about it are idle. . . . All we know is the old head of the school; we have some indications of a severe crisis in the community at a late stage, and we see the publication of the head's writings after his death."[83] Similar but more measured than Johnson and Hengel is Adele Reinhartz who thinks it perfectly valid to pursue the quest for the Johannine community provided that one remember its existence is conjectural and hypothetical rather than a historical given.[84]

Further, whereas Brown has seen distinct stages of literary composition due to the Johannine aporias, others have seen the hand of a creative storyteller and theologian.[85] Where some have seen contradictions thus necessitating the positing of redaction or literary stages,

81. Johnson, *The Real Jesus*, 100. See also Luke Timothy Johnson, "On Finding the Lukan Community: A Cautious Cautionary Essay," *SBL Seminar Papers* 18 (Missoula, MT: Scholars Press, 1979), 87–100.

82. Johnson, *The Real Jesus*, 102.

83. Hengel, *The Johannine Question*, 205 n. 85.

84. Adele Reinhartz, "The Johannine Community and Its Jewish Neighbors: A Reappraisal," in *What is John? Literary and Social Readings of the Fourth Gospel*, ed. Fernando F. Segovia (Atlanta: Scholars Press, 1998), 111–38; see her response to J. Louis Martyn, in idem, "Reading History in the Fourth Gospel," in *What We Have Heard From the Beginning*, 191–94.

85. Here Hengel *The Johannine Question*, ix, is worth citing given that he works more directly within a historical-critical (rather than literary or narrative) paradigm: "it seems to me unmistakable that the Gospel and the letters are not the expression of a community with many voices, but above all the voice of a towering theologian, the founder and head of the Johannine school."

others have argued for Johannine paradox and dialectic.[86] Others have stressed that the fourth gospel is a piece of literature that lends itself to narrative analysis and not historical reconstruction. As Alan Culpepper states with respect to the narrative analysis of the fourth gospel:

> The narrative world of the gospel is therefore neither a window on the ministry of Jesus nor a window on the history of the Johannine community. . . . According to this model, dissection and stratification have no place in the study of the gospel and may distort and confuse one's view of the text. Every element of the gospel contributes to the production of its meaning, and the experience of reading the text is more important than understanding the process of its composition.[87]

Or stated even more forcefully by Richard Bauckham:

> In the light of greater sensitivity to the literary strategies of the text, which literary criticism fosters, many of what seemed aporias to the source and redaction critics appear no longer to be so. A passage that seems awkward to the often rather prosaic mind of the source critic, whose judgment often amounts merely to observing that he or she would not have written it like that, can appear quite different to a critic attentive to the literary dynamics of the text. Thus literary criticism of the final form of the Gospel is not just an approach that can be added to source and redaction criticism, leaving their results intact, as most Johannine scholars seem still to suppose. It must pose serious questions about the interpretation of the evidence on which the older approaches were based.[88]

Furthermore, Bauckham suggests that Johannine scholarship's obsession with "the stratification of the Gospel in sources and redactional layers has distracted such scholars from the literary strategies of the Gospel as a text designed to be read sequentially and as a whole."[89] Here it must be stated that one's preference for Bauckham or the so-called prosaic source and redaction critics will almost certainly

---

86.   C. K. Barrett, "The Dialectical Theology of St. John," in *New Testament Essays* (London: SPCK, 1972), 49–69; Judith Lieu, *The Second and Third Epistles of John* (Edinburgh: T&T Clark, 1986), 214–16.

87.   R. Alan Culpepper, *Anatomy of the Fourth Gospel: A Study in Literary Design* (Philadelphia: Fortress Press, 1983), 4–5.

88.   Richard Bauckham, "The Audience of the Gospel of John," in *The Testimony of the Beloved Disciple*, 118.

89.   Bauckham, "The Audience of the Gospel of John," 121.

depend upon whether literary or diachronic solutions to the Johannine aporias prove more convincing to the interpreter.[90] And the two methods should not be seen as antithetical to one another.[91] No final solution is likely to be forthcoming here and Francis Moloney is right to indicate that, even where one supposes Brown to be wrong, interpreters would do well to recognize that:

> [Brown] exercised great discipline in pointing to the *foreignness* of a text that was written in a strange language, that followed strange literary conventions, and that took decades to assume its present shape. However much contemporary Johannine scholarship might agree or disagree with the details of Brown's analysis, and might propose methods at variance with the historical-critical paradigm, it must accept and grapple with the foreignness of the biblical text.[92]

2. Richard Bauckham and "Something Completely Different"[93]

Bauckham declares his own research on the fourth gospel to be "something completely different" to the work of Brown and Martyn, and says that in the course of his research he found himself "abandoning one by one all of these elements of the dominant approach."[94] Bauckham's different approach is clearly exemplified in his belief:

> [W]e are dealing, not with the product of an idiosyncratic community and its history, but with the work of a creative theologian who, in his long experience of teaching and on the basis of his rather special access to traditions about Jesus, developed a distinctive interpretation of the history of Jesus.[95]

Bauckham sets forth four major challenges to the dominant approach. First, the search for the Johannine community through positing distinct

---

90. Ashton, *Understanding the Fourth Gospel*, 19–22, 42–53, provides a passionate defense for diachronic solutions.
91. As indicated by the cautions of Moloney, "The Gospel of John: The Legacy of Raymond E. Brown," 118–19.
92. Moloney, "The Gospel of John: The Legacy of Raymond E. Brown," 117–18.
93. Bauckham, *The Testimony of the Beloved Disciple*, 12, uses this language to describe his opposition to the dominant approach to the fourth gospel (typified by Brown).
94. Ibid., 12.
95. Ibid., 118.

literary and redactional stages of the gospel is flawed and "largely fantasy" in that "there is no external evidence that can act as a control on imaginative reconstruction." The quest for the Johannine community is, therefore, unable to develop any set of "criteria of authenticity and critical methodological reflection."[96] Second, Bauckham is critical of the way in which the dominant approach fails to reckon with early traditions for the origins and authorship of the fourth gospel.[97] Bauckham marshals both internal and external evidence that suggests John the Elder (not the son of Zebedee or one of the 12) is the beloved disciple responsible for the gospel. Given that this John was not one of the Twelve, this may well account for his distinctive perspective on the Jesus tradition. Thus, the beloved disciple, who is with Jesus and thereby a witness of the most significant moments in his life, is uniquely perceptive in his ability to testify to the true meaning and significance of what he has seen and heard. In other words, the gospel of John reflects the uniquely creative eyewitness testimony of this disciple, rather than the collective traditions and their reworking of a community.[98]

Third, reading the gospel of John as not only the story of Jesus but also that of the Johannine community "has no basis in the literary genre of the Fourth Gospel."[99] If Richard Burridge is right that the gospel of John is understood to be a form of Greco-Roman biography, then the reader would never expect the work to "address the very specific circumstances of one particular community" through encoding the community's history through distinct literary characters.[100] The obvious significance of this generic classification is that biographies are about a person, rather than histories of communities and their theologies.[101]

---

96. Ibid., 13.

97. See here also Robert Kysar, "The Dehistoricizing of the Gospel of John," in *John, Jesus, and History, Volume 1: Critical Appraisals of Critical Views,* SBL Symposium Series 44, eds. Paul N. Anderson, Felix Just, and Tom Thatcher (Atlanta: Society of Biblical Literature, 2007), 75–101, here 77–80.

98. Bauckham, *The Testimony of the Beloved Disciple,* 33–91.

99. Ibid., 117. See here also the important study by one of Bauckham's students who also maintains that the gospel of John is a biography and would have almost certainly been intended for broad dissemination rather than for a sectarian community. Edward W. Klink III, *The Sheep of the Fold: The Audience and Origin of the Gospel of John,* SNTSMS 141 (Cambridge: Cambridge University Press, 2007), 107–15. More broadly, see Edward W. Klink III, ed., *The Audience of the Gospels: The Origin and Function of the Gospels in Early Christianity,* LNTS 353 (London: T&T Clark, 2010).

100. Bauckham, *The Testimony of the Beloved Disciple,* 117. See Richard A. Burridge, *What Are the Gospels? A Comparison with Graeco-Roman Biography,* 2nd ed. (Grand Rapids: Eerdmans, 2004). See also the critique of Martyn's claim that the fourth gospel is a gospel mixed with apocalyptic by Klink, *The Sheep of the Fold,* 115–21.

101. Richard A. Burridge, "About People, by People, for People: Gospel Genre and Audiences," in *The*

Thus, Bauckham expresses amazement that Brown's return to his major commentaries in 1998 "still lacks any discussion of genre, and the lack was neither supplied nor pointed out by the editor, Frank Moloney."[102] Furthermore, the gospel clearly and frequently distinguishes between the time of Jesus and the time of the reader, thereby demonstrating a strong interest in the past history of Jesus (e.g., John 2:22; 7:39; 12:16; 13:7). In fact, Bauckham suggests that scholars have not adequately reckoned with the way in which John's claim to present eyewitness testimony and its careful use of historiographical features (e.g., topography, chronology, narrative asides, etc.) would appear to ancient readers as an example of something like a historical biography.[103]

Fourth, Bauckham argues that the internal evidence of the fourth gospel suggests that it was not written for a single community but rather was intended for wide circulation.[104] Bauckham is rightly impressed with the sophisticated literary and theological artistry of the gospel, and sees this as *prima facie* making it incredibly unlikely that it was meant solely for specific members of one local congregation.[105] More substantively, however, Bauckham notes that (a) the author explains the meaning of difficult sayings of Jesus or aspects of his narrative the reader might not understand (John 2:21; 6:71; 7:39); (b) the misunderstandings of the literary characters have as their goal the production of deeper theological insight for the reader as it provides the occasion for Jesus to grant fuller explanation (3:3–8; 4:10–15, 31–34; 6:32–35; 8:31–36, 56–58); (c) the evangelist makes it clear to the reader that Jesus will die and be raised again (2:21–22), and by telling this to the readers John is putting them "in a better position than are any of the characters in the story for understanding a major theme in the words of Jesus."[106] Klink also appeals to Craig Koester's important work *Symbolism in the Fourth Gospel* where he argues that the symbolism is intended to "work" for a variety of readers of diverse backgrounds.[107] Koester says: "Those who read the Gospel for the

_____

    Gospels for All Christians: Rethinking the Gospel Audiences, ed. Richard Bauckham (Grand Rapids: Eerdmans, 1998), 113–45, here 120–30.

102. Bauckham, *The Testimony of the Beloved Disciple*, 17. But see here Ashton, *Understanding the Fourth Gospel*, 330–65.

103. Bauckham, *The Testimony of the Beloved Disciple*, 93–112.

104. Again, see Klink, *The Sheep of the Fold*, 251, who argues that the "common portrait of an actual JComm, a single and coherent 'group' behind the document, is historical fiction."

105. Bauckham, *The Testimony of the Beloved Disciple*, 115.

106. Ibid., 121.

107. Klink, *The Sheep of the Fold*, 149–50.

first time often find its meaning to be rather obvious; the complexity and richness become increasingly apparent with rereading."[108] Klink also provides an exegetical examination of the Nicodemus (John 3) and Samaritan woman stories (John 4) and concludes that these literary characters are representative figures for general readers of the gospel and not for one community only. John uses representative figures to represent various and different readers of the fourth gospel (i.e., a properly religious Jew, the Samaritan or non-Jew).[109] Thus, the distinctively Johannine language and symbolism is designed to facilitate communication by introducing its language to any readers who are not already familiar with it.

3. Community Hypotheses as Allegorical Interpretation

Francis Watson has argued that source and redaction critics who see the gospels as speaking primarily about communities rather than Jesus himself "practice an allegorical interpretation of the Gospels." Watson, however, wants to assert "the theological priority of an interpretation of these texts in their literal sense."[110] When gospels are read not as narratives about the historical figure of Jesus but as autobiographies of early Christian communities, this inevitably results in an allegorical reading strategy that bypasses the literal sense of the gospel and this is both hermeneutically and theologically problematic.[111] The references to historical persons and places do not serve as ciphers or symbols for contemporary ideas or persons; rather, and here Watson is relying on Hans Frei, the "realistic narrative is the narrative that means what it says."[112] Whether the gospel authors are historically accurate or not may be debated, but what cannot be denied is that the particular gospel authors intend "to refer to persons, events, and places in the world outside the text, and that this intentionality is integral to its literal meaning."[113] The intention to refer to these

---

108. Craig R. Koester, *Symbolism in the Fourth Gospel: Meaning, Mystery, Community*, 2nd ed. (Minneapolis: Fortress Press, 2003), 259.

109. Klink, *The Sheep of the Fold*, 185–203.

110. Francis Watson, "Toward a Literal Reading of the Gospels," in *The Gospels for All Christians*, 195–217, here 197.

111. Ibid., 210. See here also Tobias Hägerland, "John's Gospel: A Two-Level Drama?" *JSNT* 25 (2003): 309–22.

112. Watson, "Toward a Literal Reading of the Gospels," 212. See Hans Frei, *The Eclipse of Biblical Narrative: A Study in Eighteenth and Nineteenth Century Hermeneutics* (New Haven, CT: Yale University Press, 1974).

113. Watson, "Toward a Literal Reading of the Gospels," 211.

persons, events, and places outside of the text is fundamental for the literal meaning of the text.[114] Thus, to read the gospels as community autobiographies is a distortion and corruption of, as Klink states, "the way the text was read in the first century and has been read nearly ever since."[115] This way of reading is not only hermeneutically problematic but also theologically disastrous. I quote Watson here at length:

> Where the Word does not have the historical existence of Jesus of Nazareth as its content, the event of the divine address occurring here and now within an enclosed and self-sufficient community, then the result is an allegorical interpretation in which the text's rendering of the pastness of Jesus is systematically subordinated to the pure presence it attains as the vehicle of the divine address—in and through the proclamation of the Word that lies at the heart of the community's existence. It is, however, unclear what theological basis there could be for this act of violence to the letter of the text and to the bodiliness of Jesus's existence, to which the letter of the text bears witness.[116]

In other words, allegory is problematic if it negates the literal sense of the gospels and thereby ends up substituting something in place of the unsubstitutable realities of the life, death, and resurrection of Jesus. Watson is concerned that dispensing with the literal sense of the text will inevitably result in the significance of "this particular bodily life as rendered in this particular text," i.e., "the Word became flesh," to be taken up into "the timelessness of myth."[117]

William Wright agrees with Watson that the reading practices of these source and redaction critics (his sight is primarily set on Martyn) is allegorical given that they read the text to mean something other than its ostensible reference, but is concerned that Watson (among others) has failed to tease out the implications of Martyn's allegorical reading strategy due to his heated polemic preference for the literal sense.[118] Wright argues that both Martyn's two-level read-

---

114. Klink, *The Sheep of the Fold*, 148.
115. Ibid.
116. Watson, "Toward a Literal Reading of the Gospels," 214.
117. Ibid., 215. See also Watson's claim that "the historical existence of Jesus is mediated in the form of the Gospel narratives, and that the sole purpose of these narratives is to mediate this particular historical existence in the light of the universal and ultimate significance that is ascribed to it" (p. 216).
118. William M. Wright IV, *Rhetoric and Theology: Figural Reading of John 9*, BZNW 165 (Berlin: de Gruyter, 2009). See the criticisms of Watson's use of "allegory," in Judith Lieu, "How John Writes,"

ing strategy in John 9 and Augustine's interpretation of the same text (in *Tract. Ev. Jo.* 44) share a number of similarities. Whereas Martyn (and we can certainly include Brown here) reads John 9 in order to reconstruct *the history* of the Johannine community, Augustine reads the text mimetically as a window into the relationship between Christ and his body, particularly the way in which "catechumens are encouraged to persevere in their formation process."[119] Though the subject matter of John 9 is different, Wright shows that Augustine and Martyn share a number of similarities that justifies speaking of Martyn's approach as allegorical or figural exegesis.[120] Wright does not share Watson's concern over the validity of an allegorical interpretation, but he does question "whether the two-level reading strategy is an adequate means for reconstructing the history of a posited Johannine community."[121] This is not to say, Wright is quick to affirm, that the references to synagogue expulsion do not betray a policy from the local synagogue that would have been known to John's audience (9:22; 12:42; 16:2). But Martyn's two-level reading of John 9 for the purpose of historical reconstruction does indicate that a "category mistake has been made: the two-level reading of John 9 should more appropriately be considered figural reading rather than historical reconstruction."[122] This is not to say that identifying the historical context within which the gospel was composed is futile, but it "does suggest that alternative means of doing history should be used for this purpose."[123] Wright instead argues "the formerly blind man, instead of being a type of the Johannine Christians expelled from the synagogue, appears as an example of faith in Jesus as the Son of Man. John invites his audience to imitate the formerly blind man's faith, spiritual perception, and interpretation."[124]

---

in *The Written Gospel*, eds. Markus Bockmuehl and Donald A. Hagner (Cambridge: Cambridge University Press, 2005), 171–83, here 178.

119. Wright, *Rhetoric and Theology*, 84. Wright also examines four premodern interpretations of John 9 and concludes that whereas "Martyn reads John 9 figurally in terms of the Johannine community, the premoderns read the account figurally in terms of Christ and his work" (p. 141).

120. Ibid., 86–93. The similarities include the fact that both: (a) find multiple levels of meaning in John 9 that are found within the gospel itself and are not brought to the text by the reader, (b) read the distinct literary characters and events in light of the multiple levels of meaning, (c) employ figural reading when there are problems or anachronisms in the text, and (d) posit a particular audience within the horizon of the gospel narrative.

121. Ibid., 94.

122. Ibid., 94.

123. Ibid., 95.

124. Ibid., 210.

CONCLUSION

I do not think it an exaggeration to say that Raymond Brown's work on the fourth gospel still represents for many *the* most respected North American historical-critical scholarship.[125] "Careful," "thorough," "moderate," "critical," and "willing to change his mind in light of new evidence" are a few of the many descriptors of Brown's work on the fourth gospel. Moloney has warned that "those who do not recognize the past will not be able to create a viable future. If we are not prepared to recognize that we stand upon the shoulders of those who went before us, we will not look too far into the future."[126] Even when one wants to argue for an approach to the fourth gospel that is "something completely different" as do Bauckham, Hengel, and others, it is still the legacy of Raymond Brown with which the scholar must reckon precisely because of the clarity, incisiveness, and strong (not necessarily to say correct) answers he has provided to the origins, composition, and religious background of the fourth gospel. In other words, literary and narrative analysis, methods that I believe are indispensable, must not be used to evade these historical questions. One may not always agree with Brown's answer to these questions, but he serves as one who posed the problems as clearly as anyone in twentieth-century North America.

---

125. It is not difficult to support this claim, as many respected scholars have made similar statements.
126. Moloney, "The Gospel of John: The Legacy of Raymond E. Brown," 116.

LEON MORRIS ON JOHN'S GOSPEL: AN ASSESSMENT AND CRITICAL REFLECTION ON HIS SCHOLARSHIP

Andreas J. Köstenberger

INTRODUCTION

W hile I did not know Leon Morris personally, I have benefited significantly from his writings, especially his 1995 commentary on John's gospel and his essay collection *Studies in the Fourth Gospel* to both of which I refer rather extensively in my work on John. I stand in the conservative evangelical tradition of B. F. Westcott, Leon Morris, and D. A. Carson. Trained at Trinity Evangelical Divinity School, I taught a course in Johannine theology there in 1995–1996, twenty years after Morris did so in 1976. In any case, this paper is not primarily about Leon Morris as a person—excellent biographical entries are already available—or about Morris as a teacher, administrator, or writer—again, treatments are already available—but more specifically about Morris as a scholar commenting on John's gospel.[1] This kind of

---

1. I will not cover his work on the book of Revelation.

assessment is fitting following the centenary of his birth and twenty plus years after the publication of the revised edition of his major John commentary.[2]

BIOGRAPHY

The judgment posted on the Ridley College website at the occasion of the centenary of Morris's birth is representative of the view of many: "Leon Morris is arguably Australia's greatest biblical scholar."[3] Morris, who served as Principal of Ridley College in Melbourne from 1964 to 1979, has made a major mark on this institution. Neil Bach, graduate of Ridley, pastor for thirty-six years, and chair of the Leon and Mildred Morris Foundation, has recently completed a major biography of Morris.[4] There is an annual Leon Morris Lecture at Ridley Melbourne, and the Leon Morris Library at Ridley Melbourne is named in his honor.

Leon Lamb Morris (1914–2006) was born on March 15, 1914 in the New South Wales country town of Lithgow. He was converted at age seventeen.[5] His career took shape within Australian Reformed Anglicanism and emerging post-World War II evangelical biblical scholarship. He graduated with a Bachelor of Science (majoring in mathematics) in 1934 and served first as primary (1935) and then as high school teacher (1936–1937). Morris taught himself New Testament Greek and completed the licentiate of theology in two years, winning the Hey-Sharp Prize as top graduating student. He was ordained as deacon in the Church of England in 1938 and as priest in the Sydney diocese in 1939. From 1940 to 1945 he served as minister of the Minnipa Mission for the Bush Church Aid Society in outback South Australia.[6] During this time he married Mildred ("Millie") Dann, a trained nurse and accomplished musician, in January 1941. He earned his Bachelor of Divinity (with first-class honors) in 1943 and MTh from London University and his PhD from Cambridge

---

2. Leon Morris, *The Gospel according to John*, NICNT (Grand Rapids: Eerdmans, 1971; 2nd rev. ed., 1995).

3. See www.ridley.edu.au.

4. Neil S. Bach, *Leon Morris: One Man's Fight for Love and Truth* (Milton Keynes, UK: Paternoster, 2015). See my review at http://www.booksataglance.com/book-reviews/leon-morris-one-mans-fight-love-truth-neil-bach-constantine-tischendorf-life-work-19th-century-bible-hunter-stanley-e-porter.

5. David John Williams, "Leon Lamb Morris," in *Bible Interpreters of the 20th Century: A Selection of Evangelical Voices*, eds. Walter A. Elwell and J. D. Weaver (Grand Rapids: Baker, 1999), 272–86. The author holds a PhD from the University of Melbourne and is former Vice Principal at Ridley College, Melbourne.

6. Morris wrote about this in *Bush Parson* (Brunswick East, Victoria, Australia: Acorn, 1995).

University in 1951. His dissertation was later published as *The Apostolic Preaching of the Cross*. In this work, Morris defended the substitutionary atonement, understood as propitiation of God's wrath, and the centrality of the cross in biblical theology. The length of his Cambridge dissertation reputedly prompted new regulations in this regard![7] Morris served as Vice Principal of Ridley College Melbourne from August 1945 to 1960. During these years, Morris often put the care of souls over his academic career, engaging in parish ministry alongside his work at Ridley. He loved preaching to ordinary people; both his preaching and his writing were characterized by "simplicity, clarity, and relevance."[8] His years as Warden of Tyndale House from 1961 to 1963 were among the highlights of his career. He then made the difficult decision to return to Australia as Principal of Ridley College, where he served from 1964 to 1979.[9] He also served as editor of the Tyndale New Testament Commentary series and lectured worldwide, including at places such as Westminster, Gordon Conwell, Trinity Evangelical Divinity School, and Western. Leon and Mildred had no children, but, as D. A. Carson notes, they "were parents to many."[10] Mildred died in 2003 after sixty-two years of marriage; Leon passed away on Monday, July 25, 2006.[11]

The current Principal of Ridley College, Brian Rosner, says Morris flourished at a time "when evangelical biblical scholarship was at best marginal."[12] With a Cambridge PhD, Morris was the first Australian elected to the Society for New Testament Studies (SNTS) in 1951. He was one of the first wardens of Tyndale House (1961), a member of the NIV translation committee, and visiting lecturer around the world. He wrote more than fifty books which have sold more than two million copies. Reflecting on his own doctoral studies in Cambridge in the late 1980s, Rosner says three models of evangelical scholarly integrity stood out to him: F. F. Bruce, I. Howard Marshall, and Leon Morris. "All three wrote serious commentaries that set the gold standard for evangelical New Testament scholarship: Bruce on Acts, Marshall on Luke,

---

7. Williams, "Morris," 276.
8. Ibid., 274.
9. Ibid., 277.
10. D. A. Carson. "Brief Appreciation of the Life and Service of Leon Morris," July 31, 2006. Originally published in the online journal *Reformation21*.
11. Ibid.
12. Brian Rosner, "Remember Your Leaders," posted March 13, 2014, at https://www.ridley.edu.au/ leon-morris-centenary/remember-leaders-2.

and Morris on John."[13] Rosner remembers being "greatly encouraged by the clarity of his exegesis, the honesty with which he grappled with exegetical difficulties and the attention not only to historical matters, but also to literary and theological issues" (the hermeneutical triad!).[14] He calls Morris's treatment of John a "model of scholarship in the service of both the academy and the church" and considers him to be one of the key pioneers of serious evangelical biblical scholarship.[15] Peter Adam recalls Morris's "legendary" twin foci on the Bible and the cross, which, he says, have become his own criterion for assessing a given work: Is the Bible honored as God's Word? And is the atoning death of God's Son honored as the means of our salvation?[16] Graham Cole, former Ridley principal, refers to Morris's works as "simply written without being simplistic."[17] According to Cole, Morris first wrote his commentaries, and then consulted the secondary literature, wanting "to be exposed to the text of Scripture at a personal level before researching what others had to say about it."[18]

Peter Adam says Morris operated within the framework of three key interpretive principles: (1) biblical word studies as an expression of biblical theology (see esp. his refutation of C. H. Dodd's work on expiation); (2) a primary focus on the text of Scripture, reflecting the Reformation principle of *sola Scriptura*;[19] and (3) the centrality of the cross as the theological focal point of the Bible, which rendered his interpretation "not only christocentric but also staurocentric."[20] For Morris, the center of Scripture was not only Christ but Christ *crucified*.[21] With regard to Morris's treatment of Scripture, McLellan notes that Morris "studied the Bible with a scientist's interest in a new specimen, not with a theologian's

---

13. Rosner, "Remember Your Leaders."
14. Ibid. On the "hermeneutical triad" of history, literature, and theology see Andreas J. Köstenberger and Richard D. Patterson, *Invitation to Biblical Interpretation: Exploring the Hermeneutical Triad of History, Literature, and Theology* (Grand Rapids: Kregel, 2011).
15. Rosner, "Reflection on Leon Morris."
16. Peter Adam, "A Child Could Wade, and an Elephant Could Swim," posted April 4, 2014, at https://www.ridley.edu.au/leon-morris-centenary/child-wade-elephant-swim.
17. Graham Cole, "A Reflection on Leon Morris," posted December 5, 2014, at http://www.ridley.edu.au/leon-morris-centenary/reflection-leon-morris-graham-cole.
18. Ibid.
19. Peter Adam, "Morris, Leon Lamb (1914–2006)," in *Dictionary of Major Biblical Interpreters*, ed. Donald K. McKim (Downers Grove: IVP, 2007), 751–55. Note that Morris is not included in the *Historical Handbook of Major Biblical Interpreters*, ed. Donald K. McKim (Downers Grove: IVP, 1998).
20. Adam, "Morris," 753.
21. Ibid.

distrust."[22] In fact, David Hubbard, one-time President of Fuller Theological Seminary, observes that Morris proved inquisitive and a quick learner on any subject, whether pig farming in the Australian outback or American sports.[23] Conversely, somewhat similar to Adolf Schlatter in the German scene earlier in the twentieth century, Morris's doubt was mostly reserved for his fellow scholars, which is why he wasted little time on attempted reconstructions of earlier sources.[24] In his Matthew commentary, Morris set out to discover "the author's meaning" and to "simply take it [Matthew's gospel] as it is."[25] His focus was on "the text, the whole text and nothing but the text."[26]

MAJOR WORKS ON JOHN'S GOSPEL

The first major work on John's gospel Morris produced is his volume *Studies in the Fourth Gospel.*[27] Tom Schreiner says the book "demonstrated that a conservative reading of critical issues in the Gospel had scholarly credibility."[28] The work includes six chapters of mostly previously published essays: (1) The Relationship of the Fourth Gospel to the Synoptics (15–63); (2) History and Theology in the Fourth Gospel (65–138); (3) Was the Author of the Fourth Gospel an Eyewitness? (139–214); (4) The Authorship of the Fourth Gospel (215–92); (5) Variation: A Feature of Johannine Style (293–319); and (6) The Dead Sea Scrolls and St. John's Gospel (321–58). In the preface, Morris writes:

> The conservative evangelical who writes seriously on biblical topics is apt to find himself the target of a certain amount of criticism. If he decides simply to state the facts as he sees them, and to be silent about the works of more radical critics, he finds himself accused of obscurantism. If, on the other hand, he decides to take notice of what others have been writ-

22. Adam's words.
23. See the anecdotes referenced in Williams, "Morris," 274–75.
24. Compare Adolf Schlatter, *The History of the Christ: The Foundation for New Testament Theology,* trans. Andreas J. Köstenberger (Grand Rapids: Baker, 1997), foreword to *Das Wort Jesu* (1909), 17–20, who says the historian's task is "to perceive what actually happened" (p. 17) and who cautions against historical research that exceeds the evidence and "turn[s] out novels" (p. 19).
25. Morris, *Matthew,* Pillar New Testament Commentary (Grand Rapids: Eerdmans, 1992), x.
26. Adam, "Morris," 753. Compare the high view of Scripture enunciated by Morris in his *I Believe in Revelation* (Grand Rapids: Eerdmans, 1976).
27. Morris, *Studies in the Fourth Gospel* (Grand Rapids: Eerdmans, 1969).
28. Tom Schreiner, "Remember Your Leaders—Dr. Leon Morris," posted July 7, 2014, https://www.ridley.edu.au/leon-morris-centenary/remember-leaders-dr-leon-morris-2.

ing, and to quote them, he may find himself accused of citing authors who do not really agree with his essential position. . . . In facing this issue I fear that I am unrepentant. I unhesitatingly adopt the second-mentioned course. I read books by men of all sorts of opinions and profit not least from those with whom I disagree most fundamentally.

Morris continues, "A further disadvantage under which the conservative evangelical labors is that it is often held that his conclusions are given in his premises."[29] He says one of his critics "maintained that I imposed my pattern on the evidence; it is so incredible that I should have *found* it there that he does not even discuss the possibility."[30] Morris continues,

> Your conservative, it is held, is the slave of his presuppositions. He is bound to reach certain conclusions. Therefore his arguments need not be taken seriously. I hope that conservative evangelicals may be pardoned for wondering whether there is not perhaps a kind of radical obscurantism . . . whereby objections that evangelicals at any rate regard as really serious are simply dismissed with no attempt at a reasoned answer. Just as it seems to the radical that the conservative is simply refusing to face real objections to his position, so it seems to the conservative that the radical will not face some part of the evidence, notably that which shows that the Bible is an inspired book.[31]

Morris presents a rather feisty but, I think, not unjustified rebuttal. He concludes:

> In writing in this way I am not claiming that I have some way of resolving the conflict. Nor do I claim to have done what so many others have failed to do, namely achieve the perfect balance between recognizing the consequences of inspiration and the use of the critical method. It is rather that I, as a conservative evangelical, want to assure the reader that I have made a serious attempt to deal with the great questions raised in this book. I have not tried to defend any preconceived position or to follow a party line. As far as I am able, I have let the facts lead me where they will. I have little hope that the typical modern scholar will

---

29. Morris, *Studies in the Fourth Gospel*, 9.
30. Ibid., 10.
31. Ibid.

have much patience with this book, for I have had the temerity to argue that the Fourth Gospel was probably written by John the apostle, and that it contains good historical material. But I ask him to see this as a work meant as seriously as is his own. And I ask him to deal with the argument on its merits, and not simply to assume that I am engaging in special pleading. He is, of course, free to disagree with me fundamentally. But I want to assure him that at the least this is a sincere effort to grapple with the problems on the basis of the evidence.[32]

Stephen Smalley, in his review of *Studies in the Fourth Gospel*, says Morris "comes out strongly in favor of the 'new look' on the Fourth Gospel, and finds Johannine tradition is independent of the Synoptic tradition although parallel and complementary to it, and that it has a high claim to reliability as a result."[33]

In 1971, Morris released his commentary on John's gospel, which was published in a revised edition in 1995. Hubbard divides Morris's commentaries into his weightier and more popular ones.[34] David John Williams points out, "There is no question, however, that people most readily associate the name of Leon Morris with his commentary on John. Understandably so. It . . . is now accepted as a standard work of reference on that Gospel. It is a classic example of Morris's work. The text is clear, lucid, capable of being read and understood by the layperson no less than the scholar and of giving benefit to both."[35] Williams cites David Wenham, who writes, "The bulk of the commentary is given over to exegesis of the text. . . . Discussion of the Greek text which presupposes a knowledge of Greek on the part of the reader is limited to footnotes; and this means that the commentary will be of use to the non-specialist, not just the trained theologian."[36]

Sean Kealy's list of Morris's salient exegetical judgments is helpful:

- The Johannine prologue is not a hymn and did not exist apart from the gospel.

---

32. Ibid., 11.
33. *EvQ* 43/1 (January–March 1971): 52.
34. "Leon Lamb Morris: An Appreciation," 13, cited in Williams, "Morris," 280.
35. Williams, "Morris," 280.
36. David Wenham, Review of *The Gospel according to John*, by Leon Morris, *EvQ* 45/1 (January–March 1973): 54.

- The Johannine temple cleansing is different from the one described in the Synoptics.
- The early recognition of Jesus as Messiah and the other christological titles are historical, as is the wine miracle.
- John 6:51–59 does not refer to the Eucharist.
- John 9:22 deals with the life of Jesus, not the later church.
- The Lazarus story is historical.
- The Farewell Discourse reflects Jesus's actual words.
- Both Synoptic and Johannine chronologies are accurate.
- Both Lukan and Johannine accounts of the giving of the Spirit are accurate.
- 153 is the actual number of fish caught in John 21.
- John wrote before AD 70.
- John wrote independently of the Synoptics; any connection is through oral, not written, tradition.[37]
- The temple cleansing took place around AD 26.[38]

Another useful work on John's gospel is Morris's *Jesus Is the Christ: Studies in the Theology of John*, in which Morris made use of contributions to *Festschriften* for George Eldon Ladd and Bo Reicke as well as of articles in volume II of *The New Testament Age* edited by William Weinrich and in *Unity and Diversity in New Testament Theology* edited by Robert Guelich.[39] The book contains chapters on (1) John's Theological Purpose; (2) The Relation between the Signs and the Discourses; (3) Jesus, the Man; (4) The Christ of God; (5) The Son of God; (6) The "I Am" Sayings; (7) God the Father; (8) The Holy Spirit; (9) "That You May Believe"; and (10) Life. In the preface, Morris writes that the book is a tribute to the class of 1976 when he served as guest professor at Trinity Evangelical Divinity School and taught a class in Johannine Theology.[40] In unfolding John's theology, Morris took as his starting point John's declared aim in his purpose statement (John 20:31) and "tried to show a little of the way that aim was accomplished."[41] I. Howard Marshall, in a review, says this is "a

---

37. Morris, *The Gospel according to John*, NICNT (Grand Rapids: Eerdmans, 1971), 49–52.
38. Adapted from Sean Kealy, *John's Gospel and the History of Biblical Interpretation* (Lewiston, NY: Mellen, 2002), 773–74.
39. Morris, *Jesus Is the Christ: Studies in the Theology of John* (Grand Rapids: Eerdmans, 1989).
40. Ibid., vi.
41. Ibid.

straightforward exposition of John's teaching without too much side-glancing at scholars who interpret the texts differently."[42]

Finally, Morris's *Reflections on the Gospel of John*, originally published in four separate volumes, were released in a one-volume edition in 2000.[43]

A *Festschrift*, *Reconciliation and Hope: New Testament Essays on Atonement and Eschatology*, was presented to Morris on his sixtieth birthday, including "Leon Lamb Morris: An Appreciation" by David A. Hubbard.[44]

Morris also contributed to *An Introduction to the New Testament*, a work coauthored with D. A. Carson and Douglas J. Moo.[45] The chapter on John's gospel, presumably written by D. A. Carson, contains a handful of references to Morris. In the discussion of the internal evidence for authorship, it says: "The classic approach of Westcott, updated by Morris [*Studies in the Fourth Gospel*, 218ff.], was to establish five points: the author of the fourth gospel was (1) a Jew, (2) of Palestine, (3) an eyewitness, (4) an apostle (i.e. one of the Twelve), and (5) the apostle John."[46] A few pages later, the author remarks, "The pattern of recognition is not too surprising if the gospel of John was published toward the end of the first century. We should not then expect to find traces of it in, say, Clement of Rome (c. 95). There is more of a problem if the fourth gospel was published before 1970 (as Morris and Robinson think)."[47] Finally, the author notes that John's relation to the Synoptics and other topics are "sympathetically treated in the stream of commentaries that seeks to keep history and theology together (e.g., Westcott, Morris, Carson)."[48]

RECEPTION OF MORRIS'S WORK

Morris's work is essentially ignored by William Baird.[49] Morris is not mentioned in Stephen Neill and Tom Wright's *The Interpretation of*

---

42. *EvQ* 63/3 (July 1991): 276.
43. Morris, *Reflections on the Gospel of John* (Peabody, MA: Hendrickson, 2000).
44. Robert Banks, ed., *Reconciliation and Hope: New Testament Essays on Atonement and Eschatology* (Grand Rapids: Eerdmans, 1974).
45. D. A. Carson, Douglas J. Moo, and Leon Morris, *An Introduction to the New Testament* (Grand Rapids: Zondervan, 1992).
46. Ibid., 144.
47. Ibid., 151.
48. Ibid., 166. Other relevant works written by Morris includes his *New Testament Theology* (Grand Rapids: Zondervan, 1986) and *Testaments of Love: A Study of Love in the Bible* (Grand Rapids: Eerdmans, 1981). For bibliographies, see Williams, "Morris," 285–86; and Adam, "Morris," 754–55.
49. Though see the brief comment in *History of New Testament Research*, vol. 3: *From C. H. Dodd to Hans Dieter Betz* (Minneapolis: Fortress, 2013), 534, n. 205: "Such outstanding scholars as George E. Ladd and Leon L. Morris readily come to mind, both of whom are reviewed in substantial

the New Testament 1861–1986.[50] The entry on "Johannine Studies" by D. Moody Smith in *The New Testament and Its Modern Interpreters*, edited by Eldon Jay Epp and George W. MacRae, includes Morris among significant commentaries on John's gospel since 1945 alongside Bultmann, Dodd, Barrett, R. H. Lightfoot, Schnackenburg, Raymond Brown, J. N. Sanders, Lindars, Boismard, Becker, and Haenchen.[51] Later on, Smith writes that "most important commentaries since World War II have been written on the hypothesis of John's relative, if not complete, independence of the Synoptics," citing Schnackenburg, Brown, Sanders, Morris, Lindars, and Haenchen.[52]

Kealy mentions Morris several times in his two-volume work *John's Gospel and the History of Biblical Interpretation.*[53] He observes, "Among those who see John as 'history serving theology rather than theology serving historical fact,' Orchard includes Hoskyns (1947), Smalley (1978) and Morris (1971)."[54] He contrasts Morris with the following scholars who take a different approach: "Minear (1984) speaks of the 'obnoxious theological verbiage'; R. E. Brown (1979) comments on the general 'sense of alienation and superiority'; J. D. G. Dunn (1985) describes the synoptics as giving a portrait of Jesus, while John is more like an impressionist painting."[55] Later on in his volume, Kealy notes that C. H. Dodd's work (who challenged the notion that John is merely "pneumatic") has been followed and built upon by scholars such as Hengel, Robinson, Lindars, and Morris.[56] According to Kealy, Morris, like J. A. T. Robinson, Stephen Smalley, and D. A. Carson, took up the defense of the apostolic authorship of John beginning with his *Studies in the Fourth Gospel*:

---

articles in *DMBI* (628–33; 751–55)." Baird's virtually complete neglect of Ladd and Morris is part of a larger pattern of bias against conservative evangelical scholarship in Baird's work which more accurately could be described as a history of the historical-critical method.

50. Stephen Neill and Tom Wright, *The Interpretation of the New Testament 1861–1986,* 2nd ed. (Oxford/New York: Oxford University Press, 1988).

51. D. Moody Smith, "Johannine Studies," in *The New Testament and Its Modern Interpreters,* eds. Eldon Jay Epp and George W. MacRae (Atlanta: Scholars Press, 1989), 271.

52. Ibid., 279.

53. Kealy, *John's Gospel and the History of Biblical Interpretation.*

54. Ibid., 3. The reference is to Helen C. Orchard, *Courting Betrayal* (Sheffield: Sheffield Academic Press, 1998), chap. 1: The Disconcerting Gospel.

55. Ibid.

56. Ibid., 618. There is a certain irony in this, in light of the fact that, as mentioned earlier, Morris's work on the atonement set itself in stark contrast to Dodd's views on the matter.

The origin is unknown, the date could be before 70, the gospel is a unified and coherent composition and is reliably historical. . . . He stresses the internal evidence of the vivid "unimportant details" such as Jesus's sighs (11:33, 38), the detailed parts played by Andrew, Philip and the young boy in the feeding of the multitude account Ch. 6. He also criticizes the form-critical assumption that the gospel materials have an extensive pre-literary history. . . . He rejected the view of some critics that such vividness belongs to the mind of a good writer of fiction and not the circumstances of the narrative.[57]

The reaction of critical scholars to Morris is summarized by Kealy as follows:

Critical scholars are almost unanimous in rejecting Morris' reaction to modern Johannine interpretation. Apart from an appeal to Riesenfeld on the gospel tradition and to the Qumran documents he adds little to the stock arguments of the nineteenth and early twentieth century. He does not in fact employ a historical-critical approach to John but accepts that the scenes in John took place exactly as portrayed and that Jesus spoke most of the words attributed to him. He does not recognize the literary and artistic ingenuity of John or the theological depth of his ambiguous expressions. Morris, while conversant with modern critical approaches, is interested in drawing from John the ancient faith in the conservative evangelical tradition.[58]

CONCLUDING ASSESSMENT

It would not be fair to measure Leon Morris's contribution to biblical scholarship in general, and to Johannine scholarship in particular, by the standards of evangelical scholarship in 2018. Brian Rosner is correct when he says that Morris flourished at a time "when evangelical biblical scholarship was at best marginal." In this way, Morris, similar to George Eldon Ladd, was a pioneer who exhibited a high standard of scholarly excellence in the midst of the larger academy without denying his indebtedness to Jesus's death for him on the cross,

---

57. Ibid., 772–73; see also 881, 906.
58. Ibid., 774.

his love for the church, and his high view of Scripture.[59] As he himself testified, as such he suffered his share of ostracism from the higher critical scholarly establishment which was not so much a verdict on his scholarly contribution as it reflected the bias (if not snobbery) of critical scholars who felt they could safely ignore a conservative view despite the fact that it was based solidly on the evidence that they often brushed aside in favor of their own preferred critical viewpoints without doing adequate justice to the data Morris adduced.

On a personal level, I find myself in agreement with Morris on many Johannine fronts, such as the essential historicity of John's gospel, its Johannine apostolic authorship, his insistence that the Synoptic and John's chronology are not in inevitable conflict, and other tenets mentioned above.[60] At the same time, I differ with him on the last three items in the above-cited list: (1) that John wrote before AD 70; (2) that John wrote independently of the Synoptics and that any connection is through oral, not written, tradition; and (3) that the temple cleansing took place around AD 26. Instead, first, I believe with the vast majority of scholars that a date in the AD 80s or early 90s better coheres with the evidence (especially the Johannine temple theme in conjunction with the destruction of the Jerusalem sanctuary in AD 70).[61] Also, second, I believe there is high historical plausibility that John had read at least Mark and possibly also Matthew and Luke(-Acts) and consciously transposed many Markan themes.[62] Finally, third, I believe a strong case can be made that the temple cleansing took place in AD 29, with the likely date of crucifixion being AD 33, not AD 30.[63]

Clearly, this is not the place to adjudicate these matters. Nor do these differences in viewpoint detract from the caliber of Morris's

---

59. See John A. D'Elia, *A Place at the Table: George Eldon Ladd and the Rehabilitation of Evangelical Scholarship in America* (New York: Oxford University Press, 2008). Though note that George Ladd's personal life was different from Leon Morris's in many ways.

60. See the relevant portions in *John*, BECNT (Grand Rapids: Baker, 2004); and *A Theology of John's Gospel and Letters: The Word, the Christ, the Son of God*, BTNT (Grand Rapids: Zondervan, 2009).

61. See my essay "The Destruction of the Second Temple and the Composition of the Fourth Gospel," in *Challenging Perspectives on the Gospel of John*, WUNT 2/219, ed. John Lierman (Tübingen: Mohr Siebeck, 2006), 69–108.

62. See my essay "John's Transposition Theology: Retelling the Story of Jesus in a Different Key," in *Earliest Christian History: History, Literature, and Theology. Essays from the Tyndale Fellowship in Honor of Martin Hengel*, WUNT 2/320, eds. Michael F. Bird and Jason Maston (Tübingen: Mohr Siebeck, 2012), 191–226.

63. See Andreas Köstenberger and Justin Taylor, *The Final Days of Jesus: The Most Important Week of the Most Important Person Who Ever Lived* (Wheaton, IL: Crossway, 2014).

scholarship. In many ways, subsequent Johannine evangelical scholarship has been able to build on the work of Morris and other conservative scholars and thus been able to advance further in various areas of Johannine research. I, for one, certainly applaud the recent publication of a major biography of Morris, not least because I believe in some circles Morris has not been awarded the respect for his scholarly work that he deserves. His disdain for scholarly fads and his focus on the biblical text, not to mention his crucicentric orientation, are certainly dispositions worthy to emulate, in particular for younger evangelical scholars, who may be tempted to sacrifice scholarly integrity for academic respectability.

R. ALAN CULPEPPER AND THE LITERARY APPROACH TO JOHN'S GOSPEL

Ron C. Fay

R. Alan Culpepper is best known for his work *Anatomy of the Fourth Gospel: A Study in Literary Design*,[1] yet this volume alone does not constitute the range of his contribution to Johannine studies. Other than numerous articles, he has also written on the life of John[2] and has a commentary on the gospel and letters that bear the apostle's name.[3] Culpepper has done work exegetical, homiletical, ethical, and literary with respect to the Johannine corpus. While it is the last of these for which he is known, his other contributions should not be overlooked.

In many respects, Culpepper functions as another voice with another view on the fourth gospel (FG) within traditional historical criticism. Seen in this way, his exegesis and analysis of the text offer something

---

1. R. Alan Culpepper, *Anatomy of the Fourth Gospel: A Study in Literary Design* (Philadelphia: Fortress Press, 1983).
2. Culpepper, *John, The Son of Zebedee: The Life of a Legend* (Minneapolis: Fortress Press, 2000; originally Columbia: University of South Carolina Press, 1994). From here on, this work will be called Culpepper's *John*.
3. Culpepper, *The Gospel and Letters of John*, IBT (Nashville: Abingdon Press, 1998).

to the student of the FG simply in how he distinguishes himself from other interpreters. At the same time, his method alone appeared as an important enough departure from the approaches used by other major scholars prior to his time so as to give value to studying his work in itself. This method gained prominence in *Anatomy of the Fourth Gospel*.

BIOGRAPHY[4]

Richard Alan Culpepper, son of Hugo and Ruth Culpepper, while born in Little Rock, Arkansas, in the United States of America on March 2, 1946, always had a wider view of the world due to the mission work and expanded vision of his parents. His parents spent time in China and the Philippines prior to his birth, and this colored both their view and his view of the world. The Culpepper family lived in Chile from 1947–1951, with his brother Paul Lawrence Culpepper born there. The family returned to the United States for more than a year to continue the theological education of Hugo, and then from 1953–1958 they resided in Argentina. The family returned to the United States for Hugo to finish his doctoral work at Southern Baptist Theological Seminary (SBTS), yet he was then offered a post there, where he would stay until 1964. Alan began his own postsecondary study at Baylor University in the fall of 1963. After graduating in 1967, Alan received the call to pastor Macedonia Baptist[5] Church in Madison, Indiana. During this time, he attended SBTS and graduated with his Master of Divinity in 1970. He then attended Duke University, attaining his PhD in 1974, and was employed by SBTS from 1974 until 1991. He then moved to teach at Baylor until 1995 and finally became dean of the MacAfee School of Theology at Mercer University, until his retirement in 2015. One of the greatest and most profound influences on his life has been his father. Hugo Culpepper, in turn, had been fascinated by the life and work of Miguel de Unamuno.[6] The person of Unamuno so captured Hugo Culpepper's imagination that his life became part of Hugo's own

---

4. Most of the information in this section comes from R. Alan Culpepper, *Eternity as Sunrise: The Life of Hugo H. Culpepper* (Macon, GA: Mercer University Press, 2002) and some from personal correspondence between R. Alan Culpepper and the author.

5. According to *Eternity as Sunrise*, 277, the name of the church is as stated, but according to R. Alan Culpepper's short CV (https://theology.mercer.edu/faculty-staff/culpepper/more-culpepper.cfm, accessed June 9, 2016), the name of the church is Macedonia Bible Church.

6. See especially *Eternity as Sunrise*, 212. Dr. Hugo Culpepper wrote his dissertation on Unamuno and often quoted from or referred to him in his public speaking and writing.

story. That in turn led to the narrative form of communication that Hugo so often used in his letters: not just ideas were presented, but ideas grounded in living a life of faith within the world. This, in turn, gave Alan Culpepper a wider and more evocative view of the Christian faith, allowing him to frame the gospel message more broadly while maintaining the particulars of the orthodox Christian faith. This seems to have brought him to an understanding of John's gospel laid out in *Anatomy* that others did not at first share.

ANATOMY OF THE FOURTH GOSPEL AND THE LITERARY APPROACH

The literary approach advocated and demonstrated in *Anatomy* hit the world of Johannine scholarship as a mix of fresh air and a slap in the face. On the one hand, Culpepper deviates from the assured historical-critical method and leaves behind source and form criticism. On the other, he carries forward the revolution of bringing literary analysis into biblical studies by taking it into the realm of Johannine literature and does so with the knowledge and deftness that often escapes those whose primary focus extends to sacred texts rather than rhetorical criticism. As D. A. Carson wrote, Culpepper "breaks new ground."[7]

The Literary Approach

For literary analysis to work, the canonical form of the text needs to be assumed. Rather than seeking for layers within the text as other noted scholars have done, Culpepper begins with the finished form of the text and analyzes what lies in front of him rather than conjecturing on any other aspect. In fact, the opening paragraph of *Anatomy* highlights this trend in Johannine scholarship and, without explicitly criticizing it, notes that the character and function of the document quickly becomes overlooked through such a "dissection."[8] The goal of Culpepper in writing *Anatomy* is, simply, "to expose new considerations, explain features of the gospel, and stimulate greater appreciation for its literary design,"[9] though his work goes beyond such aims.

---

7. D. A. Carson, review of R. Alan Culpepper, *Anatomy of the Fourth Gospel: A Study in Literary Design*, *Trinity Journal* 4 N.S. (1983): 122–26, here 122.
8. Culpepper, *Anatomy*, 3.
9. Ibid., 11.

Literary criticism, or at least the branch that came to be called narrative criticism, came onto the scene of New Testament studies in the late 1960s and early '70s, with such introductory books as William A. Beardslee's *Literary Criticism of the New Testament*[10] and Norman R. Petersen's *Literary Criticism for New Testament Critics*.[11] The former begins the turn from sources and layers and begins to probe what the text conveys. However, instead of looking at conventional literary issues, Beardslee ends up with more of a genre criticism than actual literary criticism, since he explores such subjects as gospel forms, proverbs, history as form, and the function of various tropes in apocalyptic. All of this hints at the breadth that one would consider literary criticism today, yet still falls short of looking for themes, characters, plot development, and so on. The latter begins with a critique of historical-critical methods, displaying how form and source criticism ignores what the text says in order to find the historical situation that gave rise to the text, to find the community behind the text, to find how the text was assembled from disparate parts, or anything other than actually studying the text as it stands. Petersen then turns toward the constructive task, building a literary-critical model that can be used by historical-critical practitioners to inform their work. With the publication of such works as *Mark as Story*,[12] the tide had begun to turn.

How *Anatomy* Approached Literature

Instead of taking the text-as-window approach, and seeing what lies behind the Johannine narrative, *Anatomy* typifies Murray Krieger's text-as-mirror analogy[13] such that the meaning of the text is found in the interaction between the text and reader. Culpepper takes his communicative model from Seymour Chatman,[14] analyzing how the story moves from the author to the reader. Culpepper stresses this as significant: "Every story presupposes a teller, the story, and an audience."[15] The differences

---

10.   William A. Beardslee, *Literary Criticism of the New Testament*, Guides to Biblical Scholarship, New Testament Series (Philadelphia: Fortress Press, 1969).

11.   Norman R. Petersen, *Literary Criticism for New Testament Critics* (repr., Eugene, OR: Wipf and Stock Publishers, 2008; originally Philadelphia: Fortress Press, 1978).

12.   David Rhoads and Donald Michie, *Mark as Story: An Introduction to the Narrative of a Gospel* (Philadelphia: Fortress Press, 1982).

13.   Murray Krieger, *A Window to Criticism* (Princeton, NJ: Princeton University Press, 1964), 3–4; cf. Petersen, *Literary Criticism*, 19.

14.   Seymour Chatman, *Story and Discourse: Narrative Structure in Fiction and Film* (Ithaca, NY: Cornell University Press, 1978), 267.

15.   *Anatomy*, 6.

that exist between the real author and implied author will not necessarily mirror those existing between the implied reader and the real reader. As the originator of the text, *Anatomy* discusses the narrator first.

Instead of generalizing and examining the differences in definition between the real author and the implied author, Culpepper moves directly into the text of the FG to elucidate both the concepts and the narrative. Technically the narrator can be a separate element in a text, but in the case of the FG the narrator and implied author fill the same niche. The narrator in John interjects many comments and asides in order to provide clarity or background information, or even to give interpretation of what happened.[16] He functions as omniscient, omnipresent, and reliable. This means the narrative rings true no matter the location or circumstance, as the narrator knows every occurrence in every location and can interpret each correctly for the reader. Thus the reader should rely on the narrator for telling the story accurately and relaying the significance of the events as well. This also coalesces into a theological focus, since the narrator comes from a post-Easter, Holy Spirit-filled, and Old Testament-inspired point of view.[17] In taking this to be the case, the implied author and the narrator collapse into the same literary spot, thus allowing the reader to concentrate on the words of the text without needing to analyze the truthfulness or verify the perspective.[18]

One of the issues in John, more so than in the Synoptics, revolves around the use of time. Time breaks down into two main components: narrative time and story time.[19] Narrative time refers to the time of the narrative framework and the narrator, such that in John the narrator can comment on what has already happened before the beginning of the story (use of Old Testament prophecy, the history of Israel, etc.) even though it does not occur within the chronological limits of the story itself.[20] Story time is exactly what it sounds like, time as it progresses within the story itself, with John covering about two and a half years in

---

16. Culpepper (*Anatomy*, 17–18) lists the works of David W. Wead, M. C. Tenney, and John J. O'Rourke as helping him to see the significance of the narrator in the FG.

17. This is the natural conclusion stemming from Culpepper's understanding and categorization of the narrative perspective of John (*Anatomy*, 30).

18. This seems to be the reason for the various statements on the truthfulness of the witness that stands behind the FG. See Richard Bauckham, *The Testimony of the Beloved Disciple: Narrative, History, and Theology in the Gospel of John* (Grand Rapids: Baker, 2007), 73–91.

19. This is an intentional simplification. For the full taxonomy, see Culpepper, *Anatomy*, 53 n. 2.

20. Culpepper (*Anatomy*, 56) points out that the story begins in 1:19 and the opening of the FG should not be considered part of this story time. Cf. R. Alan Culpepper, "The Pivot of John's Prologue," *NTS* 27 (1980): 1–31.

the ministry of Jesus. Narrative time functions indirectly from the reader's perspective, as it most closely aligns with historical time. Story time can move linearly, as one would expect, yet the narrative comments can cause temporal dissonance within the text (e.g., John 11:2 explaining which Mary is in view, even though Mary has not appeared in the story yet). Clarifying remarks (such as speaking of the fulfillment of prophecy or Jesus referring to his own death) are typical for all of the gospels, yet John has a tendency to juxtapose chronology even more with editorial comments and asides, which explains why *Anatomy* spends a chapter focusing on the topic.[21] By differentiating between narrative time and story time, the reader understands the movement of the story alongside the interpretation of the story.

How *Anatomy* Develops Plot and Character

Stories revolve around a single main drama or tension, and this is called the plot. Plot as a term remains difficult to define yet easier to grasp, as it contains "sequence, causality, unity, and affective power of a narrative."[22] Often story and plot function as interchangeable terms in various analyses, yet the two are different since story deals with the entire conveyance of the communication, including genre, whereas plot comes down to a few basic types. These are plots of action (a change in circumstances), plots of character (a change in the moral stance of someone), and plots of thought (a change in the thinking or feeling of someone).[23] The next logical step, then, is to ask if gospels even have a plot. Rather than seeing the genre as *bios*,[24] Culpepper views the distinctive emphases of each evangelist as indicative of not only them having plots, but of those plots differing as well. For John, the plot centers on the revelation of Jesus Christ as the one who takes away sin and reveals the Father, with the latter being the distinctive element of the FG.[25] The plot of John revolves around one's response

---

21. Many of these asides clarify events, give specific interpretation, or put events into an historic context, such as believers being thrown out of the synagogues in John 9:22 and 12:42.
22. Culpepper, *Anatomy*, 80. This comes as a summary and condensed definition drawn from many sources in order to ascertain a working definition of plot.
23. Culpepper (*Anatomy*, 81) specifically links this to the protagonist in this section due to the influence of R. S. Crane ("The Concept of Plot," in *Approaches to the Novel*, rev. ed., ed. Robert Scholes [San Francisco: Chandler, 1966], 233–43), yet he moves away from this delimitation later in the book.
24. Culpepper never fully embraces any genre for the FG in *Anatomy*. With respect to classifying them as *bioi*, see Richard A. Burridge, *What Are the Gospels? A Comparison with Graeco-Roman Biography*, 2nd ed. (Grand Rapids: Eerdmans, 2004).
25. Culpepper, *Anatomy*, 88.

to Jesus: Do you believe or not?[26] Sequence seems missing in John, as the ordering follows thematic rather than chronological value. In the same way, causality and unity overlap since theme takes precedence. Finally, affective power comes to the fore as the strongest part of the FG's plot, as the narrative forces the reader to decide on how Jesus should be understood. The tension in the gospel of John is one of decision: Do you believe in Jesus? If not, this is why you should.

Stories have no way to move if there are no people in them. The second longest section of *Anatomy*, and often the most overlooked, is that on characters. Characters appear in literature in one of two ways such that they come across as their own being or else essentially function as a plot device used to carry the narrative forward in a particular manner. Culpepper argues that in the FG, characters function as extensions of the plot with the exception of Jesus. Jesus alone gets a full characterization, with his motives and personality fleshed out, since the purpose of John is to force a decision on how one understands Jesus.[27] He has both divine and human characteristics, with the former seen through his omniscience and the latter seen through his emotion.[28] The emotion, however, does not fall under the typical human reaction to events but rather showcases Jesus's otherness in that he is moved to joy at Lazarus's death and his deep emotion comes when thinking of his own death. He remains enigmatic due to his *logos*-nature introduced in the prologue and through his veiled responses to questioners. John presents Jesus as a mystery to be studied rather than as a typical protagonist.[29]

The other main character appears only on the lips of others, namely the Father, with the exception of a single spoken line (John 12:28). Jesus stands as a window to the Father, such that seeing Jesus is seeing both, and the unity of the Father and Son holds as one of the major contributions to theology from the FG. At the same time, the Son and Father serve different functions in the story and are separate characters. The descriptions of the Father appear mostly secondhand in the genitive, such as the children *of God*.[30] Jesus describes God through words, yet does so using action verbs such as "drawing" and "giving."

---

26. Ibid., 97–98. The following discussion comes mostly from these pages in terms of the analysis of the plot of John.
27. Ibid., 102.
28. Ibid., 109–10.
29. Ibid., 112.
30. "God" occurs much more frequently than "Father," yet there is clearly overlap in meaning. See Culpepper, *Anatomy*, 113–14.

The Father acts in the gospel without being seen. The focal point of the character of Jesus is to point others to the character of God.[31]

The rest of the characters in John can be grouped together under certain umbrella terms. First, the disciples include all of the named, characterized, and unnamed followers of Jesus. The disciples follow and reflect Jesus, yet they never truly understand him. The opening of the Nicodemus dialogue (John 3:2) and the level of the disciples' knowledge just before Jesus's arrest (see Peter and Jesus in 18:10–11) show strong similarities in terms of misunderstanding the person and role of Jesus. In fact, the followers of Christ orbit around the person of Christ and only understand after the resurrection. Before that, they fill the literary niche of foils, allowing both the narrator and Jesus to explain both the actions and words that they do not understand. Peter acts without thought, denies Jesus, and refuses to give up his life— the exact opposite of what Jesus portrays in the Passion. Thomas only believes upon seeing, which Jesus uses to speak of the church. The two function as opposites of each other, with Thomas drawn to the person of Jesus and Peter drawn to the position of the Messiah.[32] Andrew functions as a gate, introducing other characters to Jesus.[33] Philip, other than bringing Nathaniel, fails to understand who Jesus is, thus leading to explanations. Nathaniel represents Israel, those who hold to the teachings of the Torah and can see Jesus without blinders on. Judas is a traitor and represents all those who turn on the community and, once seeing Christ, reject the church.[34] The last named disciple actually has a title and not a name, the "Beloved Disciple." Setting aside identity and authorial aspirations, the Beloved Disciple represents the ideal follower of Jesus. He never misunderstands, he overshadows Peter (in terms of perception, not action), he is closest to Jesus both physically and emotionally, and he lives in both love and the Holy Spirit. The disciples as a group reflect the community of believers and, literarily, help move the plot forward through both positive and negative means.

The second umbrella term for a group in the FG is "the Jews." While there once was an understanding that John was anti-Jewish (and even

---

31. Ibid., 114–15.
32. Ibid., 123.
33. Ibid., 119–20. Culpepper notes how Andrew actually calls Jesus the Messiah first (John 1:41), even though Peter is the one known for his confession.
34. Culpepper (*Anatomy*, 125) links this to those who left the Johannine community and taught against John (e.g., 1 John 2:19).

anti-Semitic),[35] further research actually clouds the discussion more. John uses the term "Jews" in too many contexts and with too many possible referential groups to have a monolithic meaning attached. After looking at different taxonomies, Culpepper concludes that "Jews" stands for all Jews, those from Judea, or Jewish leaders.[36] It can function as any of those three, and therefore all are subsumed under the same term and thus are a single group. With respect to the plot, "Jews" always stand on the side of unbelief, and in that respect help move the plot along. Since the structuring of the FG includes the primacy of the author's viewpoint, the early portions of the story include virtually no opposition and therefore minimal mention of opposition groups. As the plot progresses, however, the Jews come to the forefront and their level of antagonism to Jesus increases with each encounter.[37] Class, social, and political distinctions do not hold in the designation, and thus the "Jews" confront Jesus, as both crowds who want him to begin an earthly kingdom and religious leaders who want him dead. It ends up being a blanket term for all unbelief. The Pharisees (and other religious leaders) garner their own mentions, though few. John also separates the Jews from the crowd on occasion, yet this just breaks people into those who do not believe and those who could yet fall short in understanding.[38] The crowd differs from the Jews in that they are treated without hostility and have the possibility of faith.

The third and final group in John does not fit under an umbrella term; instead they are the minor characters who appear, both named and unnamed, throughout the narrative. The named characters include Nicodemus, Mary, Martha, Lazarus, Pilate, and John the Baptist. The unnamed characters include Jesus's mother, the Samaritan woman, a royal official, a lame man, a blind man, and Jesus's brothers. John the Baptist introduces and headlines the theme of witness in the FG, and indeed becomes the example witness.[39] Nicodemus wants to believe,

---

35. E.g., Erich Grässer, "Die antijüdische Polemik im Johannesevangelium," *NTS* 11 (1964–1965): 74–90, among others.

36. See *Anatomy*, 126.

37. Ibid., though Culpepper explains that this is not a linear progression (sometimes there is more opposition and sometimes less), the general trend is a strengthening of hostilities between Jesus and the Jews.

38. Ibid., 132. The significance of this split appears in how the Pharisees and Jesus talk about the crowds in different parts of the FG.

39. Culpepper, *Anatomy*, 133. This is in contrast to Richard Bauckham, *Jesus and the Eyewitnesses: The Gospels as Eyewitness Testimony* (Grand Rapids: Eerdmans, 2008), 127, who sees the Beloved Disciple as the key eyewitness and John the Baptist as the starting point of Jesus's narratives but not at the same level of witness.

yet when pressed he never publicly confesses his faith, as one who does not want to be put out of the synagogue. Mary, Martha, and Lazarus essentially become faith, hope, and love in that they show devotion, faithful service, and the ultimate hope of resurrection. Jesus's mother occupies the strange space of being at his first sign, the wedding at Cana, and at his last moment, the crucifixion, while functioning as a narrative prop. She paves the way for Jesus's miracle in Cana and displays his compassion by being bestowed into the care of the Beloved Disciple. The Samaritan woman moves from her disadvantaged position of being an outcast among outcasts to becoming a successful missionary. The minor characters in John, whether named or anonymous, do not fit a specific mold, as each moves the story in a different direction and brings a different issue or conflict into the spotlight. While their purposes differ, each offers a unique contribution and allows the author to fill out both the characters of Jesus and the Father, as well as moving the plot along.[40]

The movement of the plot and the significance of the characters come together to give the story of Jesus meaning. Each group or individual gives a response to the call of the gospel. These range from belief and acceptance to disbelief and refusal, with varied shades in between allowing for complex rebuttals by Jesus and/or the author.[41] Some respond but refuse to commit, such as Nicodemus. Some have faith in Jesus as a miracle worker but no more. Some believe based only on the words of Christ, such as the Samaritan woman. Some commit even though misunderstanding and some move into full discipleship and belief. One defects, and of course movement from one response to another shows the movement of life itself. The FG intends to display the full range of possibilities of responding to Jesus while also prejudicing a positive reaction to Jesus, thus blending characters and plot.[42]

Commentary and the Implied Reader

John, more than the Synoptic Gospels, offers numerous asides and judgments in the midst of the story. While some of these comments

---

40. Culpepper (*Anatomy*, 145) compares the ensemble cast to the Wizard of Oz group of four, with each bringing both a special perspective and an additional plot element.

41. For example, the difficulty in assessing where the words of Jesus stop and the authorial insertion begins, if at all, in John 3.

42. Culpepper (*Anatomy*, 148) clarifies that the narrative intentionally allows the reader to respond in different ways, but it influences one toward belief.

appear obvious and stand out, many occur below a surface reading of the text and require a deeper analysis. The FG intentionally displays misunderstandings, moments of irony, and symbols to force the reader to think about the text and consider what transpires at a deeper level than just the immediate action.[43]

Misunderstandings dominate many of the dialogues in John. Some of these arise from Jesus seemingly speaking about normal matters yet actually referencing spiritual ones, some come from different definitions to words, and some appear as moments of separating the Christian community from the Jewish one.[44] The usage within John matters more than labeling or analysis of the misunderstandings. In other words, the why is more important than the how, since the why covers the purpose and therefore what the reader should be able to get from the appearances within the text.[45] The misunderstandings draw a line in the sand between insiders and outsiders. They clarify Johannine theology. Most importantly, misunderstandings teach one how to read the FG.

Irony, rather than mere coincidence or juxtaposition, results from that which is stated being opposite the intention, which the purveyor recognizes but the recipient does not. This allows both the purveyor in the story and the reader to laugh at the expense of the recipient.[46] Johannine irony typically revolves around a dualistic story, that of the earthly story and the heavenly one. The effectiveness and significance of it within the FG comes from the separation of these two, both in terms of the narrative and in terms of the awareness of the characters. Much of the irony swirls around the person of Jesus: his birth, identity, ministry, death, and the Jews' rejection of him.[47] The FG uses irony to drive the reader into agreeing with the conclusions of the evangelist, and thus not being the butt of the jokes.

---

43. The obvious comparison would be to Mark, which breathlessly moves the story from one action sequence to the next, whereas John forces the audience to take a deeper look.

44. *Anatomy* (152–54) mentions Rudolf Bultmann and C. H. Dodd as both sticking to this view as the only source of misunderstanding, yet Culpepper finds this definition too restrictive. Bultmann wants to see a specific type of content. Herbert Leroy wanted to limit the definition based on underlying riddles, and this based on form. Neither content nor form offers a convincing or convenient way to understand what the FG does.

45. Culpepper, *Anatomy*, 155.

46. Ibid., 166–67. Humor ends up being the oft-overlooked part of the definition, according to Culpepper.

47. In explaining this, Culpepper (*Anatomy*, 169–74) gives several examples for each, with the Jews' rejection being the most profound.

That symbols abound in the FG should be obvious, especially since the author explicitly mentions most of those symbols if not all and gives interpretation.[48] Light, water, and bread most heavily populate the symbolism of the FG and hold significance in its interpretation. Many characters carry symbolic weight, especially the disciples, as do many of the settings of scenes. All of the symbols, though mostly pointed toward the death and resurrection, revolve around John's exploration of the person of Jesus.[49]

Culpepper tackles the identity of the implied reader as the last major task in *Anatomy*. Essentially the task boils down to answering the question, "Who is the reader?" [50] One must recognize a few key points about the FG before continuing in this effort. First, one must understand that all of the various literary tools (irony, misunderstandings, symbolism, plot development, narrative asides) are designed to bring the reader into ideological alignment with the implied author. Second, the implied author desires for the reader to be convinced by the writing. This means that the actual audience needs to work at becoming the implied reader in order to understand and be within the sphere of the influence of the FG.[51] The question of the intended audience—a source for numerous writings on John—should be set aside in order to answer the question of the implied reader. Too often the former becomes caught up in looking at the purpose and situation of the gospel without giving thought to what the gospel asks of the reader.[52] The implied reader needs to stand as the audience sought by the writing, and therefore what every reader should seek to become.

Finding the implied reader can be tricky, as they can only be found through mirror reading and deduction.[53] One of the most important clues resides in how the author introduces characters or assumes prior knowledge. This gives the audience an idea as to what the narrator

---

48.   D. A Carson pointed this out in an email discussion about the high priest in John, when I was his student.

49.   As Culpepper (*Anatomy*, 198) states, "Always the imagery is fluid and subservient to the evangelist's exploration of Jesus's identity and the responses to him."

50.   Ibid., 205.

51.   Ibid., 208. Culpepper argues for the merging of the implied reader with the authorial audience by noting that, "The gospel is, ostensibly at least, entirely realistic." This means it should be taken as true in order to understand the meaning of the text.

52.   Culpepper (*Anatomy*, 210) is very gentle in stating this, but his frustration comes across clearly.

53.   Ibid., 212. Culpepper looks through numerous criteria to discover the identity of the implied reader, and does so very carefully. Unfortunately this summary cannot capture the care and level of detailed analysis he employs.

expects his audience to know before coming to the text. How is Jesus brought onto the scene? What political or religious groups or individuals or places elicit an explanation? Martha and Mary are known, but Lazarus needs to be introduced.[54] The geography of Israel comes across as a mixed bag, with the regions and Jerusalem assumed to be known but smaller towns and more specific locales need introduction. The audience only knows Greek, since the Hebrew or Aramaic words come with a gloss or are specifically called Hebrew words.[55] The audience should be very familiar with the Old Testament, yet they do not need to know the festivals or understand all of the Jewish ritual practices.[56] Finally, many of the events in John are retold instead of told, as if the narrator assumes the audience is familiar with the story or some details of it. Culpepper concludes that taking this all together paints a portrait of a believer who was comfortable with the Johannine community and understood their coded language, though this does not necessarily mean the person was from the group.

Conclusion of *Anatomy*

In putting all of these elements together, Culpepper argues that the literary "anatomy" of the FG opens up a different way of thinking about the book. John moves beyond being a "spiritual gospel" and becomes a wonderful piece of literature with flaws. The author gives a specific situatedness for the story, and the characters all revolve and crystallize around the person of Jesus and their responses to him. The narrative critique of the occurrences in the book, along with the way the language is aimed at a very specific type of reader, makes it clear that the author desires to move the reader from beyond a simple acceptance to an active faith in Jesus the Christ.

OTHER JOHANNINE WORKS

Though *Anatomy* certainly dominates the conversation, Culpepper has contributed many other works to the scholarly discussion on the FG.

---

54. Cf. Richard Bauckham, "John for Readers of Mark," in *The Gospels for All Christians*, ed. Richard Bauckham (Grand Rapids: Eerdmans, 1998), 147–71, here 161–65.

55. Culpepper (*Anatomy*, 219) points out that even some place names are called Hebrew words, which indeed shows that the narrator assumes a certain ignorance of the audience with respect to local place names.

56. Culpepper (*Anatomy*, 222) takes this to imply the reader is a Christian. This will be considered below.

He has a biography of John.[57] He has a commentary on the Johannine corpus, his *Gospel and Letters*. He also has numerous articles and edited works.[58] While not as seminal as *Anatomy*, these volumes have also influenced the world of Johannine studies.

Biography of John

Though denying that John the disciple wrote the FG, Culpepper spends time looking at the life of this important believer through the lens of history. The analysis surveys both various writings said to be by him and those about him. The subtitle, "The Life of a Legend," intentionally pushes beyond the historical figure of John the apostle into the realm of the mythic and legendary stories that grew around this figure.[59] This work, then, includes biblical, patristic, and other historical mentions up to the present day in order to delineate who John the apostle was and what people say about him.

With respect to the life of John, a few strands of tradition hold constant and others seem to waver. John was the brother of James, the son of Zebedee.[60] He was Jewish, and possibly from a mixed tribal background of Levi and Judah. John was a fisherman before called to a life of service. He was from Galilee. His father hired servants to help with the fishing, processing, and transport of the fish. Thus, John would not be a simple fisherman, but likely a sailor who hired fisherman. He also owned his own boats (or his family did) and sold his fish to a larger clientele. John, then, had enough wealth to not be among the poorest, and possibly could be placed in the rather small middle class of Israel.[61] He seems to be from Bethsaida, known for the richness of the fishing as it lay nestled on the shore of the shallow portion of the lake.[62]

The portrait one gleans from Scripture builds on this foundation. John lived and ministered as one of the Twelve. In fact, his prominence

---

57. Culpepper's *John*, mentioned above.
58. E.g. R. Alan Culpepper, "Reading Johannine Irony," in *Exploring the Gospel of John: In Honor of D. Moody Smith*, eds. R. Alan Culpepper and C. Clifton Black (Louisville: Westminster John Knox, 1996), 193–207. Of course, Culpepper is still writing and active, and thus he continues to contribute to Johannine scholarship.
59. Culpepper, *John*, 1.
60. All of these are common names or related to common names (Culpepper, *John*, 7–8); cf. Bauckham, *Jesus and the Eyewitnesses*, 65–91.
61. Cf. Rainer Riesner, *Jesus als Lehrer: Eine Untersuchung zum Ursprung der Evangelien-Überlieferung*, WUNT 2/7, 3rd ed. (Tübingen: Mohr-Siebeck, 1988), 412–13; and Eckhard Schnabel, *Early Christian Mission* (Downers Grove, IL: InterVarsity Press, 2004), 278.
62. Culpepper, *John*, 16–17.

places him in the inner circle of the three (along with Peter and James) who most often accompanied Jesus in special moments.[63] John obtains the name of "son of thunder," most likely for his untapped potential to be a powerful witness for Christ. John and Peter appear together in Luke's account of the preparation for the Last Supper[64] and the FG links the Beloved Disciple and Peter together throughout that Passover meal. After the resurrection and ascension, John remains paired with Peter and often functions as his silent partner in evangelism. John's last appearance in Acts counteracts one of his more brash moments, as in Acts he calls down the Holy Spirit in Samaria (8:25) just as he previously in Luke called down fire (9:54).[65] Paul names John as one of the pillars of the church in Galatians 2:9, cementing his place of authority in the early church.[66]

Ironically, the Johannine works tell little to nothing about John the apostle. In terms of being a character, John only appears briefly as one of the sons of Zebedee in the FG, while never appearing in the epistles or Revelation. The disputed authorship (or editorship) of the gospel of John has no answer, yet certainly one can rule the apostle out, Culpepper believes. In the same way, the epistles all evince no internal evidence, and the Apocalypse claims to be written by a John but not necessarily the apostle. Thus, Johannine literature does not give any added information about John.

With the beginning of Christian scholarship in the second century, John became more prominent as a possible author of the books of Scripture named after him. At the beginning of this time period, the books were not quoted or well known. The FG did not come into prominence until halfway through the century, with very few quoting it. The epistles and Revelation cropped up in later authors, and eventually all became accepted by the church only once they received apostolic attribution.[67]

---

63. Yet John's name appears in the list of the Twelve in the fourth position as often as not. See Culpepper, *John*, 29.

64. Culpepper (*John*, 46) mentions that Luke 24:24 could be a reference to John as the "some" that accompanied Peter.

65. This could entail a shift in character that Luke is trying to push, but this would be obscured by the text since so little is made of it. More likely it fulfills the mandate of Acts 1:8; cf. Darrell L. Bock, *Acts*, BECNT (Grand Rapids: Baker, 2007), 336.

66. Culpepper (*John*, 49–50) notes that John does not appear in the council of Acts 15. This could be due to his no longer being a leader, not having a speaking role, or more likely his missionary work having taken him elsewhere.

67. Humorously, the gospel of John originally appears in the writings and hands of the gnostics before the orthodox turn it against them. See Culpepper, *John*, 131 for a quick summation. For a critique of this position, see Charles E. Hill, *The Johannine Corpus in the Early Church* (New York: Oxford University Press, 2004).

The third century and those beyond moved John from the status of Apostle to that of author and legend. Tertullian names John as the author of the gospel, epistles, and Revelation. Clement, also attributing those works to the apostle, adds in more mythic episodes, such as John's hand sinking into the flesh of Jesus.[68] He mentions John along with Peter and James being those who elevated James the Just to the head of the Jerusalem church. Victorinus of Petau declares that the apostle labored in the mines of Patmos until the death of Domitian. Eusebius adds to the legend not by giving more information, but by disputing some that existed. It is in the arguing about what is true and what is untrue that the person of John begins to become the mythic character of John. According to Epiphanius, the apostle "was a model of piety and opposition to heresy."[69] Jerome includes a very long lived John, who overcame martyrdom (surviving being boiled alive), and only preached "little children, love one another" because it covered what Jesus said.[70] By 1300, Jacobus de Voragine wrote the Golden Legend (*Legenda aurea*). This compilation of legends expanded the aura around John, including his perpetual virginity (despite his marriage), being boiled alive before Domitian and surviving, raising Drusiana from the dead, among other such tales.[71] This completes the move from fisher, to follower, to apostle, to pillar, and finally to legend.

The incredible rise historically predates the inevitable fall, and so does John the apostle move from legend to lab specimen. By the time F. C. Baur popularized the idea that John did not author his namesake gospel, the debate had already gone on in scholarly circles for nearly a century.[72] David Friedrich Strauss had argued for a mythical FG and therefore not historical. C. H. Weisse, according to Albert Schweitzer, pushed further, saying Jesus could never have espoused the theology found on his lips in the FG. Baur, of course, spoke of John as the synthesis of Jewish Christianity and Paul, the book using the apostle's name to garner support and validity. A. T. Robertson argued for the traditional authorship and timeline for John, yet all of this changed

---

68. Culpepper, *John*, 141. Clement pulls in tradition from the *Acts of John*, and Eusebius adds more about Clement's view of John.

69. Culpepper, *John*, 159.

70. Ibid., 165. This very much sounds like a summation of 1 John.

71. See Culpepper, *John*, 175–77 and for an in-depth study on how *Legenda aurea* borrowed from Pseudo-Miletus, see Sherry L. Reames, *The Legenda aurea: A Reexamination of Its Paradoxical History* (Madison: University of Wisconsin Press, 1985).

72. Culpepper, *John*, 280.

in scholarly circles once Bultmann makes his entrance.[73] This has led to a three-pronged understanding in current scholarship: John the Elder wrote some or all of the Johannine corpus, the Johannine school produced the various works, or John the apostle indeed authored the works which bear his name in either title or in the opening lines. Robert Eisler theorized John the Elder as the son of a high priest who had witnessed the crucifixion as a boy and Lazarus as the Beloved Disciple. Martin Hengel postulates the Elder wrote the Apocalypse, the epistles, and then the gospel, with the longer works redacted after his death.[74] The search for the profile of the Johannine community then superseded all other considerations, as the work of C. K. Barrett led to J. Louis Martyn, Wayne Meeks, and ultimately Raymond Brown. Finally, traditional authorship finds its defense in Leon Morris, J. A. T. Robinson, Stephen S. Smalley, and D. A. Carson.

Commentary on John and the Letters

The natural outcome of so much historical and textual work is a commentary, so Culpepper finally produced one that included not only the gospel but also the epistles of John. The series Culpepper writes in, *Interpreting Biblical Texts*, has the stated aim of looking into critical issues with respect to the book or books under consideration to see how each smaller passage fits into the whole of the book.[75] This makes the introduction to the book very important, as Culpepper sets the stage for the rest of the commentary.

The introduction immediately tackles two of the most important questions about the FG: How does it fit into the categories of literature, history, and theology, and are these categories mutually exclusive? John as literature does not hide who Jesus is but confronts the reader with a faith decision about him. As history, John is more accurate with respect to timelines and geography but less accurate with respect to the actual words of Christ. In terms of theology, John's vocabulary sets the foundation for future Trinitarian language and theological concepts. Thus, the three categories work together and the FG blends them.[76]

---

73. Culpepper (*John*, 297) notes a scholarly sabbatical with respect to John, as little was published on the gospel or the man from about 1935 until 1971.
74. Hengel posits the Elder as the head of the Johannine school, per Culpepper, *John*, 305.
75. Culpepper, *Gospel and Letters*, 9.
76. This can be gleaned from *Anatomy*, but it is never stated as clearly as it is in Culpepper, *Gospel and Letters*, 17–18.

The introduction also tackles the relationship of John to the Synoptic Gospels. On the one hand, all four are gospels—a genre that had not existed before, and therefore unites them.[77] On the other hand, the style of Jesus's language (short sayings in the Synoptics, longer dialogues in John), the timelines and content of Jesus's ministry, and the Christology differ.[78] None of these answers breaks new ground, but they do set the stage for the rest of the book.

Culpepper essentially holds to an agnostic view of authorship, as he thinks the evidence points away from John the apostle but also does not really point toward anyone.[79] In this understanding, the FG addresses a specific community by using the life of Jesus. Thus, when the warnings about the synagogue casting out believers appear in the text, the actual warning goes beyond the characters in the book toward the intended readers.[80] The same holds for the connection to Petrine Christians, in that the community of the Beloved Disciple needed to assert their equality to the churches claiming Peter, and thus the FG pushes the equality of the Beloved Disciple with Peter. The letters of John display a schism within the Johannine community based on the Christology of the sides.

The theology of the Johannine works flows directly from Culpepper's analysis of the controversies within the community.[81] After a section dealing with genre (accepting Burridge's *bios* classification) and plot,[82] Culpepper wrestles with the problem of pulling theology from narrative. One the one hand, the FG clearly affirms certain key and rather typical theological truths. On the other hand, it seems to contain contradictory statements or sentiments, either spoken directly from the mouth of Jesus or else given implicit affirmation by the

---

77. Culpepper, *Gospel and Letters*, 18.
78. Culpepper, while arguing for the uniqueness of John's Christology, notes that each has an area of emphasis, which undercuts his point. Cf. Mark Strauss, *Four Portraits, One Jesus* (Grand Rapids: Zondervan, 2007).
79. *Gospel and Letters*, 40–41. Though holding to the community theory most strenuously argued by Raymond Brown, even there Culpepper wavers, saying it "may be understood" in such a way while still crediting the "genius" of the Beloved Disciple.
80. This develops directly from *Anatomy*, as seen by the identification of the implied reader.
81. Chronologically, this should be reversed, as his reading of the text gave rise to his understanding of the community conflicts, but Culpepper structured the book with the authorship before the theology and before the commentary proper.
82. In terms of genre, Culpepper (*Gospel and Letters*, 66) goes beyond what he says in *Anatomy*, whereas his section on plot reiterates it. See n. 21 above.

implied author.[83] This gives rise to the Johannine dualisms, where clear contrasts arise in order to make the theology of the book transparent.

One of the great contrasts in the gospel rises in the light-vs.-dark pairing. Darkness refers to spiritual darkness, and blindness can fit the same niche.[84] A special Johannine contribution to the gospels appears in the FG emphasis on sin, following the darkness motif. Whereas the Synoptics contain vice lists, stories about specific sins, or even details on how to fight sins (e.g., the Sermon on the Mount), the gospel of John focuses on unbelief as the only real sin.[85] Unbelief comes from living in darkness and denying the true light, namely Jesus. Living in darkness implies loving the darkness and loving one's own glory instead of God and his glory.[86]

The Christology of John centers on four titles. Jesus is the Word, and as Word he exercises the power of the creator.[87] Jesus is the Revealer, such that the primary purpose of his teaching lies in making God the Father known. Jesus is the Redeemer. Jesus is the Son, with the dual title of "Son of Man" shared with the Synoptics, while also being "Son of God," a more exalted and prophetic role.

The purpose of the gospel of John from beginning to end is to bring about faith in the readers (1:12; 20:31). Faith, then, stands as one of the most important concepts in the book. The entire question of Jesus's identity arises not to find out who he is but to imprint the importance of why his identity matters. Faith in the FG has levels. The first and lowest level equates seeing and believing (20:28–29). The second level includes those who have faith due to the words of Jesus. The highest level of faith appears in "those who know, love, and bear witness"[88] to Jesus. The church in the FG equates to the children of God, those who have faith. The church as the church does not appear yet new birth, special food, special water, a new family, and an ever-present Father occur throughout the book.

---

83. Culpepper (*Gospel and Letters*, 88) notes how John 10:30 and 14:28 stand in contrast with a surface reading.

84. Humorously, the FG uses literal blindness to show the spiritual blindness of the Pharisees in John 9; cf. Culpepper, *Gospel and Letters*, 90–91.

85. Ibid., 90.

86. Culpepper laments a lack of space to delve into these issues more fully (*Gospel and Letters*, 92), especially as the glory angle seems to fit in so well with one of the emphases of the FG.

87. This title is uniquely Johannine compared to the other gospels, whereas the other three titles crossover to different degrees.

88. Culpepper, *Gospel and Letters*, 100.

The Johannine epistles, on the other hand, focus on defending the church from a schismatic group and maintaining right doctrine.[89] Culpepper considers 1 John to be a homily directed towards those who have not split off from the Johannine church, whereas 2 and 3 John both exhibit all the characteristics of classical letters. While not advocating unified authorship, Culpepper notes that the themes, language, and commitment to orthodoxy place the composition of the letters as most likely occurring during the latter stages of the redaction and editing of the FG. He concedes that the same editor could possibly have worked on all of them, but that there exists no consensus yet.[90]

The major concern of 1 John, seen in the continuance of Johannine dualism, is the unity of the church. This unity functions more as a line of demarcation, who is in and who is out, than as a joyful community. Fellowship, not belief, lies at the heart of the book (1:3).[91] This means that the author of 1 John claims exclusivity for his community as a portion of the only true church, and therefore leaving his church means leaving salvation. The darkness, lies, and death balanced by the light, truth, and life find their fulcrum in Jesus, yet the physical instantiation of Jesus is the local church. Therefore leaving the church is tantamount to leaving Christ. The content of 2 John, while much shorter, echoes the concerns of being outside the community, and therefore warns against the false teachers that originally came from the Johannine church but now are not of the church. The last epistle, 3 John, looks for a welcome for Johannine missionaries that evidently was not granted by all churches.

CONTRIBUTIONS TO JOHANNINE STUDIES

Culpepper has left his mark and influenced all future studies in the FG due to his change of focus. While his earliest work looked behind the text,[92] subsequent publications took the text as it stood and delved into topics of structure, theme, characters, plot, and the like. By bring-

---

89. Though specifically referring to 1 John, Culpepper (*Gospel and Letters*, 251–52) reiterates these struggles and makes them more specific for 2 and 3 John.

90. Culpepper cites Raymond Brown in saying there is no consensus, yet Brown (*The Epistles of John: A New Translation with Introduction and Commentary*, AB 30 [New York: Doubleday, 1982], 30) argues quite strongly for differing authors.

91. Admittedly, belief brings about fellowship, but the assumption here is that belief needs to be reaffirmed rather than started. See Culpepper, *Gospel and Letters*, 255.

92. R. Alan Culpepper, *The Johannine School: An Evaluation of the Johannine-School Hypothesis Based on an Investigation of the Nature of Ancient Schools*, SBLDS 26 (Missoula, MT: Scholars Press, 1975).

ing the focus back to the text, Culpepper moved the stream of scholarship back to the most productive course.

Contributions to Johannine Studies by *Anatomy*

With the publication of *Anatomy*, Culpepper moved the conversation about the gospel of John from focusing on dissecting the text or looking behind it to actually looking at the text. Bultmann sifted the text to find what he wanted from John: the *kerygma* and the nature of salvation without connection to an historical event or movement. Brown and his ilk found seams in the text to discover the person, persons, community, or communities behind the words. *Anatomy* brought the spotlight back where it belonged: on the actual FG and the message it contains. Rather than using the text as window, Culpepper saw a mirror wherein the message of the text was both captured for the reader and reflected what the reader carried into the reading.[93]

Anatomy brought a new language into Johannine studies by appropriating literary techniques and introducing them into the study of the FG. While narrator and reader remain typical terms, Culpepper introduced implied reader, implied author, real author, the importance of time (analepses and prolepses),[94] plot movement, and the significance of characters. He examined commonly stated issues in John, such as misunderstandings, irony, etc., and placed them in the context of literary analysis instead of them standing alone. The analysis of characters and plot displayed how the FG revolves around not just the character of Jesus but the responses to him as well. It is in these responses that the plot, theology, and practicality of the gospel all come to light. In looking more specifically at the individual characters instead of as groups, Culpepper pulled out the significance of the groups as well. His analysis of "the Jews" highlights the importance of his work, as instead of limiting the data due to his interpretation, he broadens his conclusion because the data warrants it. This alone gives proper recognition to John's more robust use of character: instead of limiting a person or group to a specific and narrow reaction, the FG depicts the people with deft strokes that show depth and realism. Even though some of the disciples stand

---

93. In many respects this both reflected and nominally predated the entry of deconstructionism into biblical studies and the rise of post-modern reading notions in exegetical work. See Kevin Vanhoozer, *Is There a Meaning in This Text?* (Grand Rapids: Zondervan, 1998), especially 43–90 and 148–87.

94. These were introduced by Culpepper (*Anatomy*, 56) to show glimpses forward and backward in narrative time versus story time.

symbolically for a particular type of person or reaction to Jesus, none of them comes across as a cardboard cutout.[95]

The special commentary in the FG remains a major topic in Johannine scholarship, and Culpepper adds to the conversation, but his contribution in this area stems from how he applies the results to understanding the audience of this work. The commentary of the author points to an audience that has a thorough knowledge of the Old Testament but scant knowledge of the local geography of Jerusalem or the various feasts of the Jews. Many of the characters or episodes in John appear without an introduction, and thus assume a readership that already is familiar with them (e.g., John 11:2).[96] This sketches a picture of the target audience, building a portrait of the implied reader.

Anatomy is not a perfect work. The idea of reading Scripture in its final form should be able to stand alone instead of needing to assume that there was a community behind the book. The implied reader, contrary to Culpepper's conclusion, does not need to be from the Johannine community in order to have a shared vocabulary.[97] Geographic, religious, and cultural similarities would cause the same overlap instead of a shared school. Culpepper seemingly argues against this notion in his work, when he notes that many of the misunderstandings from the FG seem aimed at possible readers in order to correct them,[98] which could have been handled through teaching if they were from the same community. The thought-picture of the mirror for the act of reading seems problematic as well, since the way Culpepper communicates this image allows for the meaning to be decided by the reader instead of the text, whereas the rest of *Anatomy* argues for the meaning coming directly from the narrator to the implied reader. This in itself seems self-defeating. Finally, Carson argues convincingly that *Anatomy* never makes the case for applying the standards of current literary critical methods for novels to the gospel of John.[99] In fact, the issue of genre stands out as a slightly neglected issue— a true problem in a work on literary design![100]

---

95. Cf. the essays in Christopher W. Skinner, ed., *Characters and Characterization in the Gospel of John*, LNTS 461 (New York: Bloomsbury, 2013).

96. Culpepper, *Anatomy*, 223.

97. Ibid., 226.

98. Ibid.

99. Carson, review of *Anatomy of the Fourth Gospel*, 126.

100. Culpepper, *Anatomy*, 84. Though here Culpepper seems to answer the question, the truth is he calls them gospels and then talks about the work of each evangelist without coming to a specific conclusion. He changes this position in later works.

Contributions of Other Works

Culpepper has numerous other publications that contribute to the study of the FG as well. His biography of John and his commentary highlight his contributions outside of *Anatomy*. The biography does a great service in tracing the impact of John the Apostle both textually and chronologically. While much of the text dealing with authorship arguments and the identity of the Beloved Disciple occur in other works in a much stronger fashion, *John, The Son of Zebedee* contributes much to the historical study of the person of John by chronologically and systematically surveying authors from throughout the history of the church to access their writings. Culpepper does not take what fits his own theories of John, instead he carefully moves through the Synoptics, Acts, and Galatians to record the data. He looks at the Johannine corpus and notes the paucity of data, especially discounting John as the author of any of the works. The unique contribution of his book comes from the middle to the end of the work, where Culpepper gleans information from enormous amounts of historical authors from the second century until the end of the twentieth.

In *The Gospel and Letters of John*, Culpepper moves from the historical to the textual. With respect to his scholarly trajectory, this should be where his contributions in literary theory and structure meet the exegetical road. The introductory sections restate the findings of his research and the commentary does a strong job of promoting literary preaching of the FG. In other words, instead of a word-by-word or even phrase-by-phrase approach, Culpepper's work forces the teacher to engage the part in light of the whole, making sure that the narrative forest is not lost for the exegetical trees. While the commentary itself does not make any groundbreaking claims in understanding John's gospel, it does correct the natural inclination to focus on the details of the text and miss the larger issues. For example, by seeing Thomas as a character, the preacher is less likely to miss the development of deep attachment he has for Jesus, and therefore "let us also go that we may die with him" is not seen as giving up but a statement of love and a challenge to the other disciples.[101] Culpepper also compares John to the Synoptics, noting that sin in the Synoptics is found in vice lists and pronouncements, whereas sin in John boils down to unbelief. This makes preaching John starker, in that one must move directly to the question of belief since that is

---

101. Culpepper, *Gospel and Letters*, 187.

what the FG asks. Who is Jesus, and why does he matter function as
the central questions the FG asks of the reader, and Culpepper uses his
commentary to flesh out the answers to both questions. In turn, he then
encourages the preacher to posit those questions to his congregation.
With respect to those who belong to the church, Culpepper reads the
gospel of John as looking for unity within the body. This also becomes
a major theme in the epistles, as 1 John looks to warn about false teachings, 2 John about specific false teachers, and 3 John about not welcoming those doing God's work.

CRITIQUE AND CONCLUSION

Culpepper has truly helped lead a renaissance in Johannine studies. While
John was overlooked for Paul and the Synoptics for years, Bultmann
brought the FG back to the fore of scholarship. However, instead of looking at the content, the typical theologian from the time looked for seams
or inconsistencies in the narrative to find the redactor or sources behind
the text itself. Culpepper changed the focus from looking at authorship
or sociological issues to the text itself. He did this by reading John as a
story, focusing on the narrative elements, tracing out the plot, studying
the characters, and finally recognizing that the FG is brilliant literature.
In doing so, he moved the discussion from behind the text to the text.

In making this movement, however, Culpepper conceded a lot of
ground. He argued for a Johannine community as author of the book,
and therefore he found seams in the text, argued for various layers of
tradition, and assumed fabrication and embellishment in the text. The
problem with this approach stems from his method: If one is reading
the FG as literature, if one is arguing for an implied author, then the
considerations of Johannine schools and redactors should be eliminated from comments on the text itself since those ideas counter one
another. One can hardly speak of the genius of the author in weaving
a story together on the one hand, then point out seams that cause a
discontinuity of thought on the other. Instead, a canonical approach
could be implemented, such as Brevard Childs has argued for and
utilized.[102] This allows the text to speak for itself, alleviates issues of

---

102. Brevard Childs, *Biblical Theology in Crisis* (Philadelphia: Westminster, 1970); idem, *Introduction to
the Old Testament as Scripture* (Philadelphia: Fortress Press, 1979); and idem, *The New Testament as
Canon: An Introduction* (Philadelphia: Fortress Press, 1985).

authorship, and lets the reader handle the text as literature. Another problem in Culpepper's approach stems from his metaphor. If the text functions as a mirror, then is it not that one only gleans what one has already brought to the text? The text may set boundaries on the meaning, but the product of meaning relies too heavily on the beholder.[103]

R. Alan Culpepper will continue to influence the trajectory of Johannine studies by forcing all interpreters to wrestle with the literary nature of the FG. No commentary or study will be complete without mentioning *Anatomy of the Fourth Gospel* or some of his other publications. His work should reinvigorate narrative preaching, looking at the larger story in the midst of speaking about the smaller sections of Scripture. While many will focus on history or theology, Culpepper's works will not allow anyone to forget that the gospel of John is literature aimed at forcing a response of faith from the reader.

---

103. A criticism Carson (review of *Anatomy of the Fourth Gospel*, 124–25) levels.

Stanley E. Porter and Ron C. Fay

A milestone in Roman times was a stone marker erected to indicate distances between locations, originally used to indicate the distance from Rome, the center of the Roman empire. This volume has been concerned with milestones in Johannine scholarship. By use of that term, we mean to indicate an admittedly incomplete and only partial group of scholars whose work has marked significant epochs in Johannine scholarship. We have studied eight such milestone figures in this volume, with numerous others who might equally well be discussed in other volumes of this sort. Now that we have reached another milestone in Johannine scholarship—the end of this volume about milestones—it is appropriate to draw our journey to a conclusion by reflecting back on some of the observations that have been made along the way. As with the scholars included, we do not pretend that these are the only observations that may be made, but we believe that at least this set is worth making.

The following conclusions capture some perspectives on the basis of reading the preceding eight essays about milestone figures in Johannine scholarship, along with our introductory essay that has attempted to establish the major trends in Johannine scholarship, into which these figures may be placed. The first observation is that John's gospel has long been a source of Christian theology and thus it has been a source of theological controversy in New Testament scholarship. Whether the fourth gospel is accused of being gnostic, Jewish, or Hellenistic, a case can be made for it opposing the same as well. John contains an extremely exalted Christology, one that must have taken at least a century to develop (so it has been argued), unless of course his words fit easily within the first-century milieu and thus place the composition in the middle of the first century. Second, John often serves as a battleground over historical issues. John clearly gives an easy-to-follow timeline of about three years for the ministry of Jesus—except that his gospel also has relatively little interest in earthly matters and emphatically focuses on theological issues. The fourth gospel displays the itinerant movement of Jesus and his followers throughout the story, except that the book groups the stories based upon thematic and not chronological grounds. The third observation is that, no matter the argument or point to be made, the gospel of John functions as a crux of the Christian narrative, and various theories have grown up around it, sometimes in positive relationship and sometimes in opposition to its emphases.

B. F. Westcott, Adolf Schlatter, and C. H. Dodd all worked in the Johannine material before the turning point of the magisterial commentary of Rudolf Bultmann. Westcott focused primarily on the text. He based his comments on the Greek text (no matter the type of commentary) and eschewed overreliance on secondary literature. His preferred method of comment began with looking at other passages within the book, then the corpus, then the Bible as a whole before moving to other scholars. This allowed his comments to be succinct and textually driven, and for him to ignore arguments he considered to be irrelevant. Schlatter combined two specific traits in his work on the fourth gospel. First, he emphasized and focused on the Jewish flavor that permeates the book. The significance of this observation—now readily accepted—comes from how this view stood in contrast to most of the works of his German contemporaries. Second, Schlatter read John as a theological and historical document instead of assuming a lack of history and that the theology was to be found either behind or in spite of the text. Dodd's reputation with respect to Johannine studies begins and ends with his focus on eschatology, explicitly his understanding of realized eschatology as revealed in John's gospel. However,

Dodd's influence can be felt in numerous other areas, even though most scholars do not trace the thoughts back to him. Dodd pushed the idea of oral tradition behind John's work. He examined Hellenistic Jewish, Greek, and Old Testament backgrounds to the language and structure of the fourth gospel. These three scholars all published prior to the meteoric impact of Bultmann.

Rudolf Bultmann functions within Johannine studies like the place of Alexander the Great in history: There is a time before (BB = Before Bultmann) and a time after (AB = After Bultmann), since that one person initiated a new era in Johannine scholarship, quite possibly New Testament scholarship. Whereas before Bultmann scholars focused on the text, its historicity, the tradition behind it, and the theology proposed by it, after Bultmann the Johannine questions completely changed. Bultmann saw John's gospel not as a way to know Jesus and his time but as a way to begin to understand God and religion once the implausible elements were disregarded. This began with his adoption and implementation of the tools of the history-of-religion approach (*religionsgeschichtliche Schule*), specifically focusing on the impact of Wilhelm Bousset. In appropriating these ideas, Bultmann sees Christianity (and therefore John) as a natural development of the religions and ideas both surrounding and within Judaism of the first century. This gave Bultmann a lens through which he understood Christianity and the language of the Bible: a lens that assumed syncretism in belief and appropriated mythology in word. It is specifically this mythological word that Bultmann sought to strip away using various critical tools in his famous demythologizing of the New Testament. By removing the mythological language and stories, the true heart of Christianity could be discerned in its *kerygma*. In a strange way, Bultmann turned on the liberal theology of his day by noting how the central message of the New Testament in theological liberalism became a list of moral platitudes instead of a life-changing encounter. Liberal theology focused on humankind, whereas Bultmann held that true theology and the New Testament focus on God. Bultmann's existential understanding of reading Scripture comes to the fore at this point, since he holds that experiencing God ultimately determines one's actual religious self, and one experiences God through an intentional recognition of God as "wholly other" and the self-determined step to have faith. Ironically, in his attempt to demythologize and then focus on one's experience of God, Bultmann falls victim to his own criticism of liberal theology. Since the emphasis of Bultmann's thought falls on experience and necessarily ends up an individualistic instead of universal faith, the human being again becomes the focus. With respect to Johannine studies, Bultmann pushed the gnostic interpretation of John, and thus the need to strip John of such language. He emphasized how John constantly pushes again and again for the reader to make a faith decision. This comes from the fact that Jesus is the Revealer. The lasting influence of Bultmann comes not from his many followers; indeed, he has few today. Rather, his influence stems from every scholar's need to interact with the questions he raises and his emphases on the importance of Jesus and the need to have an authentic faith that the fourth gospel proclaims.

The next three scholars were all subsequent to Bultmann and born at about the same time, and yet they diverge widely in their approach to Johannine studies. Leon Morris was a conservative scholar focused on the historicity and theology of the text, such that one can learn who Christ crucified was from a close reading of the fourth gospel. Morris helped lead the resurgence of conservative (and evangelical) thought into the academy, with his essays on John spearheading the effort to defend many traditional views of the fourth gospel while arguing within the milieu of modern scholarship. Looking at his works in total, Morris argues for the historical reliability of John, its composition independently of the Synoptics (though with possible oral crossovers), and for John the apostle as the author of the fourth gospel. John A. T. Robinson also argues for some conservative positions for John, including dating the composition of the gospel to AD 50–55 and the final redaction (inclusion of prologue and epilogue) to a bit after AD 65. This conclusion naturally progresses from his earlier work on John that emphasizes the fourth gospel's historicity, reliability, and independence from the Synoptic tradition. Robinson eventually settles on the fall of Jerusalem and the destruction of the temple as the major turning point for dating the gospels, yet this only later became the telling blow for him. What makes Robinson stand out from most other Johannine scholars is his liberal theological beliefs that are wedded to a more conservative dating and defense of the historicity of the gospels. This makes Robinson the inverse of Raymond Brown, who has more progressive ideas on the text while leaning more conservatively in his theology. Brown's notoriety stems from his hypothesis of a Johannine community being behind the text of John and its primary audience. At the same time, he force-fully argues for the independence of John from the Synoptics, the significance of the Jewishness of the fourth gospel, a complete rejec-tion of gnostic overtones, and the assertion that John was written to believers in order to strengthen their faith instead of for the purpose of converting nonbelievers. This in turn sets the table for his under-standing of John's gospel having multiple layers of development. By using only redaction and source criticism, Brown limits the way a text can be understood. For Brown, therefore, any time a seam or aporia appears, it becomes evidence of editing or altering the text in some way by an additional hand. These three scholars, Morris, Robinson, and Brown, together offer a wide view of the majority of Johannine scholarship of the second half of the twentieth century.

The final scholar reviewed in this work, even if to a lesser degree, overturns some of the previous paradigms much as Bultmann changed the tide of New Testament studies as a whole. Brown constructed a view of John through the lens of a specific community that wrote, redacted, edited, and finally finished the gospel of John for itself. R. Alan Culpepper's work in literary and narrative criticism explains and hence removes much of the evidence for such a view. Coupled with the work of other major scholars interested in literary and theo-logical interpretations of the New Testament, Culpepper's literary views remove the need for a large group of redactors and editors and brought with them a major change in approach to Johannine criti-cism. John's gospel was now read as John's gospel, with no need for historical emendation or complicated schemata. A literary view of John allowed the characters to speak for themselves, the major themes of John to shine through, and the previously identified "errors" to be understood as intentional literary devices. In many respects, we can see a unified pattern to scholarly discussion of John's gospel: Study of John's gospel began with a deep look at the text by earliest scholars, moved into dating and authorship issues in the modern era, shifted into the realm of demythologizing, and then slowly made its way back to being read once more as a literary text. The difference in approaches, however, is profound, as each of these scholars reflects the issues of their time as they wrestle with the biblical text.

After more than two centuries of study, John's gospel itself has not changed but the approaches to the text and the interpretive presup-positions brought to the text have. The pre-critical notion of John as the spiritual gospel that did not interact with the Synoptics but carried the memories of a then-ancient John the apostle slowly changed over time. To simplify some of the major trends in Johannine scholarship, the dating of the fourth gospel has moved from the 90s, to the mid-to-late second century, to the mid 60s, and back to the 90s again. Views of authorship have similarly shifted from the apostle, to the Elder, to a disciple of a church leader, to a collaborative and complex community, and back to an individual author who may or may not be John the apostle. The different tools used to analyze the gospel (redaction criticism, form criticism, demythologizing) have ended up telling us at least as much about the person doing the work, what they wanted to find, and the era in which they worked as they have explained the actual text. While much of this scholarly discussion may at times seem circular or even reductive, the work of centuries has produced great creative scholarship that has provided some answers, but it has also produced many further questions—some of them new ones and others deeper versions of the previous questions. These are the kinds of issues that the authors represented in this volume have addressed and that contemporary Johannine scholars will continue to address in further study of John's gospel.

SCRIPTURE INDEX

AUTHOR INDEX